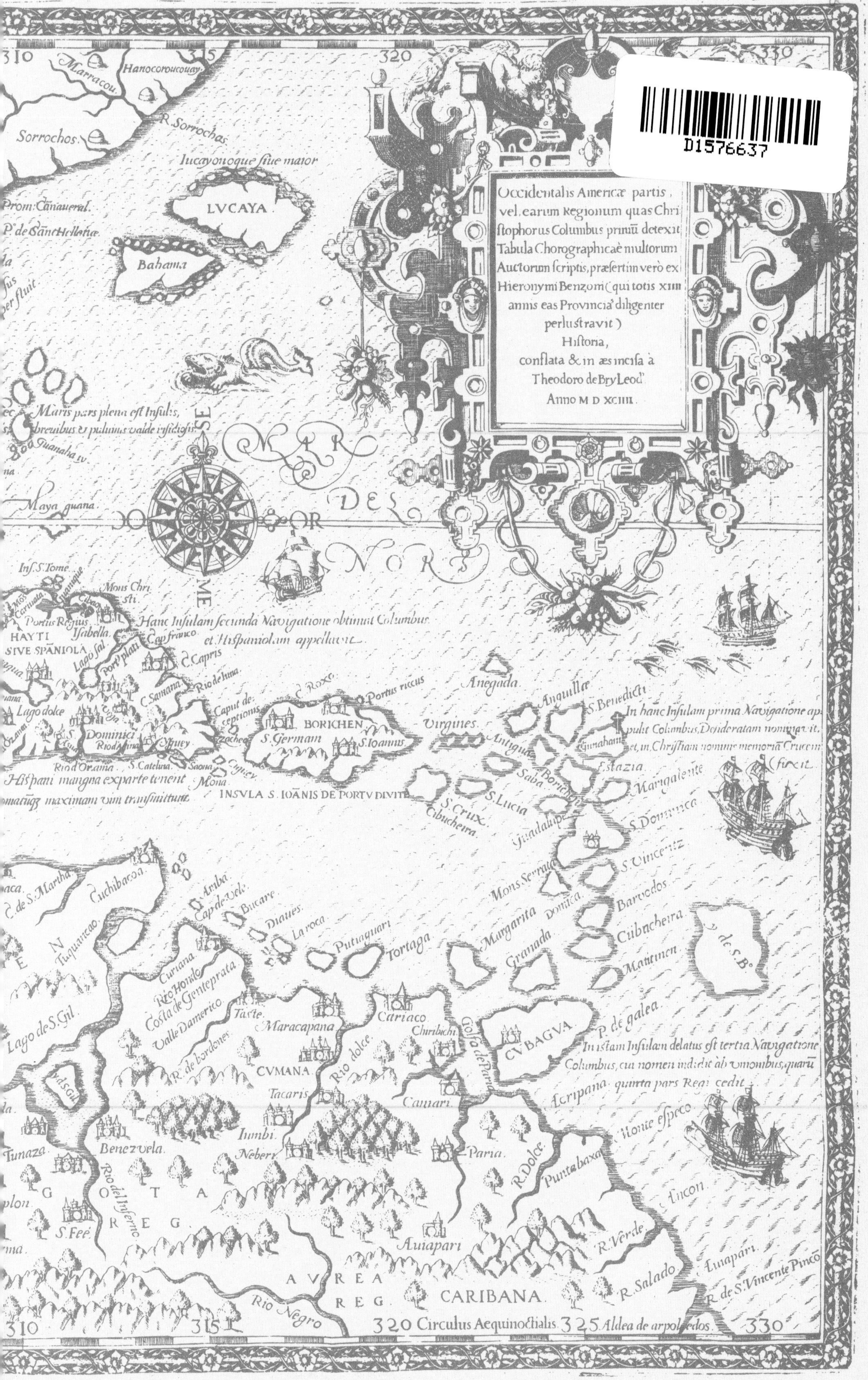
Occidentalis Americæ partis, vel, earum Regionum quas Christophorus Columbus primũ detexit Tabula Chorographicaè multorum Auctorum scriptis, præsertim verò ex Hieronymi Benzoni (qui totis XIIII annis eas Provincia diligenter perlustravit) Historia, conflata & in æs incisa à Theodoro de Bry Leod. Anno M D XCIIII.
310
315
320
330
Marracou
Hanocoroucouay
Sorrochos
R. Sorrochas
Iucayonoque siue maior
LVCAYA
Prom: Canaueral.
P. de Sanct Hellenæ.
Bahama
Maris pars plena est Insulis, breuibus & paludibus valde insidiosis.
Guanaha
Maya guana
MAR DEL NORT
SE
ME
Ins. S. Tome.
Mons Christi.
Portus Regius
Isabella.
HAYTI SIVE SPANIOLA
Lago sal.
Hanc Insulam secunda Navigatione obtinuit Columbus, et Hispaniolam appellauit.
Capfranco
port plati
C. Capris
Rio de luna
C. Samana
Lago dolce
Dominici
Rio de Ozama
Higuey
Rio d'Orama
S. Catelina
Saona
Mona
Hispani mangna exparte tenent
Caput de ceptionis
C. Roxo
Portus riccus
BORICHEN
S. Germani
S. Ioannis
INSVLA S. IOANIS DE PORTV DIVIT
Anegada
Virgines
Anguillæ
S. Benedicti
In hanc Insulam prima Navigatione appulit Columbus, Desideratam nominauit, et, in Christiani nominis memoria Crucem fixit.
Antigua
Saba
S. Crux
Cibucheira
S. Lucia
Estazia
Margalante
S. Dominica
Guadalupe
S. Vincentz
Mons Serrat
Barvodos
Cibucheira
Matinino
Aruba
Cap de Vele
Bucare
Diaues
La roca
Putiaguari
Tortaga
Margarita
Granada
Dominica
C. de S. Martha
Cuchibacoa
Tuquracao
Curiana
Rio Hondo
Costa de Genteprata
Valle Damerico
Taste
Maracapana
Cariaco
Churibichi
Golfo de Paria
CVBAGVA
P. de galea
In istam Insulam delatus est tertia Navigatione Columbus, cui nomen indidit ab unionibus, quarũ quinta pars Regi cedit.
Acripana
Lago de S. Gil
R. de bordones
CVMANA
Rio dolce
Camari
Tacaris
Iumbi
Neberi
Paria
Benezuela
Tunaza
R. Dolce
Punta baxa
Monte espeço
Rio del Inferno
S. Feé
G O T A
R E G
Auiapari
R. Verde
R. Salado
Auiapari
R. de S. Vincente Pinco
AVREA REG
CARIBANA
Rio Negro
Uncon
310
315
320 Circulus Aequinoctialis 325 Aldea de arpoledos 330

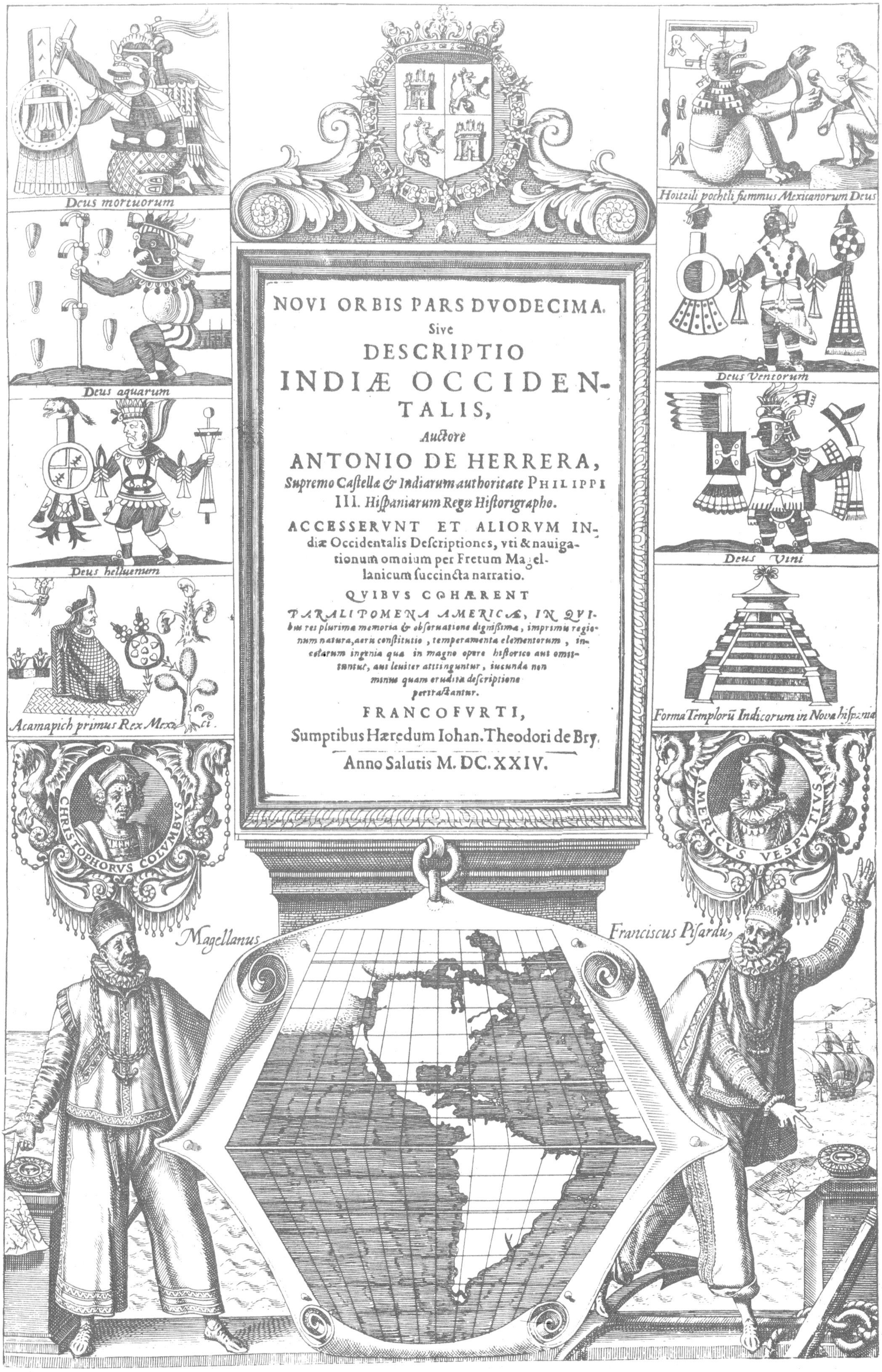

NOVI ORBIS PARS DVODECIMA.

Sive

DESCRIPTIO INDIÆ OCCIDENTALIS,

Auctore

ANTONIO DE HERRERA,

Supremo Castellæ & Indiarum authoritate PHILIPPI III. *Hispaniarum Regis Historigrapho.*

ACCESSERVNT ET ALIORVM Indiæ Occidentalis Descriptiones, vti & nauigationum omnium per Fretum Magellanicum succincta narratio.

QVIBVS COHÆRENT

PARALIPOMENA AMERICÆ, IN QVIbus res plurimæ memoria & obseruatione dignissimæ, imprimis regionum natura, aeris constitutio, temperamenta elementorum, incolarum ingenia quæ in magno opere historico aut omittuntur, aut leuiter attinguntur, iucunda non minus quam erudita descriptione pertractantur.

FRANCOFVRTI,

Sumptibus Hæredum Iohan. Theodori de Bry.

Anno Salutis M. DC. XXIV.

DISCOVERING THE NEW WORLD

based on the works of
THEODORE DE BRY

edited by
Michael Alexander

Harper & Row, Publishers

New York, Hagerstown, San Francisco, London

Printed in England

Published in the United States of America
by Harper & Row, Publishers, Inc., 10 East 53rd Street,
New York, New York 10022

First U.S. Edition
Library of Congress Catalog Card Number: 74-25021
ISBN: 0-06-010043-5

This book was designed and produced by
London Editions Limited,
30 Uxbridge Road, London W12 8ND

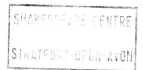

Contents

THEODORVS DE BRY LEODIENSIS,
ANNO ÆTATIS SVÆ LXIX, A° CHRI. 1597.
DOMINE
doce me ita reliquos vitæ meæ dies
transigere vt in vera pietate vitam & moriar
NVL SANS SOVCY
DE BRY

Introduction

Theodore de Bry (1528–98) was the first to illustrate the literature of American travel with any degree of accuracy or elegance. His great series of printed books, with their large number of beautiful copper-plate engravings, brought to the European public the first realistic visualization of the exotic world opened up across the Atlantic by the explorers, conquerors and settlers.

Historia Americae, a series that was to run to fourteen volumes, was launched in 1590. Thus it was not until a hundred years after Columbus, by which time the globe had been circumnavigated three times and the oceans were bustling with European shipping, that an effective picture book was to be published on the New World. Though the renaissance of science and learning was in full spate and printing and engraving techniques, in those days of Plantin, Aldus and Dürer, were highly efficient, well-illustrated travel books did not make their appearance until late in the century with the productions of de Bry and his inferior imitator Hondius.

The main reason was lack of good material. In the beginning of the century information was available to those concerned only from the unpublished reports or 'relations' of the sea captains, the log-books and charts of the pilots and the romantically embellished maps of the cartographers. In addition, expansionist monarchs liked to keep their discoveries secret: John II of Portugal had made betrayal punishable by death. As a result, for the first twenty-five years there was little travel literature on the market and books that were obtainable gave no idea of how things actually *looked* in those distant lands where an increasing number of people might have wished to invest, adventure, settle, or simply travel in the mind.

The best known early works about the New World were Oviedo's *Historia general y natural de las Indias* (1537–47), Peter Martyr's *De Orbe Novo Decades* (1525), and later the popular collection of voyages compiled by Richard Hakluyt *Divers voyages touching the discoverie of America* (1582). These publications contained vivid verbal descriptions but, with the exception of some crude representations in Oviedo's *Historia*, no illustrations. Of lesser works, Ramusio's collected *Navigationi e Viaggi* (1550–59), Benzoni's *Historia del Mondo Nuovo* (1565), Thevet's *Singularitez de la France Antarctique* (1558) and de Léry's *Histoire d'un voyage faict en la Terre du Brésil* (1578) did carry rough attempts to picture the Indians and their artefacts, but in general it can be said that before de Bry travel books featured only the crudest cuts based on the imagination of the artist or the untutored sketches of travellers. Though there was some good first-hand material lodged in the archives of Spain it was not made available to publishers.

Despite the example of Sir Francis Drake who, according to his Portuguese pilot, was 'an adept at painting' and used to shut himself up with his cabin boy and work away at such items as 'birds, trees and sea lions', the English were backward in graphic recording. Richard Hakluyt the elder, an ardent promoter of merchant adventure, as late as 1585 thus instructed a projected North American expedition: 'A skilful painter is to be carried with you, which the Spaniards used commonly in all their discoveries to bring the descriptions of all beasts, fishes, trees, towns etc.' There is no mention, it may be noted, of people, though another abortive English expedition was counselled to 'drawe the figures and shapes of men in their apparell and also their manner of wepons.' The 'figures and shapes' of primitive people seem to have presented some difficulty to artists brought up in the European tradition: Jean de Léry, finding problems with the anatomy of the Brazilian Indian, complained: 'Although I diligently perused and marked those barbarian people, for a whole year together, wherein I lived amongst them, so as I might conceive in my mind a certain proportion of them, yet I say, by reason of their

An Indian woman with a plantain leaf, from Ramusio's Navigationi e Viaggi

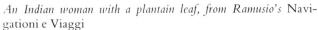

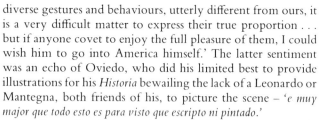

An ugly Indian woman at Cumana, from Benzoni's Historia del Mondo Nuovo *(see p. 127)*

diverse gestures and behaviours, utterly different from ours, it is a very difficult matter to express their true proportion . . . but if anyone covet to enjoy the full pleasure of them, I could wish him to go into America himself.' The latter sentiment was an echo of Oviedo, who did his limited best to provide illustrations for his *Historia* bewailing the lack of a Leonardo or Mantegna, both friends of his, to picture the scene – *'e muy major que todo esto es para visto que escripto ni pintado.'*

The first really efficient artist to record the American people was the French Huguenot Jacques le Moyne de Morgues, who was attached as artist to the disastrous French settlement in Florida and barely escaped massacre by the Spaniards in 1564. Le Moyne had since lived in London as a religious refugee and had worked up his sketches into a series of what must have been exquisite water colours if we are to judge from the only example that remains. The next useful set of pictures was not to appear until 1590, when John White was sent to Virginia with specific instructions from Sir Walter Raleigh to record local life around the newly-founded Roanoke settlement. White, who was to return as governor (his daughter Elinor Dare gave birth to Virginia, the first child born to English parents in America), produced a wonderful set of paintings of Indians, birds, insects and fishes, the originals of which are now in the British Museum. It was the knowledge of the availability of these two splendid series that gave Theodore de Bry his great idea: to produce a comprehensive set of travels based on original texts and generously illustrated with accurate engravings. He had a third source to hand: the twenty-eight woodcuts published in Marburg in 1557, accompanying the remarkable story of Hans Staden. Staden had spent nine months as prisoner of the Tupinamba cannibals of Brazil. His clearly authentic account was illustrated by crude but informative woodcuts made under his supervision. De Bry's adaptation of them was to result in the most sensational section of his project.

Theodore de Bry was born in Liège in 1528, a Protestant at a disadvantageous time when the Duke of Alva and the Spanish Catholics were rampaging through the Netherlands. In 1570 he was forced to flee to Strasbourg where he opened up a goldsmith's shop and like others of that trade doubled as an engraver. We have a glimpse of him in the foreword to *Icones quinquaginta virorum illustrium* (1597), a book of lives of worthy men, which he illustrated: 'I was the offspring of parents born to an honourable station and in the first rank among the more honoured citizens of Liège. But stripped of all these belongings by accidents, cheats, and ill luck and by the depredations of robbers, I had to contend against adverse fortune so that only by my art could I fend for myself. Art alone remained to me of the ample patrimony left me by my parents. On that neither robbers nor the rapacious bands of thieves could lay hands. Art restored my former wealth and reputation, and has never failed me, its tireless devotee.'

Later in the same work his homily to the reader gives further indication of his puritan temperament: 'I would specially prevail on parents to attend diligently to the upbringing of their children that they melt not away in detestable ease, which is indeed the pillow of Satan, and so at last bring upon themselves the extremity of sorrow. . . . For it is not by sleep or idle hours that these famous men have won such a name as to shine forth amongst the illustrious luminaries of the world. But unwearied pains, indefatigable labour and the most burning love of truth in the investigation of the abstruse have brought them these honours.'

De Bry materializes more precisely in an engraved self-portrait published a year before his death. He looks prosperous enough in his merchant's coat trimmed with fur; his hair is white and sparse, and his eyes seem strained at peering too closely over his plates; map-makers' dividers are in one hand

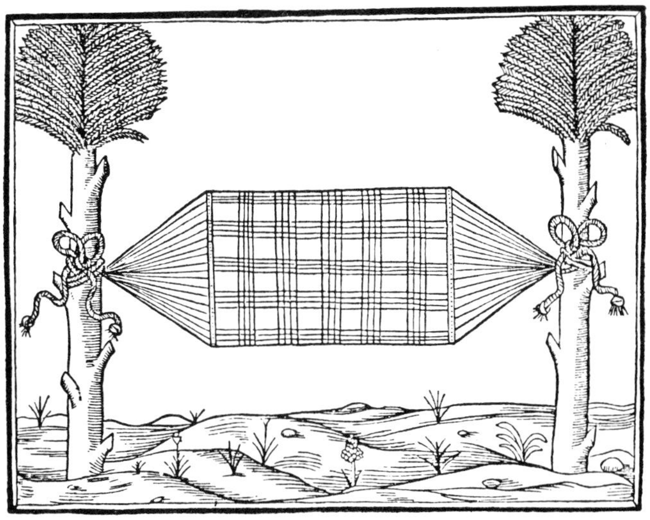

An Indian hammock, from Oviedo's La historia general y natural de las Indias

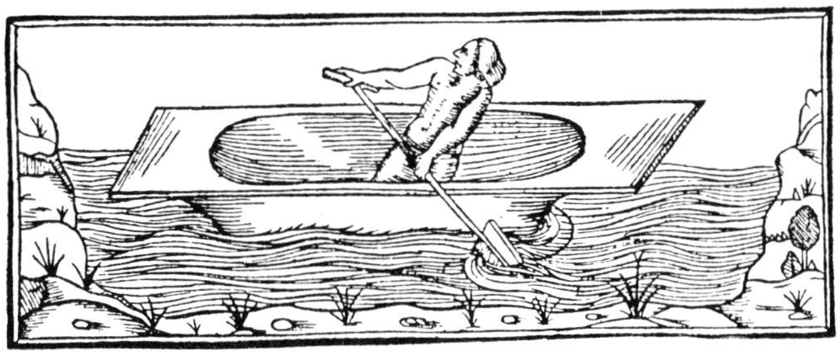

A canoe, from Oviedo's La historia general y natural de las Indias

and in the other a skull. His motto *Nul sans Souci* conveys that nothing good can be achieved without painstaking effort, a principle he seems to have kept in mind to the end of his days if we are to believe his friend the French antiquary Jean-Jacques Boissard who wrote, apropos the illustrated voyages: 'He is especially to be praised in this, that though now almost seventy years of age, and at a time of life when men are unfitted for more laborious actions, yet he, pursuing his former skill, and lest he grow benumbed with unfruitful ease spends his whole day on his engraving and typographical work, although he is daily weakened with gout, and his hands and fingers are contracted into knots. He draws assiduously and delineates everything with such perfection, that a young man of thirty could not do it with more precision.' This intense dedication, considerable skill as an engraver, money in the bank, and now access to good material made de Bry well-equipped to carry out his ambitious project.

Richard Hakluyt, scholarly Englishman, friend of Sir Walter Raleigh, had long had the idea of putting together the narratives of explorers for the inspiration of English readers. His great work *The Principall Navigations, Voiages and Discoveries of the English nation* was taking shape and in 1587 he published an English translation of René de Laudonnière's account of the French adventure in Florida. In the margin of the dedication to Raleigh, Hakluyt remarks that 'The chiefe things worthie observation in Florida are drawen in colours by James Morgues painter sometime living in the Black fryers in London.' This was none other than Jacques le Moyne, referred to above, who twenty years earlier had been recording the New World for the French. Perhaps de Bry saw this reference in Hakluyt's publication, for in that year he came to London to see if he could obtain the drawings for his own purpose. Though a brother Huguenot, le Moyne would not sell; a publisher, engraver and bookseller himself he may have had the idea of producing a book on his own account. Before returning home de Bry started on a commission to engrave thirty plates for Lant's drawings of the funeral procession of Sir Philip Sidney. News of le Moyne's death and a commission to illustrate Sir Anthony Ashley's translation of the Dutch work *The Mariner's Mirrour*, brought him back to London the following year and he was able to buy the coveted pictures. 'Filled with joy, therefore', he wrote in the preface to the Florida story he was soon to publish, 'at having obtained it, I have spared no expense to commit the work to the press, and I and my children have spent diligent pains in engraving the pictures on copper plates, to render them clearer, although little durable, because that kind of engraving being more delicate is easily worn.'

De Bry probably met Hakluyt on his first visit to London; in any case on his return the two of them were deep in discussions over publishing matters. The artist John White, now governor of Virginia, was in London, and on Hakluyt's introduction de Bry was able to obtain his drawings of Roanoke and its environs. Hakluyt must have realized that he himself was technically incapable of producing illustrated books otherwise it is difficult to understand his apparent generosity in giving ideas and material to a rival in the same field of publishing. But Hakluyt had one request to make: that de Bry should open his series with the Virginia story rather than Florida, even though it happened later. Hakluyt and his friend Raleigh were not concerned with de Bry's chronology: they had in mind to publicize as quickly as possible a vindication and further promotion of the discredited English colony for which White was at that time desperately trying to obtain relief. De Bry could but agree: it may even have been a condition of the deal. As he wrote somewhat wistfully in the foreword to the English edition of *Virginia*, published in 1590 and dedicated to Sir Walter Raleigh: 'being there unto

Tupinamba cannibals, from Hans Staden's Wahrhaftige Historia und beschreibung eyner Landtschafft der Wilden *(see p. 117)*

requested by my friends, by reason of the late performance thereof, albeyt I have in hand the Historye of Florida which should bee first set foorthe because it was discovered by the Frenchmen long before the discovery of Virginia, yet I hope shortly also to publish the same, a Historye doubtless so Rare, as I think the like has not been heard nor seene.'

De Bry's monumental series falls into two sections known to bibliophiles as the *Grands et Petits Voyages*, and comprising a total of twenty-five parts. The *Grands Voyages*, so called because the size of the volumes in the series was larger than that of the *Petits Voyages*, are concerned almost entirely with the Americas; the *Petits Voyages* cover Africa and the East Indies. Theodore de Bry lived to publish the first six volumes of the *Grands Voyages*. Thereafter the venture, which had become the main family business, was continued by his widow and sons and grandsons-in-law until 1634, when the final volume of the *Grands Voyages* was published. The pictures should be looked into carefully, for they may contain many telling details and one plate may be a serial story in itself. As well as conveying information about the native way of life there is something to be learned about the customs, costumes, weapons, and the enormous canoes of the European savages who so ruthlessly hacked their way through the American Arcadia. If scale and perspective are often eccentric and if the savages sometimes look like European ecclesiastics we must try and see them through the eyes of the time and remember that the traditions of the illustrators were not so far removed from the illuminators. Though a *mannerist* in the heyday of mannerism, as his other engraved work reveals, de Bry did not let his decorative urge overwhelm his historical integrity: if prepared to let fancy run free in spendidly florid title pages and allegorical glorifications of great explorers, he saw to it that when an original was available it was adapted seriously and without indulgence; where imagination was called for it was kept in check. In any event, the historical, anthropological and ethnological content of the plates and their sheer artistic interest – and surely many of the pictures have a compelling aesthetic appeal – produce a treasure trove that has lain for far too long in the confines of a few exclusive libraries. As his friend Boissard expressed it: 'Undoubtedly posterity will have cause to be grateful to Theodore de Bry of Liège. He has spent the whole of his past life with these objects always before his eyes – the promotion of literature by his studies and the increase of the public good by his infinite labours, combining pleasing entertainment with useful instruction. In all this I know not whether we should admire most his art, his genius, or his diligence. For there is nothing done by him in which accurate industry and ingenious invention are not apparent; whereby not only does he feed the minds of his readers, but delights the eyes of those who gaze on his work.'

Editorial note

Though agreeable, the task of presenting de Bry's *America* in a single manageable volume is intricate. The work runs to fourteen folio volumes and contains the narratives of thirty-five explorations and 'relations' over a period of one hundred and fifty years, illustrated by over two hundred and fifty engravings. It is not arranged in chronological order and its issue spread over forty-eight years. *America* was written in German and Latin (Hariot's *Virginia* also appeared in English and French), and there are enough variants to have inspired ten published bibliographies.

In addition, the de Bry system is editorially inconsistent: in the early volumes each plate has its related text, generally a summary or re-write of the relevant part of the original; later the plates may be scattered sporadically and more sparsely amid a general account. The de Bry picture-texts are often tantalizingly superficial, even if enlarged upon in the narratives that precede them: to include these narratives here would take as many volumes as the original! I have substituted a brief historical introduction to the main series, and it is hoped that too little learning has not been assumed in the reader – I am acquainted with a French Academician who was unaware that his countrymen had ever colonized Florida!

In the main I have worked from German texts (set in Gothic type) from the many different editions available in the British Museum and the National Maritime Museum, and have thought it best to present them almost literally, in the somewhat naive style of the original. A more elegant modernization would seem to detract from the *Geist* of the period and the personality of the writers. In the case of the Hariot captions to *Virginia*, originally published in English, I have modernized virtually only his punctuation and spelling, which was necessary because de Bry, perhaps in his haste to publish, seems to have been negligent in his proof-reading. In the Benzoni *Historia* I have infiltrated a few telling passages from his original text, and where the author is personally concerned, I have concentrated on this aspect of the work and have transposed it to the first person singular. I have also re-arranged the Staden text to include his additional material where appropriate. The various Dutch voyages through the Straits of Magellan, which appear in various volumes, have been placed together in a single section.

In the notes I have retained the sometimes difficult syntax and often inconsistent orthography of my sources. To resist excessive digression, quotations are generally of the period and I have abstained from excursions into comparative anthropology. An unwillingness to paraphrase is due to an affection for Elizabethan English, which I hope is shared.

The most useful sources for the notes have been those great, if occasionally uneven, editors Hakluyt and Purchas, whose poetic translations and adaptations were also drawn on by de Bry in the formulation of his texts. I have preferred to use their versions rather than make my own translations of such foreign-language originals as Oviedo and Acosta. Let us ride what Purchas called 'Rhetorickes Full sea and spring tide'!

As regards the plates, it will be noticed that quality and content languish a little after the death of Theodore de Bry: they are also less profuse and do not fall together so neatly as in the earlier series. To bring them into bounds I have had to take liberties with their arrangement and have omitted, for example, the story of Pizarro's conquests and the rather tedious internecine strife between the Spaniards which followed, as well as some of the later, and more fanciful, material. For the de Bry enthusiast, however, I have thrown in such addenda as the spendidly florid title pages, the unexpected Pictish couple who appear at the end of the *Virginia* volume, and various maps and topographical plates. These make up the most complete set of *America* engravings to be published since the beginning of the seventeenth century.

I

The French adventures in Florida 1562–5

In April 1513 Ponce de Leon, searching from Puerto Rico for the fabled 'Fountain of Youth', sighted an unknown coast. It was Easter Week, so he named it 'Pasqua Florida.' Taking it to be an island, he landed in the area of the St John's River where he saw an Indian settlement. Two of his men were wounded by arrows. Ponce de Leon sailed on, noting for the first time the powerful current that swept northwards between the mainland and the Bahamas. On its full flood he passed Cabo de las Corrientes, the Cape of Currents, re-named a few years later Canaveral. He followed the Florida Keys and is thought to have reached as far as Pensacola. The Indians everywhere were hostile, attacking his ships in fleets of canoes. Ponce de Leon returned nervously to Cuba without having explored the new territory, still uncertain if it was an island. Eight years later he attempted to find out, but again the Indians frustrated his plans, attacking and killing many of his men. Ponce de Leon was badly wounded and died a few days after reaching Cuba.

In the next forty years the Spaniards made various attempts to explore or settle the area – men such as de Soto, Narváez, Ayllón, Nuñez Cabeza de Vaca and Tristan de Luna came and went and found no gold. In 1561, seeing nothing in the way of profit, Philip II proclaimed that no further expeditions would be undertaken. The French had other ideas: at that very moment two small ships were being fitted out at Le Havre. In February 1562 they sailed: their purpose was to explore the coast and challenge the presumptions of Spain in the northern hemisphere, and their destination was 'la Florida'.

France, like England, resented the papal Treaty of Tordesillas which divided the New World between Spain and Portugal: 'Je voudrai bien', François I had said, 'qu'on me montrât l'article du testament d'Adam qui partage le Nouveau Monde entre mes frères Charles V et le roi du Portugal.' French ships probed and pirated the South American trade routes; in 1552 Villegagnon established a Protestant colony in Brazil under the noses of the Portuguese, vaingloriously referring to the south as 'La France Antarctique' and himself as 'King of America'; in the north Verrazano, before being eaten by Caribs in 1528, had followed the coast from North Carolina to Newfoundland in the name of France and had become the first man to sail up the Hudson River; Cartier and de la Roque de Roberval had looked for riches in the colder parallels; innumerable ships operated from the ports of Brittany and Normandy on the North Atlantic fishing banks. Even if 'La France Antarctique' was not to last long, 'La Nouvelle France', as they liked to call almost the whole of North America, was taking on a vague reality.

The Florida venture was conceived by Gaspard Coligny de Chatillon, Admiral of France and the most influential Protestant in the country. Catherine de Medici, the Queen Regent, holding a delicate balance between Huguenots and Catholics, had given her support. The expedition was commanded by Jean Ribaut, one of the greatest sailors of his day; like him the crew were Protestants. Its official object was a reconnaissance from Florida to Cape Breton so that, in the words of Ribaut, France might one day 'receave, by meanes of contynewall trafficque, riche and inestimable comodities, as other nations have don.'

Like Ponce de Leon they landed at the St John's River, which they named the Mai because they discovered it on the first of May. The enraptured Ribaut 'veewed the coast all along with an inspeakable pleasure of thodiferous smell and bewtye of the same.' This time the Indians were friendly, paragons of the *bon sauvage*, 'all naked and of a goodly stature, mighty, faire, and as well shapen and proportioned of bodye as any people in all the worlde, very gentill, curtious and of a good nature'.

Ribaut and his men explored the vicinity, naming rivers and erecting columns to claim the land for France. Ribaut described the country as 'the fairest and frutefullest and plesentest of all the worlde, habonding in honney, veneson, wildfoule, forrestes'. And then, more interesting to his employers, he mentioned gold, silver, turquoises and a 'great abundance of perrles'. This first expedition was more in the nature of a reconnaissance, but most of the men wanted to remain in so Arcadian a spot. Leaving thirty volunteers in the newly-constructed fort they named Charlesfort (near Beaufort S.C.), Ribaut sailed back to France on June 11 having promised to return in six months with settlers and supplies.

But Ribaut could not fulfill his undertaking: France was in the throes of a religious civil war. As a Protestant he fought in the defense of Dieppe against the Catholics; when it fell he fled to England. In London he published a book, from which extracts have been quoted above. It appeared in the spring of 1563 and its full title was:

> The whole and true discoverye of Terra Florida, (englished the Flourishing Lande.) Conteyning as well the wonderfull straunge natures and maners of the people, with the merveylous commodities and treasures of the country: As also the pleasaunt Portes, Havens, and wayes thereunto Never founde out before the last yere 1562.

This small volume of twenty-three pages soon came into the hands of Queen Elizabeth, who was captivated, as her courtiers intended, by the description of a strategically sited land of milk and honey. Ribaut was summoned to an interview and his story generated further ideas of English involvment. Master-minded by the notorious adventurer Thomas Stukeley a plot was hatched, with the Queen's backing, to take possession of Florida in her name. Ribaut, who is said to have been offered a salary of 300 ducats and a house, agreed to co-operate and lead the expedition. But he must have had second and more patriotic thoughts now that the religious wars were ended and his patron Admiral Coligny was back at court, for he reneged

BREVIS NARRATIO
EORVM QVÆ IN FLORIDA AMERICÆ PROVĪCIA
Gallis acciderunt, secunda in illam Nauigatione, du-
ce Renato de Laudōniere classis Præfecto:
Anno M D LXIIII.
QVAE EST SECVNDA PARS AMERICAE.
Additæ figuræ & Incolarum eicones ibidem ad vivū expressæ:
brevis item Declaratio Religionis, rituum, vivendique
ratione ipsorum.
Auctore
Iacobo le Moyne, cui cognomen de Morgues, Laudōnierum
in ea Navigatione sequuto.
Nunc primùm Gallico sermone à Theodoro de Bry Leodiense
in lucem edita: latio verò donata a C.C.A.
Cum gratia & privil. Cæs. Maiest. ad quadriennium.
FRANCOFORTI AD MOENVM
Typis Ioãnis Wecheli, Sumtibus vero Theodori
de Bry ANNO M D XCI.
Venales reperiūtur in officina Sigismundi Feirabēdii

Montes Apalatci, in quibus aurum

Apalatci

In hoc lacu Indigenægenti grana

Ouſtaca

Onatheaqua

Appalou

Potanou

Ehiamana

Anouala

Hica

FLORIDA PROV

AB INDIGENIS DICTA IAQVAZA

Aſtina

Choja

Vtina.

Patchica

Enrca
Timoga
Melona

Eloquale

Aquouma

Edelano

Eclanou

Cadica

Chilili

Omitaqua

Mocoſo.

Calanay.

Onachaquara.

Mathiaca.

Mayarca.

Maira.

Marracou

Laudon

Hanocorou:couai:

Rib.

Hauiguata

Lacus
aquæ dulc

Sorrochos

F. Sorrochos

Hic defendit
Pamphilus Vernaez.

Sinus Moquiu.

Adeo magnus eſt hic lacus
ut ex una ripa conſpici altera
non poſſit. Diſtat a Charles
fort 180 leucis.

Prom: Can

Oathaqua

Mocoſſou

Lacus ɛ
Inſula Sarrope

Mexicani Sinus pars.

Sinus Ioan
nis Ponce

F. Canoer

F. Pacis

Iardines

Æſtuaria.

Bipini

Baha

Aquatio

F. Iethiopum
Portus Ioanis
Proxach Conſum.
Natiuitatis
F. Florinj
F. Nations
F. Cuſk

CALOS

Calos

Prom: Florida

Rupes

Hæc maris p

Inſula dicta
Teſtudines.

Scopuli dicti
Martyres

Hauana

F. Marien

Portus
Mataneas

Xeqia

Guanagnarico

Cuba inſula.

Cuſpis. S.
Antonij

Inſula
Pinorii

Iardines ſcopuli, na:

FLORIDAE AMERICAE PROVINCIAE
Recens & exactissima descriptio
Auctore Iacobo le Moyne cui cognomen de Morgues, Qui Laudonierum, Altera Gallorum in eam Prouinciam Nauigatione comitat⁹ est, Atque adhibitis aliquot militibus, Ob pericula, Regionis illius interiora & Maritima diligentissime Lustrauit, & Exactissime dimensus est, Obseruata etiam singulorum Fluminum inter se distantia, ut ipsemet redux Carolo. IX. Galliarum Regi, demonstrauit.
Chicola
Terra plana
S. Michael
Portus Principis
Stalame.
Prom. Lupi
Charlefort
F. Iordanis
Littus rectum
Siccum
Humile
Prom. S. Romani
Portus Regalis, siue
S. Helenæ
Magnum
Bellum
Gironda
F. Garumna
Charenta
F. ligeris
Axona, Iracana
Sequana
Hiouacara
Sarrauahi
Alimacani
Maij
Zagareo.
Lucaya.
est Insulis, scopulis, breuibus et puluinis valde insidiosis.
SEPTENTRIO
OCCIDENS
ORIENS
MERIDIES
Pars Maris Antillarum
Mons Christi
Isabella
Portus Patris

on the plan and attempted to escape to France with the French pilots. Ribaut was caught aboard a Flemish ship at Gravesend and thrown into prison.

Meanwhile in Florida the men of Charlesfort were desperately awaiting their long-overdue leader. Morale was low: they had planted no food in the expectation of early relief and the local Indians, though friendly, were unable to provide it, while a fire at the fort destroyed what little they had been able to obtain from more distant tribes. The officer left in charge by Ribaut, a ruthless disciplinarian, had hanged a soldier for 'a smal fault' and exiled another to an island where he was starving to death. The soldiers, 'seeing his madnes to increase from day to day', resolved to kill their officer. Then they appointed a new leader and decided to return to France. Having no boat, they built one – 'a smal Pinnesse'. The Indians provided rope for rigging, rough planks were caulked with moss, shirts and sheets made do for sail. The story of the voyage of this frail, over-loaded and under-provisoned craft is dramatic: shoes and leather jackets were eaten; urine was drunk in the absence of water, and by the time they were picked up by an English ship they had drawn lots among themselves and eaten the loser.

Florida was now empty of Frenchmen except for a sixteen-year-old boy who had opted to stay with the Indians. But the Spaniards were not aware of this; by now they had received detailed reports of the French settlement and were making strong diplomatic representations for its withdrawal. Though they could not make good use of the territory themselves, the Spaniards by no means wished to have Frenchmen commanding the route through the narrow straits between the Bahamas and the mainland up which their richly-laden galleons rode the Gulf Stream on the way home. To add insult to potential injury the interlopers were Protestants and heretics. While Catherine de Medici temporized with feigned innocence, the exasperated Spaniards acted. Philip II ordered the governor of Cuba to remove Ribaut's impertinent columns, destroy the French fort, and deal with the settlers as he saw fit. By the time the Spaniards arrived, in May 1564, the pathetic French boatload had already sailed and there was only the boy to show them the location of Charlesfort and one of the Ribaut columns. Charlesfort was burned down; column and boy were carried back in triumph to Havana.

The Spaniards had not at first realized that another French fleet was even at that moment en route for Florida. The Peace of Amboise in 1563 had temporarily ended the religious war and Admiral Coligny, 'seeking new means of traffic and profit in strange lands', had set up a second Huguenot expedition. As Ribaut was still in an English prison, command had been given to a subordinate on the previous voyage, René de Laudonnière. On 2 June 1564, a month after the punitive visit of the Spaniards to Charlesfort, three hundred men and four women were disembarked about forty miles south of the original landfall. A member of the expedition was Jacques le Moyne de Morgues, whose instructions were 'to map the sea coast, and harbours, indicate the position of towns, plot the depth and course of rivers, and portray the dwellings of the natives and anything else in the land worthy of observation'.

Laudonnière built another fort he named Caroline and made friends with the local Timacua Indians, promising them support against rival tribes. His real objective was to have access to the auriferous Appalachians inland and to achieve this he made alliances with their enemies and generally incurred the distrust of all. The Indians stopped supplying food and soon the French were starving. Laudonnière was accused of failing to invest sufficient money in stores and of hoarding food for his own use. Some of his officers mutinied and forced him to allocate ships in which they could sail to the Spanish main. The men in the fort would have starved to death had it not been for the timely arrival of Sir John Hawkins, returning from a slaving expedition, who sold them one of his ships and gallantly gave them supplies. They were about to sail for home when a fleet of seven ships appeared on the horizon. It was Ribaut, released from prison and now sent by Coligny to relieve the discredited Laudonnière of his command.

The departure from France of the Ribaut fleet had not gone unreported to the Spaniards, who by now saw that the French intentions on Florida were in earnest. 'Act promptly before the Admiral of France can forestall you,' the Spanish ambassador advised his master, 'and seeing that they are Lutherans it is not needful to leave a man alive, but to inflict an exemplary punishment that they may remember it forever.' After contentious diplomatic exchanges with Catherine de Medici, Philip acted for the second time. Eight warships under the command of the great admiral Pedro Menendez de Avilez were sent out and on 4 September, a week after Ribaut's arrival, appeared off the French settlement. The Spaniards landed about thirty miles to the south and immediately constructed a fort which they named St Augustine, site of the 'oldest city' in the United States. The story of the Spanish attack on Fort Caroline is told at length by Laudonnière in Hakluyt's *Voyages*, a tale of cunning and ruthless cruelty which ended in a massacre of almost all the French in Florida, including Ribaut, whose beard is said to have been cut off and sent to Spain. Laudonnière and le Moyne managed to escape and reach England. Laudonnière returned to France where he died in obscurity; le Moyne, under the name of James Morgues came to live in London until his death in 1585; Admiral Coligny was killed in the massacre on Saint Bartholomew's Day, 1572. The French had some satisfaction from the dashing action of a Catholic corsair named de Gourgues who, on his own initiative, took three ships and 180 men and in 1567 attacked Fort Caroline, re-named Fort San Mateo, and put all its defenders to death. As Menendez had displayed the legend: 'I do this not as to Frenchmen but as to Lutherans', so de Gourgues burned onto a wooden board 'I do this not as to Spaniards or as to Marranos (converted Jews), but as to traitors, robbers and murderers.'

Le Moyne's pictures of Florida have been lost, except for one beautiful water-colour, found in 1901 in a château near Paris. From this single example, now in the New York Public Library, which represents the visit by Laudonnière to the column set up by the French on their first expedition (page 24), it can be seen that de Bry's translation to a copper plate is almost immaculately precise. It can be assumed that le Moyne's representations of the Timacua Indians, with whom the French had intimate and complex dealings, are accurate in detail; it is with these Indians that most of the pictures are concerned. Together with le Moyne's text they give a unique record of this now extinct people. Le Moyne undoubtedly produced, as de Bry claimed, 'a Historye doubtless so Rare, as I think the like has not been heard or seene'.

Pages 14–15 Map of Florida, from de Bry's *America*, Part II

The promontory of Florida, named the French Promontory

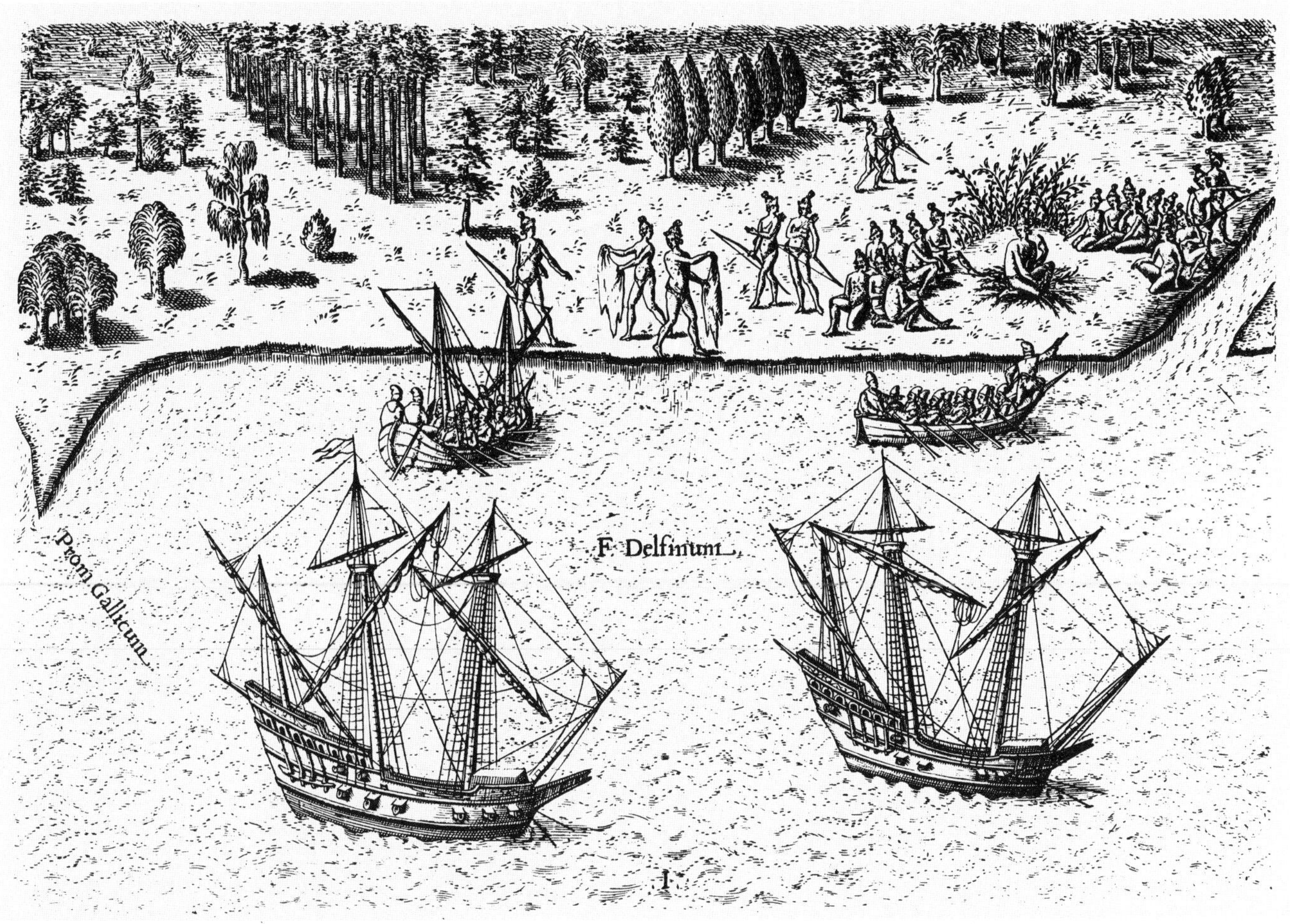

DURING their first voyage to Florida, the French landed near a well wooded headland, slightly raised from the surrounding flat coastline. In honour of France the commander of the fleet named this place, which is about thirty degrees from the equator, the French Cape. Coasting northward, they discovered a deep and beautiful river at whose mouth they cast anchor in order to examine it in more detail the next day. On his second expedition Laudonnière called it the river of Dolphins because he had seen large numbers swimming there. When they disembarked they saw many Indians coming to give them a kind and friendly welcome, even making them presents of the skins they wore. After accepting many gifts from the commander of the expedition the Indians brought them to their king, who had not risen up, but remained seated on branches of laurels and palms. This king made our captain a present of a large animal skin decorated all over with very lifelike drawings of animals of the forest.

The French sail up the river of May

RE-EMBARKING, the French sailed on further. As they came in to land they were greeted by another tribe of Indians, some of whom waded in the water up to their shoulders offering up little baskets of maize full of red and white mulberries, while others offered to help them come ashore. Having landed, the Frenchmen saw the Indian chief, who was accompanied by his two sons and a company of his men armed with bows and quivers of arrows. After exchanging greetings our men proceeded into the forest hoping to discover many wonderful things. But they saw nothing except for some trees bearing red and white mulberries whose tops were covered with innumerable silk worms. The French named this river the May, because they sighted it on the first day of that month.

Leaving the river of May the French discover two other rivers

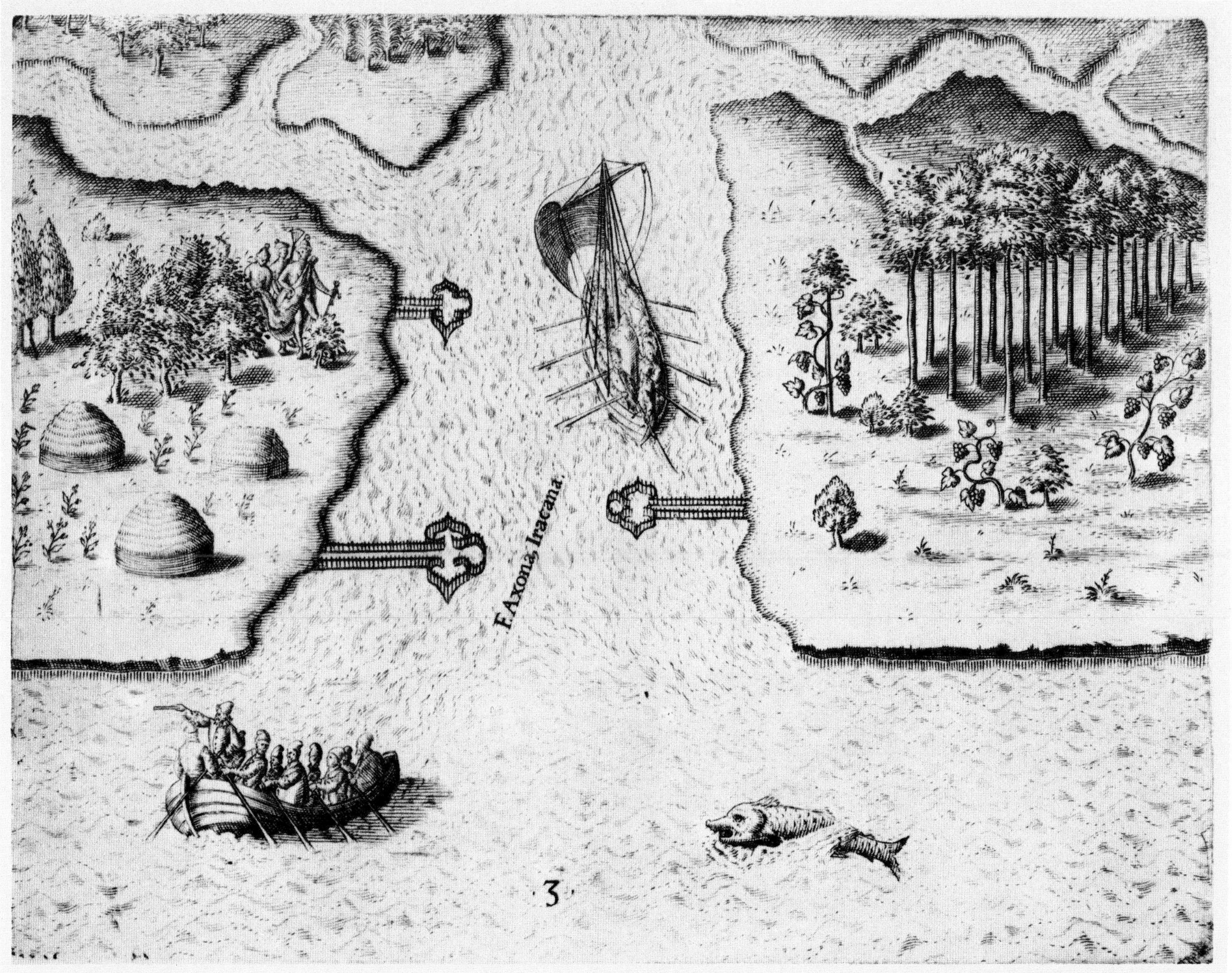

THEY returned on board and having raised anchor navigated along the coast until they came to a beautiful river which the commander himself wished to explore with the chief of that vicinity and some of the natives. Captain Ribaut named it the Seine because it was like the river in France. It is about fourteen leagues from the river of May. Having re-embarked they continued sailing towards the north, but not far away they discovered another river just as pretty and sent off two boats to explore it. In it they found an island whose chief was no less friendly than the others. They named this river the Aisne (Axona). It is about six miles from the Seine.

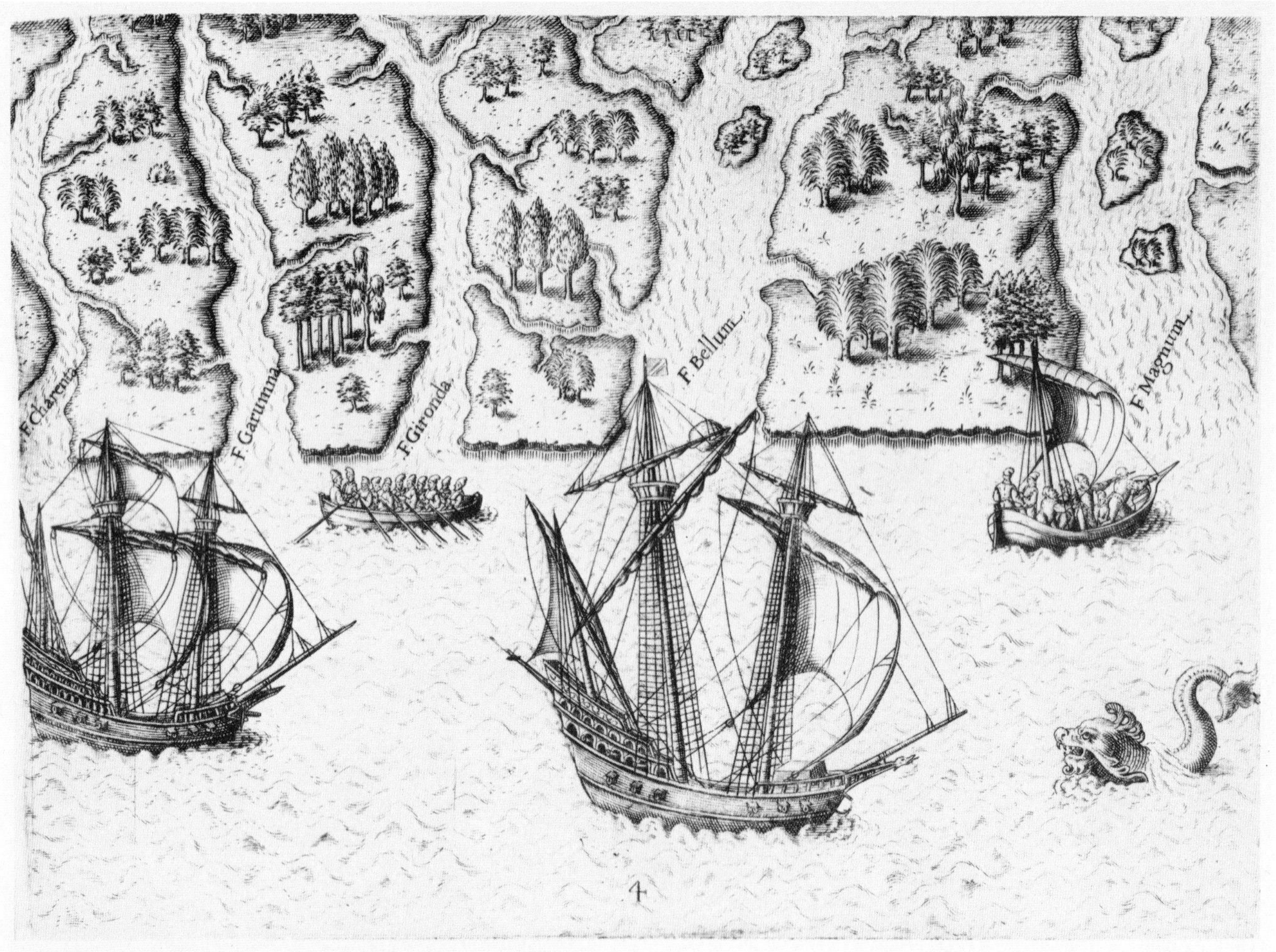

SAILING hence, about six miles further on they discovered another river which they called the Loire and subsequently five others, of which the first was named Charente, the second Garonne, the third Gironde, the fourth Belle, and the fifth Grande. After exploring them thoroughly they made many observations in an area of less than sixty miles, finding many singular things. However, not being content with that, they advanced further north, following the route which would lead them to the river Jordan, perhaps the most beautiful of all the seven rivers.

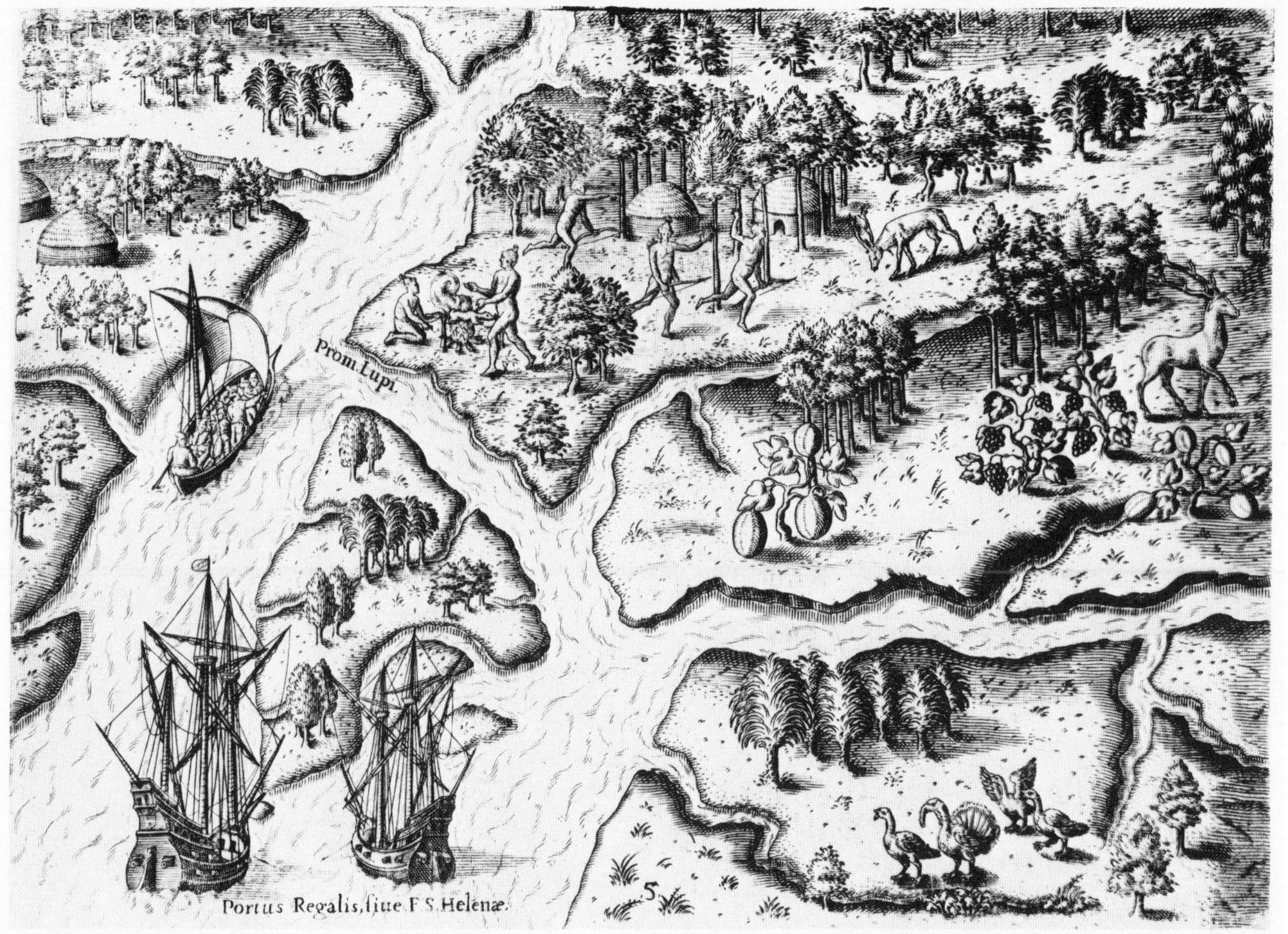

Resuming their route, the French found a river which they called Bellevue. Three or four miles further on they were told that there was another deep river not far away which surpassed all the others in size and beauty. When they reached it they found it so magnificent and great a stream that they called it Port Royal. Here they lowered the sail and dropped anchor at ten fathoms. The commander of the expedition and the soldiers that went ashore with him found it a very pleasant place, well wooded with oak, cedar and other types of tree As they walked in the forest they saw turkeys flying and stags wandering. The mouth of this river is three miles wide and splits into two arms, one towards the west and the other to the north. This latter (according to the opinion of some) penetrates deep into the interior towards the river Jordan. The other, as has been observed, throws itself westwards into the sea. Midway between the two branches is an island whose point faces the mouth of the river. The French re-embarked and took the northern branch in order to see what advantages it might have. After about twelve miles, they saw a company of Indians who, at the sight of the boats, fled, leaving behind a wolf's whelp which they were in the middle of eating. For this reason they called the place Wolf's Point. Sailing further, they came across another branch of the river, which came from the east. The commander decided to leave the main stream and continue along this other arm.

The captain of the French raises a column bearing the arms of the King of France

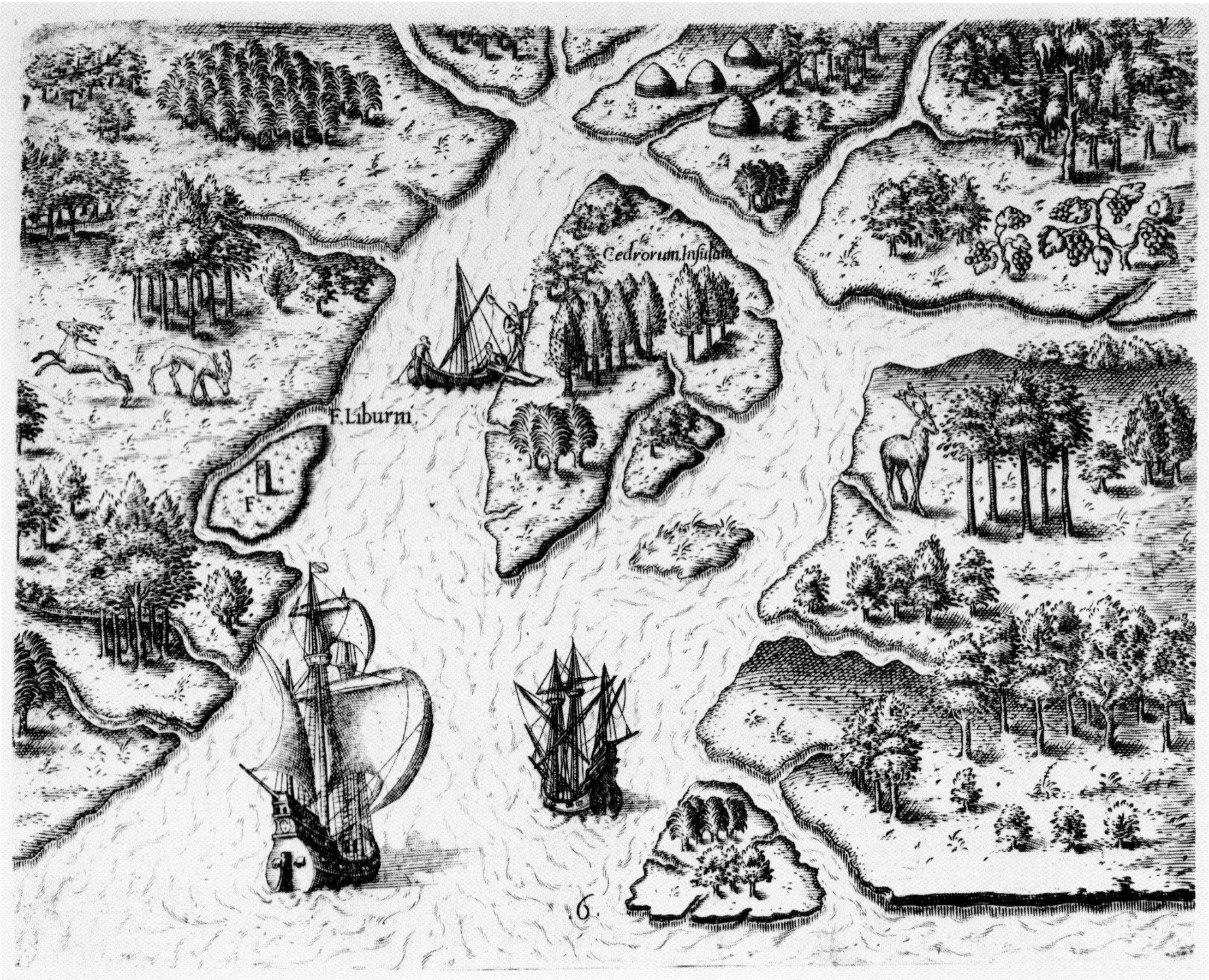

We returned on board and spent the night there. The captain of the expedition had the arms of the King of France engraved on a column and ordered it to be loaded on a small boat, ready to be erected in some pleasant and well chosen spot. The French sailed on three miles further where they noticed a small stream, and continued until they saw that this little creek joined the bigger one, thus forming a small island. They disembarked and finding it a pleasant place, the commander ordered the column to be placed on a bare mound. They saw two stags of a gigantic size, larger than any they had seen before. They could easily have killed them with their arquebuses, but the captain, who was impressed by their extraordinary size, forbade it. Before re-embarking they gave the river that surrounded this little island the name of Libourne. They continued their explorations on another island, not far from the first. Here they discovered some very high cedars, taller than they had seen anywhere else in this region, so they called it the island of Cedars. They then returned aboard. The little island in which the column was erected is marked by a letter F in this engraving.

The French left in Charlesfort suffer from a scarcity of provisions

NOT long after Captain Ribaut's departure from Florida, the French whom he left at Charlesfort began to suffer from lack of provisions. After considering how best to overcome this, they decided the best plan would be to turn for help to King Ovadé and his brother Covexis. They delegated a certain number among themselves to go off in an Indian canoe. After travelling about ten miles they discovered a beautiful river of fresh water where they noticed numerous crocodiles, much larger than those of the Nile. The banks of this river were covered with lofty cypresses. After a short stop they continued further and found Chief Ovadé who received them with great kindness. They explained their predicament to him and begged him not to abandon them in their need. Chief Ovadé was friendly and understanding and sent to his brother, requesting beans and maize. Covexis responded promptly and Ovadé's messengers, on their return next morning, carried the provisions to the boat. The French, grateful for the king's generosity, wished to take leave of him but he would not allow it and detained them with him that day, entertaining them kindly. The next day he showed them his fields and said that they would not want for grain while his crop lasted. After leaving the king the French returned by the same way they had come.

The natives of Florida worship the column erected by Captain Ribaut

DURING the second voyage in Florida under Laudonnière's command, that leader went ashore with twenty-five arquebusiers. He was greeted by the Indians who had gathered in crowds to see the new arrivals. Their king, Athore, who lived five or six miles inland from there, welcomed them with great kindness and presented Laudonnière with gifts. He then gave the French to understand that he wished to show them something remarkable and begged them to follow him. They agreed, but seeing how many natives surrounded them, proceeded with caution. He conducted them to the island where Ribaut had erected on a hillock the stone column engraved with the arms of the king of France. On approaching the French saw the Indians worshipping the stone as an idol. The chief, having saluted it with the respect that his subjects were used to accord him, kissed it and the other Indians then did likewise. Afterwards the French were encouraged to do the same. Before the monument lay baskets filled with the country's fruit, vases full of perfumed oils, roots both edible and medicinal, and a bow and arrows. From top to bottom the stone was wreathed with flowers of all kinds and branches of the rarest trees. After watching the rituals of these wretched barbarians, the French rejoined their companions in looking for the most suitable place to build a small fort. The king, Athore, is a handsome man, wise, honourable and strong, more than half a foot taller than even the tallest of our men. His modest gravity lends majesty to his already noble bearing. He married his mother and had by her several children of both sexes whom he proudly introduced to us, striking his thigh as he did so. It might be added that after he married his mother his father, Satourioua, ceased to live with her.

The French select a place to build a fort

HAVING explored the numerous rivers of this region, it was decided that it would be better to build on the river of May than on any other. It had, in fact, been noticed that millet and maize were more abundant there than elsewhere, and besides, gold and silver had been found there during the first voyage. The French went, therefore, to this river and while sailing upstream they arrived at a place, close to a mountain, which seemed to them, of all the places they had seen up till then, the most fitting for the establishment of a fort. The next day, at sunrise, they prayed to God and gave thanks for their fortunate arrival in this province and they all went to work with a will. The outline of a triangle was measured on the ground and everyone got to work; some dug the soil, some put up wood fences, and others made entrenchments. Each person had his tool, spade, saw, axe, bill-hook and hatchet for cutting the trees and raising the fort. They put so much zeal into this work that it was finished in a short time.

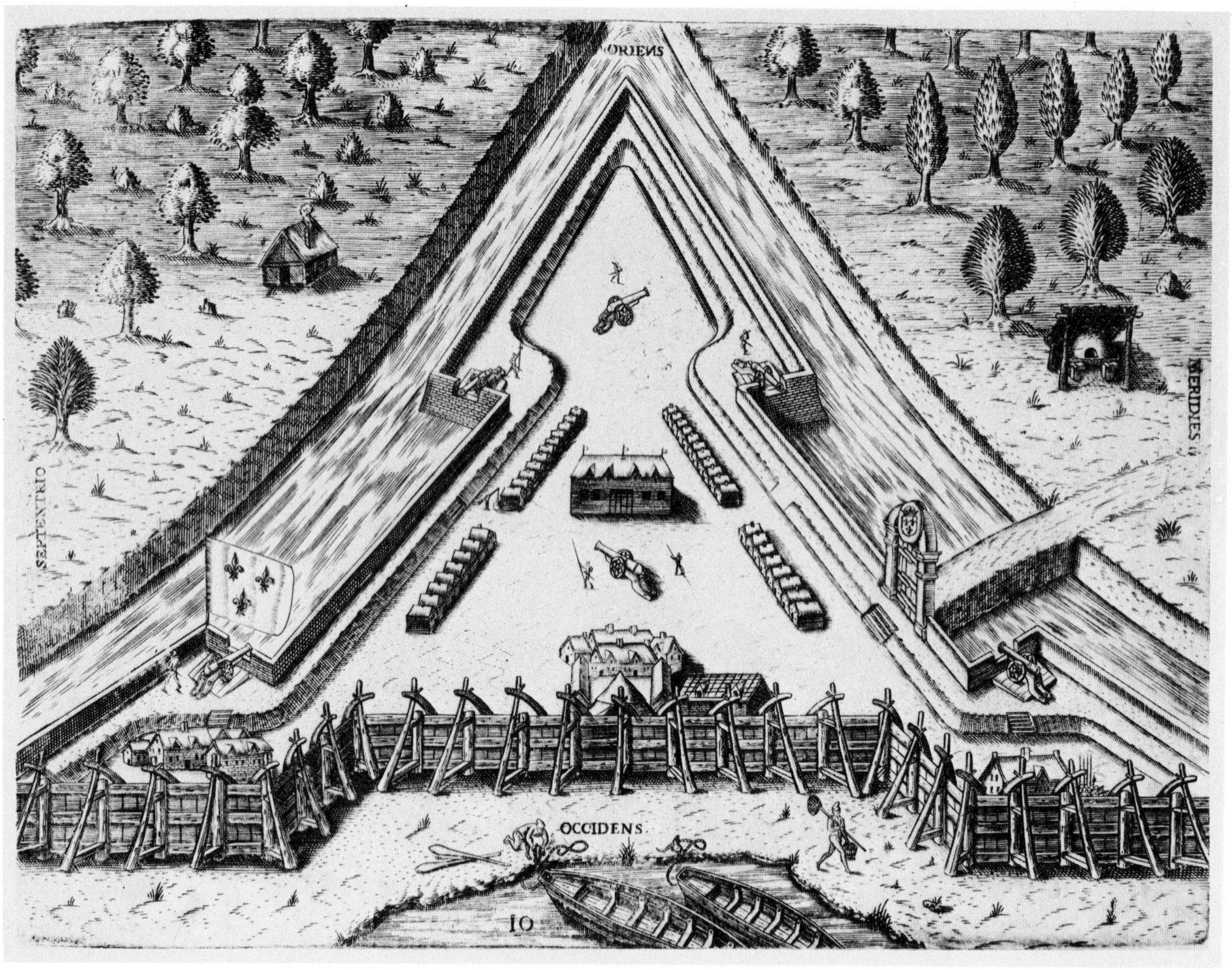

Erected in the shape of a triangle, the fort was afterwards named Caroline. The west side, facing the land, was closed by a small ditch and an entrenchment made of sods of earth nine feet high. The other side, facing the river, was surrounded by planks and brushwood. On the south front, like a citadel, a sort of granary was erected for provisions. For this construction branches and gravel were used except for the top part of the entrenchment which was made of sods of earth two or three feet high. In the middle of the fort lay a roomy courtyard, eighteen yards square and entirely level, which was the soldiers' place of assembly, their quarters being on the southern side. On the north side a construction was raised too high and in consequence soon collapsed in the wind. Thus, experience taught us that in this country, where winds are so furious, buildings must be made lower. There was also another quite spacious site, one of whose walls was contiguous to the granary, mentioned above, while opposite, overlooking the river, was Laudonnière's residence, surrounded on all sides by a gallery. The front door of this house opened onto the courtyard, the back door onto the river. To avoid fires, an oven was built at quite a distance from the fort because the houses, roofed with branches, would have caught fire very easily.

Ceremonies performed by Satourioua before setting off for war

It is reported in the account of the second expedition, that the French made a treaty of alliance and friendship with the powerful king of the vicinity called Satourioua, in order to be able to erect a fort on his territory. It was agreed that their friends and their enemies must be the same, and in time of need they must lend each other support. Now, about three months after this treaty was made the king sent to Laudonnière for arquebusiers as he wanted to make war on a neighbour. Laudonnière despatched Captain Caillot with several soldiers to him, telling the captain to say that at the moment he could not supply him with men because he hoped he would be able to make a reconciliation with this enemy. Indignant with this reply, the king decided to leave immediately (he could not defer his expedition because he had collected all the necessary provisions and summoned the neighbouring kings). So, in the presence of the soldiers sent by Laudonnière, he assembled his men, all decked out in feathers and other ornaments of Indian fashion, and they sat down in a circle around him. A log fire was lit at his left, and at his right two big vases of water were placed. As if seized by a violent anger, the king, rolling his eyes terribly, began making a deep throaty sound and then, gesticulating wildly, let out some horrible cries which his soldiers repeated, striking their hips and rattling their weapons. Next, the king took a wooden bowl full of water and turning towards the sun worshipped it and asked it for victory over his enemies; that he might spill their blood as he was going to spill the water with which he had filled his bowl. With a quick movement he threw the water in the air and as it fell upon his soldiers he cried out 'May you do with my enemies' blood the same as I have just done with this water.' The water from the second bowl was thrown in the fire and the king cried out 'May you thus extinguish my enemies and return with their scalps.' Then they got up and set off on their expedition.

At the beginning of a campaign Outina consults his sorcerer

LAUDONNIERE sent several Indian prisoners back to their king, Outina, who lived about forty miles south of the French fort. These men had been captured by Satourioua during the previous expedition. As a result of the French action a solemn treaty was concluded with Outina and reciprocal friendship promised. The reason for the French wanting this treaty was that this king's territory could offer access, both by land and by river, to the Appalachian mountains where gold, silver and copper was found. Having the friendship of this king (which scarcely lasted a year), the French could easily reach these mountains. Under the terms of this alliance he asked Laudonnière for a few arquebusiers to help him to make war on his enemy. He was sent twenty-five men under the command of Ottigny. He received them with great pleasure, counting on victory because of their co-operation, for the fame of their weapons had spread into the neighbouring countries and inspired terror. Now the king was ready and they departed. On the first day the going was easy, on the second more difficult, across swampy ground, covered with thorny scrub. The Indians carried the French on their shoulders which was a great relief to them in the strong heat. At last they arrived at the frontier. The king then halted his army and called an ancient magician who was more than a hundred years old, bidding him reveal the enemies' dispositions. The magician cleared a space in the middle of the army and on seeing Ottigny, he asked for the shield his page was brandishing. This he put on the ground and drawing a circle of five feet diameter around it, he inscribed some letters and signs in the circle. Kneeling with his heels on the shield, he sat in such a way that he was not touching the ground anywhere. Mumbling unintelligibly, he gesticulated as if he was engaged in a vehement discourse. After a quarter of an hour he looked so terrifying that his face no longer seemed human. He contorted himself until his bones could be heard cracking and he did many other things besides that were most unnatural. At last, exhausted and as if confused, he resumed his original aspect. Then he left the circle, saluted the king and informed him of the number of enemies and in which place they were awaiting him.

Thanks to the French Outina gains a victory over his enemy Potanou

So frightened was the chief by the sorcerer's words, that he no longer thought of attacking, but rather of how he might return home safely. However, Ottigny, indignant at having gone to such trouble without results, told him he would take him for a lowborn man and not a king if he did not dare risk his luck. At length these threats and insults forced him to attack. With their consent, he put the French in the front line, and indeed it is certain that had they not sustained the whole brunt of the battle and massacred so many of the enemy, causing King Potanou's army to flee, Outina would have been beaten. The magician was surely inspired by a spirit, for all he predicted was correct. Outina, content with the flight of his enemy, recalled his men and ordered them to return home, much to the irritation of Ottigny, who would have preferred to follow up his victory.

The military discipline observed by Outina when leaving for war

When King Satourioua left for war, his soldiers advanced in no particular order, scattered on all sides. On the other hand his enemy Olata Outina, of whom I have already spoken, and who is considered the king of kings, superior to all others in his number of subjects and his riches, marches with his troops in military formation. He goes alone in the middle of his ranks, painted red. The wings of the army, in the order of march, are composed of young men, the fittest of whom, also painted red, are used as runners and scouts to reconnoitre the enemy troops. Like dogs after wild beasts, they hunt the enemy by scent, and when they find traces of them they run back to their army to report. In the same way that our soldiers pass orders by trumpets and drums, they use heralds who have certain cries for when to halt, or to advance, or to attack or make some other manoeuvre. They stop at sunset and never fight at night. When they set up camp, they divide up into squads of ten, the bravest apart. The king chooses a place in the fields or in the forest to pass the night and after he has eaten and gone to rest the masters of the camp place ten squads of the bravest men in a circle around him. About ten yards away some twenty other squads form another circle around the first. Twenty yards further away there is another circle of forty and this formation continues enlarging according to the size of the army.

How Outina's soldiers treated their slain enemies

DURING all the time that the French had dealings with the great chief Olata Outina in the war against his enemies, no pitched battle was fought. It all happened in ambushes and skirmishes, fresh troops constantly replacing those who retired. Whoever put the enemy to flight first was credited with victory, even when the number of his losses was very large. In these skirmishes those who fall are immediately dragged off by men especially charged with this duty. With a sliver of reed, sharper than any steel blade, they cut the skin with the hair from the skull all the way round, the longest hairs being twisted into a plait, the hair from the forehead being rolled up for the length of two fingers with that of the back of the head in the manner of the ribbon of a bonnet. Immediately afterwards (if they have time), they dig a hole where they make a fire of smouldering moss which they carry around in their leather breechclouts. The fire lit, they dry the scalp until it becomes hard like parchment. At the end of the battle, they are accustomed to cut the arms of their victims off at the shoulder and their legs at the thighs. The bones laid bare are crushed and the pieces, still dripping with blood, are dried on the same fire. Then they return home triumphantly with the skin of the heads at the ends of their spears. What astonished me (for I was one of the men sent by Laudonnière under Ottigny's command), was that they never left the place of battle without piercing the mutilated corpses of their enemies right through the anus with an arrow. During this task a protective force always surrounded them.

R. Holata Outina.

Functions of the hermaphrodites

In this country there are numerous hermaphrodites, a mixture of both sexes. They are considered odious by the Indians, but as they are robust and strong they are used to carry loads instead of beasts of burden. When the kings set out to war, it is the hermaphrodites who transport the supplies. They place the Indians, dead from either wounds or sickness, on a stretcher made of two stout poles covered with a mat woven of thin canes. The head rests on a fur; a second fur is wound around the stomach; a third around the hips; a fourth is placed around the calves. (I did not ask the reason for this custom, but I suppose it is for show, for sometimes they do not do all this and simply bind one leg.) Next they take belts of leather, about three or four fingers wide and fix them at both ends of the poles and put them on their heads, which are very hard; then they carry their dead to the place of burial. Persons with infectious diseases are carried to places reserved for them on the shoulders of the hermaphrodites who supply them with food until they are well again.

The erection of trophies and the ceremonies intended to celebrate the defeat of the enemy *see previous page*

On their return home from a military expedition they reunite in a place selected for that purpose. There they pile up the arms and legs and scalps of their enemies with solemn ceremony on rows of tall poles set in the ground. The men and women sit in a circle around the sorcerer who, clutching a small image, mutters a thousand imprecations, cursing the enemy. Over on the far side three men are kneeling. One of them, holding a club in both hands, strikes a flat stone, as if in time to the words of the sorcerer. On his left and on his right two other men are seated. They hold in their hands the fruit of a certain plant which grows like a gourd or melon. This fruit has been pierced at both ends, hollowed out and dried. The Indians fill this container with small stones or seeds; they attach a stick handle and shake it to make a noise like hand-bells. All this is accompanied by chanting in the national manner. These ceremonies are celebrated each time they take prisoners.

Petitions addressed to the king by the wives whose husbands have died

THE women whose husbands have succumbed in battle or have died from illness have the custom of assembling on a day that seems to them most suitable to appear before their king. They approach him, overcome with grief, sit down on their heels, and covering their faces with their hands, they cry out and moan. They ask the king to avenge their dead husbands, to provide them with means to live during their widowhood and to permit them to remarry after the time laid down by law. The king, taking pity on them, grants their requests. They return home, weeping and wailing, as proof of the love they felt for their husbands. After having spent several days in mourning they carry their husbands' weapons and drinking cups to their tombs, then they start to weep again and celebrate other funereal ceremonies.

Ceremonies of the women in mourning for their husbands

AFTER arriving at their husbands' burial place, in memory of these brave men they cut their hair below their ears and scatter it on the graves where they have already thrown their husbands' shell drinking-cups and weapons. Then they return home, but are forbidden to remarry until their hair has regrown long enough to cover their shoulders. They also let their toe and finger nails grow, filing the sides to make them pointed. But it is above all the men who practise this custom. Whenever they can grab hold of an enemy, they sink their nails deep into his forehead and tear the skin, leaving him blinded and bloody.

How the Indians cure their sick

As can be seen from this engraving, the Indians make a long wide platform where they lay the sick person, with his face up or down according to his complaint. With the help of a pointed instrument, a hole is made in the forehead from where blood is sucked through the mouth and spat into an earthen vessel or gourd bottle. Women who are suckling boys or who are with child or suffering from some disease come and drink this blood, especially when it is that of a strong young man, so that it may improve their milk and make their offspring stronger and more energetic. To others, lying face down, they administer fumigations by throwing certain seeds on the fire. The smoke, entering by the mouth and nose, circulates the entire body and induces vomiting and so expels the cause of the sickness. The Indians possess a certain plant whose name is *petum* in Brazil and which the Spanish call *tapaco*. The dried leaves of this plant are put in the widest part of a pipe. The Indians set it on fire and inhale the smoke so deeply from the narrowest part of the pipe that it comes out through the mouth and nose at the same time dispelling the humors. They are also extremely subject to venereal diseases, to cure which they have special remedies provided by nature.

Cultivation and sowing

The Indians cultivate the earth with diligence. They have learnt to make hoes with fish bones and to fit them with wooden handles. With these they can dig the soil quite easily as it is not heavy. Once the earth has been well broken up and levelled, the women sow beans or millet or maize. To do this they are helped by people who precede them with a stick, and make holes in the soil where the grain or bean or millet is thrown. The sowing completed, they leave the field alone. It is, in fact, then their winter season which is quite cold in this region and which lasts three months, from 24 December to 15 March. Being always naked, the Indians then seek shelter in the forests. The winter over, they return to their houses, anticipating the ripening of the crops. The harvest gathered, they store the corn for the year's use, and do not trade with any of it except perhaps for some exchange of household articles.

The industry of the Floridians in storing the products of the harvest

THERE are in this country many islands that produce an abundance of various fruits which they harvest twice a year. These fruits the Indians take home in boats. Then they stack them up in storehouses which are simple yet large and built of mud and small stones. They are roofed with thick branches and soft earth, suitable for this purpose. Usually these storehouses are built under a hill or rock close to a river. In order to prevent the fruit from rotting, the sun's rays must not penetrate the building. Apart from the fruit, the Indians put there other food that they wish to keep. They go and take it whenever they need it without any disagreement among themselves. It could be wished that such a lack of avarice prevailed among Christians and then their minds would be less tormented.

Bringing in game, fish and other provisions

AT a certain time of year the Indians collect all kinds of game, fish and even crocodiles. Baskets are filled with these creatures and put on the shoulders of curly-haired hermaphrodites whom we have already described. All this is taken to storehouses where it is not touched except in cases of extreme need, when, to avoid disputes, the Indians come to an agreement among themselves, which illustrates the harmony that exists among them. However, the king is at liberty to take what he chooses.

Mode of drying fish, game and other provisions

In order to preserve the flesh of animals, they prepare them in the following way: four strong forked stakes are planted in the ground over which are laid more sticks, forming a grating to take the animals and fish. A fire is lit underneath in such a way that the meat may be dried by the smoke. As the picture shows, the Indians take great care with this procedure so that the provisions do not spoil. I suppose that they prepare all this for the winter months when they are in the forests since at this time we were never able to obtain anything from them. As we have said before, the storehouse is on a rock or some shelter, near a river and not far from a big forest so that they can take provisions there in canoes whenever necessary.

Stag hunting

NOWHERE have we seen stag hunting as the Indians do it. They put themselves inside the skins of the largest stags they have been able to kill, so that their heads are in those of the animals. As with a mask they see out through the holes of the eyes. Thus dressed they can approach the deer closely without frightening them. Beforehand they find out the time when the animals come to the river to drink. Bow and arrow to hand, it is easy for them to aim, especially since stags are numerous in this country. Experience has taught them to protect their left arm with a piece of bark to avoid being hurt by the string of the bow. They know how to prepare the skins in a wonderful way, without iron instruments, using shells. In my opinion, no one in Europe could rival their skill.

The Indians' method of killing crocodiles is as follows: on the edge of a river they erect a small hut, full of holes and slits, where a watchman is stationed so that he is able to see and hear the crocodiles from afar. These creatures, driven by hunger, climb up out of the rivers and crawl about on the islands in search of prey. When they find none they make such a ghastly noise that it can be heard half a mile away. At this moment the watchman calls the hunters who are in readiness. Grasping a pointed tree trunk ten or twelve feet long, they advance towards the animal, who usually crawls along with open mouth, and when he opens his mouth they quickly plunge the thinnest part of the pole into it in such a way that he cannot get it out because of the roughness and irregularity of the bark. Turning the crocodile over, they then pound and pierce his belly, which is the softest part of his body, with blows from clubs and arrows. The backs of these animals, particularly those of the old ones, are impenetrable, covered as they are with hard scales. Such is the Indians' method of hunting crocodile. These animals trouble them so much that they have to keep a watch against them at night and sometimes even in the day, as if they were guarding against some dreadful enemy.

The Indians' amusements when they cross to the islands

As can be seen from the preceding illustrations, this area abounds with very agreeable little islands. The rivers are not deep; the pure, clear water scarcely reaches the chest. When the Indians want to make an enjoyable excursion with their wives and children, they go to these islands. They either swim across the river (for they are excellent swimmers) or they wade across carrying the little children. In fact the mothers can manage three children at once, the smallest on a shoulder clutching its hand, and the other two under her arms. With the free hand, the women carry a basket full of fruit or other food for the occasion. For fear of meeting enemies the men carry bows and arrows. In order not to wet them, they attach the quiver to their hair and hold their bows stretched and ready with an arrow, prepared instantly to defend themselves, as can be seen in our engraving.

Preparations for a feast

AT a certain time of the year, the Indians are accustomed to celebrate feasts among themselves, and for this purpose they have specially chosen cooks. They begin by putting a large, round, clay pot (so well made that water can boil in it just as well as in our vessels) on some logs which they light, while one of them holds a fan to encourage the flames. The chief cook throws what has to be cooked into the great pot; others pour water which has been brought to them in a vessel shaped like a bucket into a hole for washing; another uses a flat stone to crush the herbs to season the food; and meanwhile women are busy sorting out what is necessary for the cooking. In spite of these great feasts the Indians are very moderate in their eating, thanks to which they live to a great age. One of their chiefs asserted to me that he was three hundred years old and that his father, whom he pointed out to me, was fifty years older than he. It is true to say that on looking at him, he seemed all skin and bones. The Indians put us Christians to shame, for we, by over-indulgence in food and drink, shorten our lives considerably. We should attend the Barbarian school in order to learn temperance.

How the Floridians deliberate on important matters

On certain days of the year the king usually assembles with his nobles in a place specially prepared for this. There, there is a large bench constructed in a semi-circle with a projection made of nine tree trunks in the centre, which serves as the throne of the king. He sits here, all alone, so he can look distinguished and the others come, in turn, to salute him. First the oldest make their obeisances, by twice raising their hands to their head and saying *'Ha, he, ya, ha, he'* to which the others reply, *'ha, ha.'* After saluting the king, everyone goes and sits down on the bench. If any question of importance is to be discussed, the chief calls first upon the *jawas* (that is, the priests) and upon the elders to each give their opinion. The Indians, in fact, never make any decisions without first having listened to all the various opinions and discussed them. Then the king orders the women to prepare some *casina* which is a beverage made from the leaves of a certain plant passed through a strainer. Then, an Indian, stretching out his arms, says some prayers to the king and those who are going to partake of this hot drink, which is then passed round in a big shell, first to the king and afterwards, in strict order of protocol, to the others. This drink is so highly esteemed, that no one is allowed to drink it in council unless he has proved his courage in battle. Moreover it causes sweating almost immediately after it has been swallowed. Also those who cannot keep it down and throw it up are never confided with any difficult task or military responsibility, being considered useless; for on campaigns the Indians often have to go three or four days without food, but having once managed to drink this liquor, it is possible to go twenty-four hours afterwards without food or drink. When setting out on an expedition, the hermaphrodites carry nothing but this drink, contained in gourds or wooden receptacles. This is because *casina* nourishes and fortifies the body without causing drunkenness, as we have observed on occasions.

How the Floridians construct their fortified towns

THIS is how the Indians construct their towns: they choose a place near a swift stream and level it as much as possible. Next they make a circular ditch and fix in the ground, very close together, thick round palings the height of two men. At the town's entrance they make the opening of the circle narrower, in the form of a spiral so that this entrance does not admit more than two men abreast at a time. The course of the stream is diverted to this point. At the beginning and end of this passage a round edifice is erected, full of holes and slits which, considering their means, are constructed very elegantly. In each, sentinels who are expert at smelling the enemy from afar are stationed. As soon as they detect the scent of the enemy, they rush out, shrieking, to find him. At this alarm the inhabitants of the town run out to defend their fortress, armed with bows and arrows and clubs. The king's dwelling is in the middle, and has been a little sunk into the ground to avoid the sun's heat. All around it are grouped the nobles' houses, lightly constructed and roofed with palm branches. As has been mentioned earlier, they only spend nine months of the year here, emigrating to the forest for the rest of the time. They make new houses with the same materials, if, on their return, they find they have been burnt down by the enemy. Thus magnificent are the palaces of the Indians.

How they destroy the enemy's towns during the night

BURNING with revenge, the enemy will sometimes creep up at night, as silently as possible, to see if the sentinels are asleep. If they hear nothing, they approach the town. The points of their arrows are already trimmed with dry moss which they set alight and then shoot the arrows at the roofs of the houses which are made of branches, dried out by the heat of the summer. When they see the roofs in flames, they quickly withdraw, before the inhabitants have noticed anything. They run so fast that it is difficult to catch them. In any case the people in the town have enough to do trying to extinguish the fire and make it easy for the incendiaries to escape. Such is the strategy used by the Indians to destroy a town of an enemy. The loss is not very great, though, because the construction of new houses merely requires some extra work.

Punishments inflicted on negligent sentinels

WHEN a town is burnt due to the negligence of the sentinels, they are punished in the following manner: the chief is seated alone on his chair with the most senior Indians sitting on a semi-circular bench and the executioner forces the guilty men to kneel down before them. Taking a club of ebony or some other hard wood filed to an edge on both sides, he puts his left foot on their backs and strikes them such a blow with both hands on the club that he almost splits their skulls in two. This same penalty is meted out to any who are accused of what is considered to be a capital offence. We were, in fact, present at two such executions.

How the Indians declare war

WHEN a king wishes to declare war on his enemy, he does not send heralds to announce his intentions. He orders arrows with locks of hair attached to the notches to be stuck along the public ways. We observed this practice when we conducted King Outina, as a prisoner, through villages that he governed, to make them supply us with provisions. These arrows were later carried back to the fort by Ottigny.

First-born children sacrificed with solemn ceremonies

THE Indian custom is to offer as a sacrifice to their chief, their first-born son. On the appointed day the chief goes to a place specially assigned for the purpose and there sits down on a bench. In the middle of this area there is a tree trunk which is two feet high. The mother of the child squats in front of this, her face covered by her hands, lamenting the death of her first-born. The most distinguished of her relations or friends offers the child respectfully to the king. The women who have accompanied the mother sit in a circle, then they get up and dance and sing joyously, without joining hands. The one who holds the baby goes into the middle of the dancing women, also dancing and singing praises. On another side of the place six specially chosen Indians are standing round the sacrificer, who is magnificently decorated and solemnly holds a club. When the ceremonies are over, he seizes the child and, in honour of the chief, slays it on the wooden stump, in the presence of the assembled company. We saw this sacrifice carried out.

The solemn consecration of the skin of a stag to the sun

EVERY year, a little before spring, that is to say at the end of February, King Outina's subjects take the skin of the largest stag they have been able to capture. Leaving on its antlers, they stuff this skin full of the most delicate plants which grow there and sew it up. At the antlers, the neck and the stomach they hang the best of their fruit, made into wreaths or garlands. Thus decorated, this effigy is carried to the sound of flutes and harmonious songs, to a special place, large and level. Here it is put on a high tree with its head and breast facing the rising sun. Then the Indians say prayers to the sun so that it will give them again good fruit similar to the ones offered to it. The king and his sorcerer stand near the tree singing chants to which the people, standing apart, make the responses. Then the king and all his retinue salute the sun and depart, leaving the deer's hide where it is until the following year. They repeat this ceremony annually.

The exercises of the youth

THE young are trained at running. He who runs the longest without stopping receives a prize chosen by the competitors themselves. They also frequently practise with the bow. They have a ball game they plays as follows: in the middle of an open space they set up a tree trunk eight or nine fathoms high, and at the top they fix a sort of hurdle. He who manages to hit it is declared the winner. They also enjoy hunting and fishing.

The pomp with which the queen-elect is brought to the king

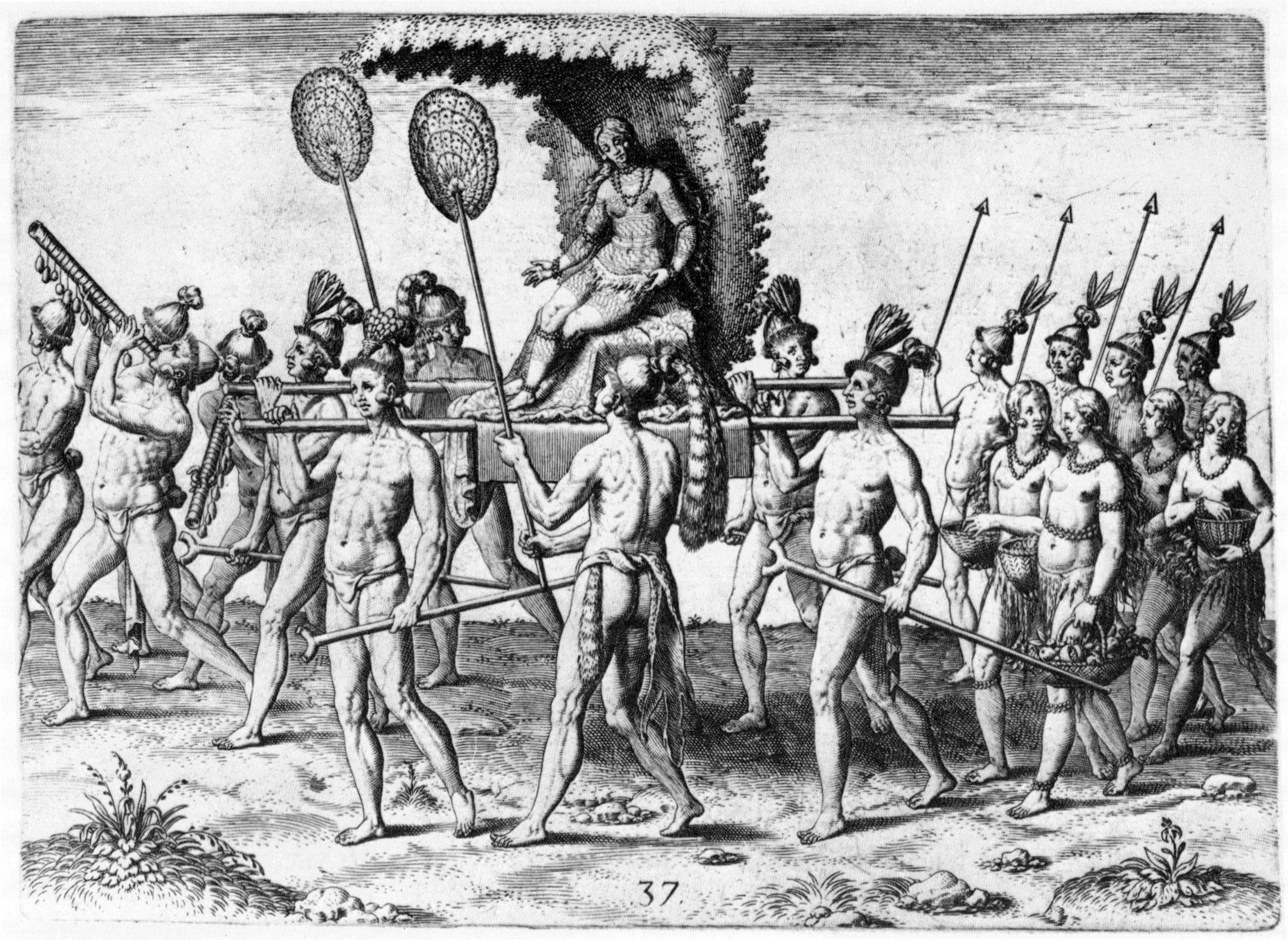

When the king wishes to get married, he orders the most beautiful and the tallest girl from among the most noble families to be chosen. Then a seat is fixed on two stout poles and covered with the skin of some rare animals. Behind the seat a structure of branches is made so as to shade the head of the sitter. The queen-elect is put on this chair and four strong men take up the poles and carry them on their shoulders. They each carry a wooden fork on which to put the poles when they halt. On each side of the queen walk two men waving elegant fans, attached on long handles, to protect her from the ardors of the sun. Other men go before, blowing trumpets made of tree bark. These instruments have only two holes, one at the top and one at the bottom; they are narrower at the mouth end than at the other end. Hanging from them are oval balls of gold, silver and copper which are designed to make a very harmonious sound as they knock against each other. Then follow the most beautiful of the young girls, all decked out with necklaces and bracelets of pearls. Each carries a basket full of the choicest fruit. For the sake of decency they hang moss from their navel to their thighs. After them come the bodyguards.

The solemn reception of the queen by the king

IT is with great pomp that the queen is led to the king in a place specially designed for that purpose. There a large platform made of logs has been erected, and on each side of it are benches for the nobles. Seated on the right, the king welcomes the queen who takes her place on his left, and he tells her the reasons he has chosen her to be his wife. The queen, a fan in her hand and full of majestic reserve, answers the king as graciously as her education has taught her. Next the young girls, now wearing a different costume, form a circle without touching each other. Their hair floats over their shoulders and down their backs, a wide belt encircles their hips and a sort of purse hides their intimate parts; pendants of gold and silver are attached to their belts and tinkle when the girls dance and sing the praises of their king and queen. When one of them raises her hand the others copy her, they do likewise when she lowers it. Men and women have the ends of their ears pierced in which they put little inflated fish bladders, bright as pearls, painted red and looking like carbuncles. It is astonishing that such savage people should have created such tasteful devices.

SOMETIMES, in the evening the king goes for a walk in the neighbouring forest with his first wife. He wears a stag skin, most elegantly prepared and painted in incomparable colours. At his sides two youths wave fans to make a breeze for him; a third, his belt ornamented with little gold and silver balls, holds the king's robes up to prevent them touching the ground. The queen and her handmaidens wear a kind of moss that grows on trees falling from their shoulders. This moss is interlaced into delicate tresses which make chains of an azur blue; they are so pretty that one would say they were filaments of silk. The trees that have this moss look very beautiful for it often falls from their tops right down to the ground. We have often seen it while on hunting expeditions with our companions in the forests near where Satourioua lives and I saw him and his Queen thus decorated. All these chiefs and their wives have their bodies pricked with certain pictures which sometimes make them ill for seven or eight days. They rub the pricked places with a special herb whose sap gives an indelible stain. They believe they embellish themselves by letting their finger and toe nails grow and by filing them with a shell into sharp points. They also outline their mouths in azur blue paint.

Funeral ceremonies in honour of kings and priests

WHEN a chief from that country dies, he is buried with great solemnity. The cup from which he used to drink is placed on his tomb which is surrounded by arrows stuck in the ground. His subjects mourn him for three days and three nights without eating or drinking. All his friends do the same, and in testimony of the affection they held for the deceased, both men and women cut off more than half their hair. During the next six moons, women specially chosen for the task lament the death of their king at dawn, midday and twilight with great howls. All the king's personal property is carried to his house where it is burnt. They do the same thing for priests.

How gold is collected in the rivers running from the Appalachian mountains

SOME considerable distance from the place where we have constructed our fort, rise some high mountains called Apalatcy in the Indian tongue. As can be seen from our map, these mountains give birth to three rivers in whose sand there is much gold, silver and copper. The natives dig trenches near the banks of the rivers so as to catch the sand brought down by the current. The water rapidly fills these up and goes on further. A short time later the Indians remove the sand which has gathered there with hollow reeds and convey it by canoe down the great river which runs into the sea and which we named the river of May. The Spaniards have taken great advantages of the riches coming from these places.

The murder of the Frenchman, Pierre Gambié

We have spoken in our account of a certain Pierre Gambié, a delegate of Laudonnière. In carrying his merchandise across the country to sell it, he had traded so honestly that not only had he enriched himself but he had also married into the family of one of the kings of the region. This king allowed him to leave to pay us a visit on condition that he returned after a certain number of moons. He gave him a canoe and two Indians to accompany him. Thus he embarked with his riches, but his travelling companions slew him while he was poking the fire. They had two motives for this: the first was revenge (Gambié, who during the king's absence was managing his affairs, had killed one of their tribe by hitting him with a stick); and the second was greed. Having seized the riches stored in the boat, they fled and the deed remained unknown for a a long time. This picture has been put in at the end so as not to disturb the order of the preceding series. We would not have reproduced it had not the author of this narrative recalled the event.

2

The First English in Virginia 1584–8

'I marvel not a little,' wrote Richard Hakluyt, arch-promoter of Elizabethan expansion, 'that since the first discovery of America (which is now full fourscore-and-ten years), after so great a conquest and plantings of the Spaniards and Portugals there, that we of England could never have the grace to set fast footing in such fertile and temperate places as are left as yet unpossessed by them'. While the Spaniards and Portuguese were enjoying the immense wealth of the Pope's arbitrary allocation of America, the excluded Elizabethans, many of whom felt like Hakluyt, had to make do with the crumbs of piracy and half-hearted excursions into the intemperate and unprofitable north lands. England had made her first expedition across the Atlantic in 1497 when Henry VII sent John Cabot to search, like Columbus, for the 'land of the Great Khan'. Seeking a 'northwest passage', he sailed halfway down the coast of North America, possibly as far as Chesapeake Bay, before he turned for home. By virtue of his voyage the English pretended to themselves that they had a claim to all America north of Carolina, but fifty years later their only successful land settlement, won by the sword, was in Ireland. And yet Frobisher, Gilbert, Hawkins, Grenville, Drake and Raleigh showed that England could provide the captains; the merchants of London and Bristol had the cash; Queen Elizabeth was anxious to encourage with patronage and letters patent; and there were plenty of her impoverished or dissident subjects looking for opportunities abroad. Even the French, having abandoned their colony in Brazil under Villegagnon, were now consolidating their place in the sun – Florida.

As has been outlined in the previous section the French captain, Jean Ribaut, arrived in London in 1563, a refugee from the religious wars. The publication of his book *The Whole and True discoverye of Terra Florida* in May of that year, with its honeyed descriptions of fertile lands, game-filled forests and tractable natives, not to mention hints of pearls and precious metals, acted as catalyst to English aspirations. Thomas Stukeley, one of the most irrepressible and irresponsible of Elizabethan adventurers, plotted with Ribaut and the great at court to take over Florida in the name of the Queen. Ribaut defected on the day of sailing and Stukeley's fleet took to piracy. But this fiasco and the subsequent annihilation of the French of Fort Caroline, did not dampen England's American ambitions. Sir Humphrey Gilbert, scourge of Ireland, was the new champion of colonialism. The publication of his *A Discourse of a Discoverie for a New Passage to Cataia* (1576) had marked him as a man with a mission; and in 1578 Queen Elizabeth, in diplomatic phraseology designed to accomodate the Spaniards, authorized him to 'inhabit and possess at his choice all remote and heathen lands not in actual possession of any Christian prince or people'. But Gilbert's powerful fleet, like Stukeley's, showed more interest in the immediate profits of piracy and an Atlantic crossing was never made. He tried again in 1580, sending out the renegade Portuguese pilot Simon Fernandez to investigate the north American coast in the *Squirrel*. Fernandez, who had become a Protestant and married in England, returned with nothing more valuable than a buffalo hide. Three years later Gilbert assembled a more practical expedition, complete with artisans and artefacts such as 'toys, hoby horses, and Maylike conceits to delight the Savage people'. They sailed the northern route, gratuitously taking possession of the international fishing base at St Johns, Newfoundland. But the warmer land they sought hid behind banks of cloud and contrary winds; the fleet turned back, and Gilbert went down in the tiny *Squirrel* off the Azores.

'The time approacheth and now is', Hakluyt wrote in 1582, 'that we of England may share and part stakes (if we will ourselves) both with the Spaniard and with the Portugal in part of America and other regions as yet undiscovered.' Basing his fanciful case on the discovery of America by the Welsh Prince Madoc in the twelfth century, he went even further by claiming that 'the Queen of England's title to all the West Indies, or at least to as much as is from Florida to the arctic circle, is more lawful and right than the Spaniards, or any other Christian Princes.' Hakluyt's hope for the future lay in Sir Walter Raleigh, Gilbert's brother-in-law, and next to put on the colonial mantle. Raleigh obtained a new patent in 1584 and, forbidden by the Queen to go himself, sent his excellent captains, Barlowe and Amadas, to make a reconnaissance. On 13 July their pilot, again Simon Fernandez, came upon the coast of North Carolina and after sailing along the Banks that Verrazano had taken to be an isthmus dividing Atlantic from Pacific, found a gap at Hatterask, opposite a small island called by the Indians Roanoke. They claimed the land in the name of Queen Elizabeth, unaware that they were not yet on the mainland. A string of sandy islands, a shallow harbourless sea, no hint of mineral riches; yet for Arthur Barlowe it might have been an earthly paradise. His account, which was published by Hakluyt, outdid even Ribaut's, telling of beaches covered with delicious grapes, woods filled with game, splendid timber and noble savages 'most gentle, loving, and faithful, void of all guile, and treason, such as lived after the manner of the golden age'; the soil, Barlowe claimed, was 'the most plentiful, sweete, fruitful and wholsome in all the worlde'. The English met the aimiable chief of the place, Wingina, and learned that it was called Wingandacoa, which Raleigh duly pointed out was not in fact the name of the place, but the local way of saying 'you weare good clothes'. Barlowe and Amadas brought home two Indians, Manteo and Wanchese, whom Raleigh adopted, dressing them up in brown taffeta; a German visitor to the Elizabethan court reported that they looked like 'white Moors', that no one was able to understand them, and that they made 'a most childish and silly figure'.

Some animal skins, two savages, a few pearls and inferences in high places that a base might be established from which to prey on Spanish shipping, encouraged Raleigh's backers. In 1585 the Virgin Queen knighted him and allowed him to call his strip of sand 'Virginia' in her honour. Plans for a colony went ahead, with help from Richard Hakluyt whose *A Discourse concerning Western Planting* (1584) set out the case for colonization and collated the experience of Spaniards, Portuguese and French. Raleigh was to take farmers, masons, alchemists, geologers, physicians and Cornish miners; as chief scientist he appointed his friend the brilliant Oxford mathematician Thomas Hariot, who had been learning the Algonquin language from Manteo and Wanchese. Hariot's brief was to study Indian customs and make observations on

ADMIRANDA NARRATIO
FIDA TAMEN, DE COMMODIS ET
INCOLARVM RITIBVS VIRGINIÆ, NVPER
ADMODVM AB ANGLIS, QVI À DN. RICHARDO
GREINVILE EQVESTRIS ORDINIS VIRO EÒ IN
COLONIAM ANNO. M.D.LXXXV. DEDVCTI SVNT
INVENTÆ, SVMTVS FACIENTE DN. VVALTERO
RALEIGH EQVESTRIS ORDINIS VIRO FODINARV̄
STANNI PRÆFECTO EX AVCTORITATE
SERENISSIMÆ REGINÆ ANGLIÆ.

ANGLICO SCRIPTA SERMONE
À THOMA HARIOT, EIVSDEM WALTERI DOMESTI-
CO, IN EAM COLONIAM MISSO VT REGIONIS SI-
TVM DILIGENTER OBSERVARET

NVNC AVTEM PRIMVM LATIO DONATA À
C. C. A.

Cum gratia & priuilegio Cæs. Maiest. ad quadriennium.

FRANCOFORTI AD MOENVM
TYPIS IOANNIS WECHELI, SVMTIBVS VERO THEODORI
DE BRY ANNO CIↃ IↃ XC.
VENALES REPERIVNTVR IN OFFICINA SIGISMVNDI FEIRABENDII

HONI SOIT QVI MAL Y PENSE
Autore Ioanne With
Sculptore Theodoro
de Brÿ, Qui et excud
V
I
Mongoack
N
SECOTAN
Cwareuuoc
Panauuaioc
Neuustooc
Secota
Sectuooc
Cotan
Aquscogoc
Paquuip
Pomeiock
Wokokon
Croatoan
Paquiwoc
Meguope
Tramasque
Dasamonquepe
Hatore
Scala leucarum 25
5 10 15 20 25

Americæ pars, Nunc Virginia dicta, primum ab Anglis inuenta, sumtibus Dn. Walteri Raleigh, Equestris ordinis Viri Anno Dñi M.D LXXXV regni Vero Serenifs: nostræ Reginæ Elisabethæ XXVII
Hujus vero Historia peculiari Libro descripta est, additis etiam Indigenarum Iconibus
C H A W A
N O
R G I
O K
I A
Ramushowũg
Ohaumoock
Catokinge
nuc Metpcuuem
Waratan
Mascoming
Skicoak
W E A P E
M E O C
Chepanuu
Chesepiooc
Apasus
Chesepiooc sinus
Comoke
Pasquenoke
Trinety harbor
OCCIDENS
MERIDIES
SEPTENTRIO
ORIENS

the natural resources of the country. On Hakluyt's recommendation the 'skilful painter' John White, who had already delineated Frobisher's esquimaux, was designated surveyor and artist. In charge of the military was Ralph Lane, recalled from the Irish wars; Sir Richard Grenville was in overall command. Orders were given to protect the natives: 'non shall stryke or mysuse any Indian' – the punishment for so doing was 'to haue XX blows with a cuggell In the presentz of the Indian strucken.'

After various adventures on the Spanish Main, the expedition reached the Carolina Outer Banks on 20 June 1585. Having first landed at the wrong place and run their largest ship aground on the bar, they explored Pamlico sound. They found the Indian village of Pomeiooc, which White duly sketched, and saw the lake the Indians called Paquippe (Lake Mattamuskeet); they visited Secota, also sketched by White. At Aquascogoc a silver cup was thought to have been stolen by the Indians and the odious Grenville ordered the village and its corn field to be burned. The fleet then sailed sixty miles northwards and on 21 July anchored off the gap named Port Ferdinando, after Simon Fernandez, who was again the pilot and whose original point of entry this had been. At the invitation of the Indians they chose Roanoke, an island ten miles long by two miles across, for their first settlement, where they built a fort to Hariot's design and prepared to spend the winter. Grenville returned home leaving the 107 men of the garrison under Lane's command.

Sorties were carried out into the interior, contacts were made with local chiefs with the help of Manteo and Wanchese and that autumn Lane sent a patrol a hundred miles north to Chesapeake Bay, which he realized was an altogether more suitable place for a settlement. Supplies ran out in the winter and following English indiscretions the gentle Indians of White's drawings began to show hostility. Lane, used to dealing with recalcitrant Irishmen, tried rough treatment. The chief, Wingina, now called Pemispan, could not be said to be 'void of all guile', for he witheld supplies and planned an attack. Lane moved first and during the fighting the chief, according to Lane's account, was 'shot athwart the buttocks by mine Irish boy' and ran off into the woods pursued by a soldier who returned carrying Wingina-Pemispan's head.

Lack of food, trouble with the Indians, a conspicuous absence of gold and silver, delayed relief, and dissatisfaction among the 'gallant gentlemen' of the expedition who had bullied the Indians and had, as Hariot put it, 'little or no care of any other but to pamper their bellies', caused distress and disillusion. They were happy to see the large fleet of Sir Francis Drake, who was calling in after a great raiding sweep of the Spanish Main, which had included the razing of Fort Augustine, in former French Florida. Drake had intended leaving supplies and slaves, but the sea was rough and the main store ship was sunk. By now the settlers were so eager to return home that he took all of them on board except for three men who were out with the Indians. After only a year of occupation, Raleigh's Virginia was abandoned with only the potato and tobacco plants, already known in Europe, brought back by Hariot and the drawings of John White, some of which had been damaged in the sea, to show for it.

But Raleigh still believed in the viability of a Virginia colony and he was not the man to abandon an *idée fixe*. Further to promote the idea and to counter the malicious reports of the 'gallant gentlemen', he hurried the publication, in February 1588, of Hariot's *A briefe and true report of the new found land of Virginia*. After a dig at the detractors, to whom 'the whole countrey was miserable', because they did not find 'their olde accustomed daintie food, nor any soft beds of downe or feathers', Hariot addressed himself to potential mercantile sponsors, covering such matters as 'marchantable commodities', 'Commodities for Building', 'Roots', 'Fruites', 'Beasts', 'Foule', 'Fish', and 'the nature and manner of the people'. Under the latter heading, having given useful anthropological information about their social organization, villages, weapons, and religous aptitude, he made a guarded reference to Lane's 'trouble': 'some of our companie . . . shewed themselves too fierce, in slaying some of the people, in some towns, upon causes that on our part might easily enough have bene borne withall: yet notwithstanding because it was on their part iustly deserved'. All things considered, Hariot recommended settlement, especially in the richer lands in the interior, adding as an inducement that Sir Walter Raleigh would grant 500 acres to any man 'onely for the adventure of his person'.

In fact, even without Hariot's propaganda, Raleigh had managed to get together another expedition in the spring of the previous year to plant the 'City of Raleigh' in the area of Chesapeake Bay. Under command of John White, 89 men, 17 women and 11 children landed at familiar Roanoke and, owing to the passing of the planting season, decided to remain there for the winter rather than move on to Chesapeake. On 18 August White's daughter, Elinor Dare, gave birth to the girl they christened Virginia; a few days later Governor White was persuaded by his fellows to return to England to use his influence in London in obtaining further supplies and assistance for the infant colony. The reluctant White arrived at Southampton on 8 November 1586, having spent no more than a month in Virginia.

Raleigh, puffing away at his pipe of tobacco, soon arranged relief ships, but war with Spain prevented their departure. Even after the defeat of the Armada in August 1588 English ships were held back in anticipation of further Spanish action, and it was not until two years later that White was able to return to his colony. But of course there was nobody to be seen: Roanoke was deserted, with only the letters CRO carved on a tree to indicate they might have moved to Croatoan Island, thirty miles to the south. White was not to meet his grand-daughter, now aged three, or any other member of the colony: bad weather prevented a landing and he was forced to return to England without even establishing whether they were there. The fate of the first Virginians remains a mystery.

Before White left England on this last unfruitful trip Raleigh and Hakluyt had been more than ever anxious to maintain public interest in the Virginia project. It was during this period that Theodore de Bry, in London on his own affairs and in the pursuit of le Moyne's paintings, was offered White's paintings. Hakluyt, as we have told, persuaded him to publish them together with Hariot's *A briefe and true report* and his additional picture notes. The book appeared in 1590, in German, French and Latin, with a special English edition dedicated to Raleigh and carrying his florid arms. The title page reads:

> The true pictures and fashions of the people in that parte of America now called Virginia, discowred by Englishmen sent thither in the years of our Lorde 1585. att the speciall charge and direction of the Honourable Sir Walter Ralegh Knigt Lord Warden of the stanneries in the duchies of Corenwal and Oxford who therin hath bynne favored and auctorised by her Maaiestie and her letters patents.
>
> Translated out of Latin into English by Richard Hackluit. Diligentlye Collected and Draowne by Ihon White who was sent thither speciallye and for the same purpose by the said Sir Walter Ralegh the year abovesaid 1585, and also the year 1588. now cutt in copper and first published by Theodore de Bry att his wone chardges.

Pages 62–3 Map of Virginia from de Bry's *America*, Part I

The arrival of the Englishmen in Virginia

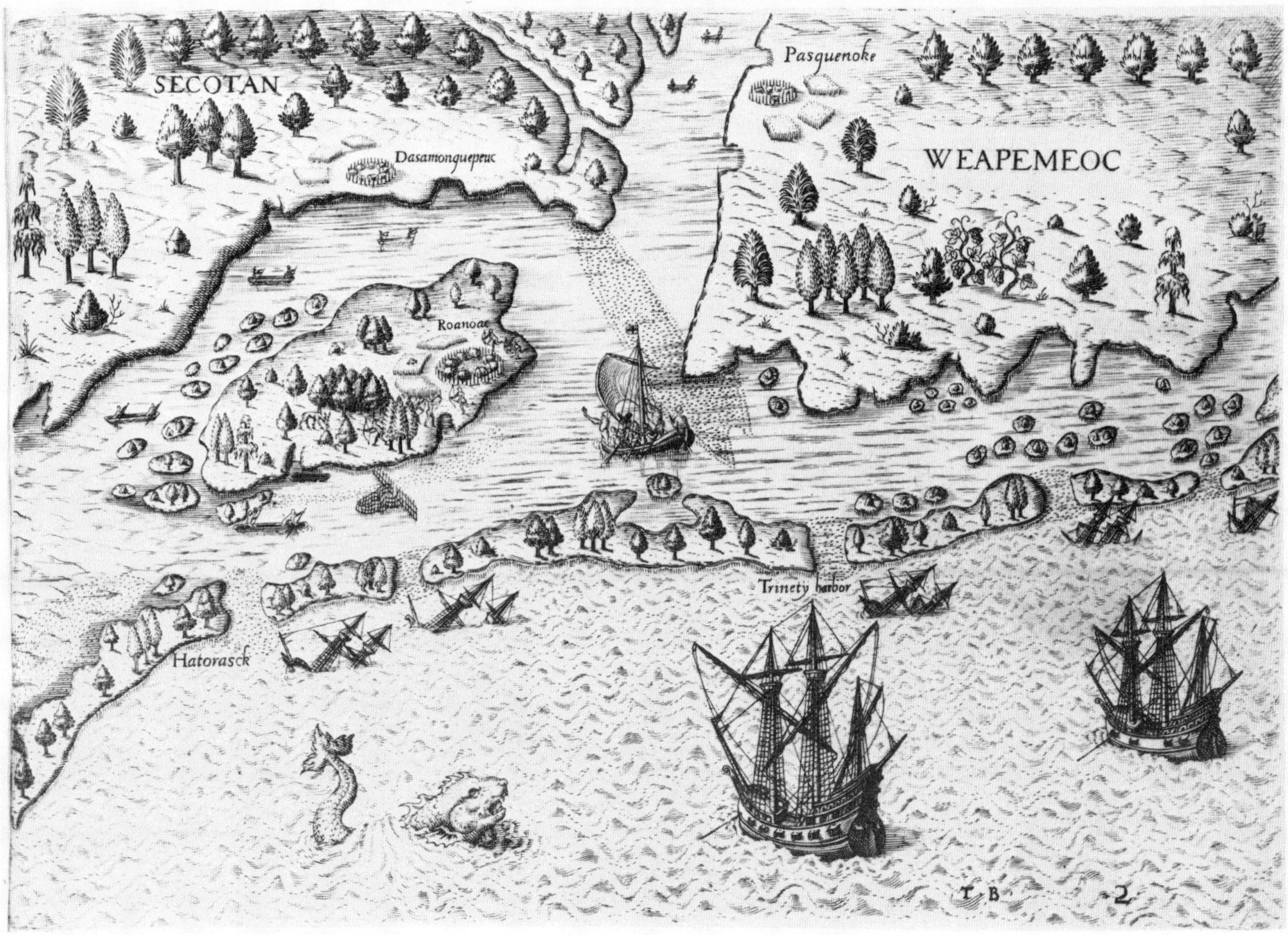

THE sea coasts of Virginia are full of islands, whereby the entrance into the mainland is hard to find. For although they be separated with divers and sundry large divisions which seem to yield convenient entrance, yet to our great peril we proved that they were shallow and full of dangerous flats, and so we could never pierce up into the mainland until we made trials in many places with our small pinnace. At length after diligent search we found an entrance and after we had passed up and sailed therein for a short space, we discovered a mighty river falling down into the sound over against those islands; nevertheless we could not sail up far by reason of the shallowness, the mouth thereof being annoyed with sands driven in with the tide. Therefore sailing further, we came unto a good big island, whose inhabitants, as soon as they saw us, began to make a great and horrible cry, as people which never before had seen men apparelled like us, and made away giving out cries like wild beasts or men out of their wits. But being gently called back, we offered them of our wares, such as glasses, knives, babies, and other trifles, which we thought they delighted in. So they stood still, and perceiving our good-will and courtesy came fawning upon us, and bade us welcome. Then they brought us to their village in the island called Roanoke, and unto their *Weroans* or Prince, and entertained us with reasonable courtesy, although they were amazed at the first sight of us. Such was our arrival into the part of the world which we call Virginia. The stature of body of this people, their attire, and manner of living, their feasts, and banquets, I will particularly declare unto you.

A weroans or great Lord of Virginia

THE princes of Virginia are attired in such manner as is expressed in this figure. They wear the hair of their heads long and bind up the end in a knot under their ears. Yet they cut the top of their heads from the forehead to the nape of the neck in manner of a cockscomb, sticking a fair long feather of some bird at the beginning of the crest upon their foreheads, and another short one on both sides about their ears. They hang at their ears either thick pearls, or something else, as the claw of some great bird, as cometh into their fancy. Moreover they either pounce or paint their forehead, cheeks, chin, body, arms, and legs, yet in another manner than the inhabitants of Florida. They wear a chain about their necks of pearls or beads of copper, which they much esteem, and thereof wear they also bracelets on their arms. Under their breasts about their bellies appear certain spots, where they use to let themselves blood when they are sick. They hang before them the skin of some beast very finely dressed in such a way that the tail hangeth down behind. They carry a quiver made of small rushes, holding their bow ready bent in one hand and an arrow in the other, ready to defend themselves. In this manner they go to war, or to their solemn feasts and banquets. They take much pleasure in hunting of deer, whereof there is great store in the country, for it is fruitful, pleasant, and full of goodly woods. It hath also store of rivers full of divers sorts of fish. When they go to battle they paint their bodies in the most terrible manner that they can devise.

One of the chief ladies of Secota

The women of Secota are of reasonable good proportion. In their going they carry their hands dangling down, and wear a deer skin very excellently well dressed hanging down from their navel unto the middle of their thighs, which also covereth their hinder parts. The rest of their bodies are all bare. The fore part of their hair is cut short, the rest is not over long, thin, and soft, and falling down about their shoulders. They wear a wreath about their heads. Their foreheads, cheeks, chins, arms and legs are pounced. About their necks they wear a chain, either pricked or painted. They have small eyes, plain and flat noses, narrow foreheads, and broad mouths. For the most part they hang at their ears chains of long pearls, and of some smooth bones. Yet their nails are not long, as the women of Florida. They are also delighted with walking into the fields, and beside the rivers, to see the hunting of deer and catching of fish.

One of the religious men in the town of Secota

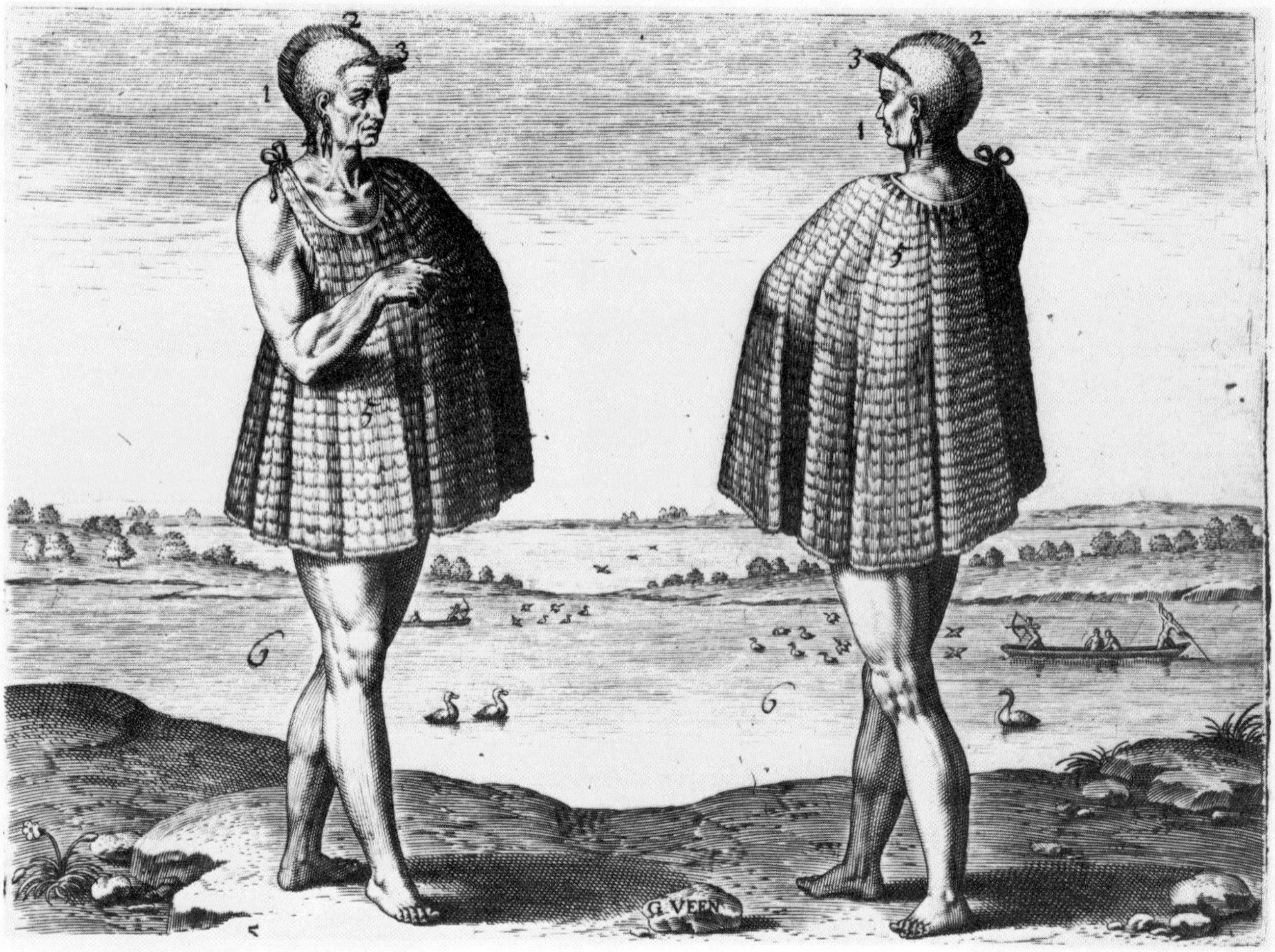

THE priests of the aforesaid town of Secota are well stricken in years, and as it seemeth of more experience than the common sort. They wear their hair cut like a crest on the tops of their heads as others do, but the rest are cut short, saving those which grow about their foreheads in manner of a periwig. They also have something hanging in their ears. They wear a short cloak made of fine hares' skins quilted with the hair outward. The rest of their body is naked. They are notable enchanters, and for their pleasure they frequent the rivers, to kill with their bows, and catch wild ducks, swans, and other fowls.

A young gentle woman daughter of Secota

VIRGINS of good parentage are apparelled altogether like the women of Secota above mentioned, saving that they wear hanging about their necks instead of a chain certain thick and round pearls, with little beads of copper, or polished bones, between them. They pounce their foreheads, cheeks, arms and legs. Their hair is cut with two ridges above their foreheads, the rest is trussed up on a knot behind. They have broad mouths, reasonable fair black eyes. They lay their hands often upon their shoulders and cover their breasts in token of maiden-like modesty. The rest of their bodies are naked, as in the picture is to be seen. They delight also in seeing fish taken in the rivers.

A chief lord of Roanoke

THE chief men of the island and town of Roanoke shave the hair of the crowns of their heads cut like a cockscomb, as these others do. The rest they wear long as women and truss them up in a knot on the nape of their necks. They hang pearls and string copper on thread at their ears, and wear bracelets on their arms of pearls, or small beads of copper or of smooth bone called *minsal*, neither painting nor pouncing of themselves. But in token of authority and honour, they wear a chain of great pearls, or copper beads or smooth bones about their necks, and a plate of copper hung upon a string. They cover themselves before and behind, from the navel unto the midst of their thighs as the women do, with a deer's skin handsomely dressed and fringed. Moreover they fold their arms together as they walk, or as they talk one with another, in sign of wisdom. The isle of Roanoke is very pleasant, and hath plenty of fish by reason of the water that environeth the same.

A chief lady of Pomeiooc

ABOUT twenty miles from that island, near the lake of Paquippe, there is another town called Pomeiooc hard by the sea. The apparel of the chief ladies of that town differeth but little from the attire of those which live in Roanoke. For they wear their hair trussed up in a knot, as the maidens do which we spake of before, and have their skins pounced in the same manner, yet they wear a chain of great pearls, or beads of copper, or smooth bones, five or six folds about their necks, bearing one arm in the same, and in the other they carry a gourd full of some kind of pleasant liquor. They tie deers' skin doubled about them crossing higher about their breasts and hanging down before almost to their knees, and are almost altogether naked behind. Commonly their young daughters of seven or eight years old do wait upon them wearing about them a girdle of skin, which hangeth down behind, and is drawn underneath between their twist and bound about their navel with moss of trees between that and their skins to cover their privities withall. After they be once past ten years of age, they wear deer skins as the older sort do. They are greatly delighted with puppets and babes which were brought out of England.

An aged man in his winter garment

The aged men of Pomeiooc are covered with a large skin which is tied upon their shoulders on one side and hangeth down beneath their knees. They wear their other arm naked out of the skin, that they may be at more liberty. Those skins are dressed with the hair on, and lined with other furred skins. The young men suffer no hair at all to grow upon their faces but as soon as they grow up they put them away, but when they come to older years they suffer them to grow although to say truth they come up very thin. They also wear their hair bound up behind, and have a crest on their heads like the others. The country about this place is so fruitful and good that England is not to be compared to it.

Their manner of carrying their children and attire of the chief ladies of the town of Dasemonquepeuc

In the town of Dasemonquepeuc, distant from Roanoke four or five miles, the women are attired, and pounced, in such sort as the women of Roanoke are, yet they wear no wreaths upon their heads, neither have they their thighs painted with small pricks. They have a strange manner of bearing their children, and quite contrary to ours. For our women carry their children in their arms before their breasts, but they, taking their son by the right hand, bear him on their backs, holding the left thigh in their left arm after a strange, and unusual fashion, as in the picture is to be seen.

The conjurer

THEY have commonly conjurers or jugglers which use strange gestures, often contrary to nature, in their enchantments. For they be very familiar with devils, of whom they enquire what their enemies do, or other such things. They shave all their heads saving their crest which they wear as others do, and fasten a small black bird above one of their ears as a badge of their office. They wear nothing but a skin which hangeth down from their girdle, and covereth their privities. They wear a bag by their side as is expressed in the figure. The inhabitants give great credit unto their speech, which oftentimes they find to be true.

The manner of making their boats

THE manner of making their boats in Virginia is very wonderful. For whereas they want instruments of iron, or others like unto ours, yet they know how to make them as handsomely, to sail with where they list in their rivers, and to fish withall, as ours. First they choose some long and thick tree, according to the bigness of the boat which they would frame. Then they make a fire on the ground about the root thereof, kindling the same by little and little with dry moss of trees and chips of wood, that the flame should not mount up too high and burn too much of the length of the tree. When it is almost burnt through and ready to fall they make a new fire, which they suffer to burn until the tree fall of its own accord. Then burning off the top and boughs of the tree, in suchwise that the body of the same may retain his just length, they raise it upon posts laid over crosswise upon forked posts, at such a reasonable height as they may handsomely work upon it. Then they take off the bark with certain shells, reserving the innermost part of the trunk for the nethermost part of the boat. On the other side they make a fire according to the length of the body of the tree, saving at both the ends. That which they think is sufficiently burned they quench and scrape away with shells, and making a new fire they burn it again, and so they continue, sometimes burning and sometimes scraping, until the boat have sufficient bottom. Thus god induceth these savage people with sufficient reason to make things necessary to serve their turns.

The broiling of their fish over the flame

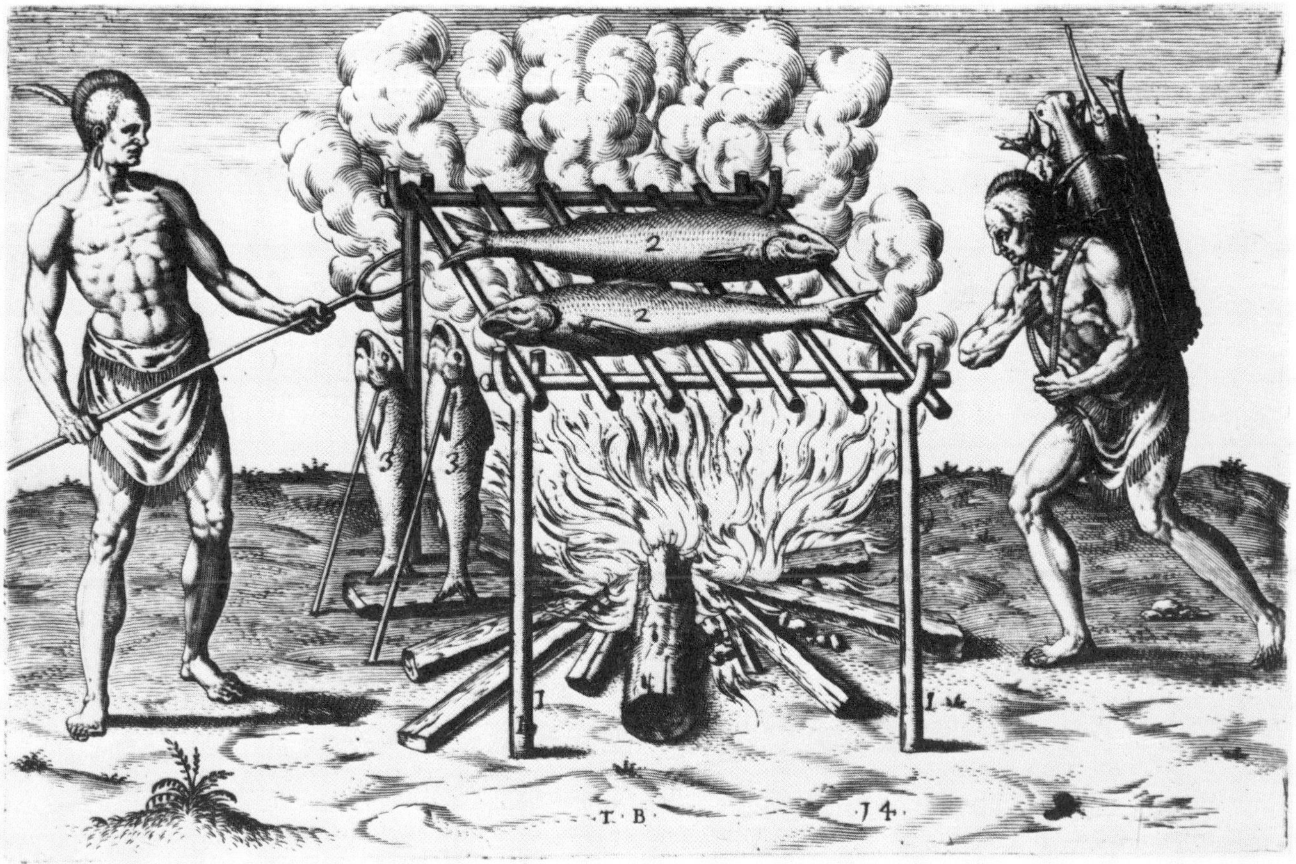

AFTER they have taken a store of fish, they get them unto a place fit to dress it. There they stick up in the ground four stakes in a square room, and lay four posts upon them, and others athwart the same like unto an hurdle. And laying their fish upon this hurdle, they make a fire underneath to broil the same, not after the manner of the people of Florida, which do but scorch and harden their meat in the smoke only to reserve the same during all winter. For this people, reserving nothing for store, they do broil, and spend away all at once, and when they have further need they roast or seethe fresh, as we shall see hereafter. And when the hurdle cannot hold all the fishes, they hang the rest by the fire on sticks set up in the ground against the fire, and then they finish the rest of their cookery. They take good heed that they be not burnt. When the first are broiled they lay others on that were newly brought, continuing the dressing of their meat in this way until they think they have sufficient.

Their manner of fishing in Virginia *left*

THEY have likewise a notable way to catch fish in their rivers. For whereas they lack both iron and steel, they fasten unto their reeds or long rods the hollow tail of a certain fish like to a sea crab instead of a point, wherewith by night or day they strike fishes and take them up into their boats. They also know how to use the prickles and pricks of other fishes. They also make weirs, with setting up reeds or twigs in the water, which they so plant one within another that they grow still narrower and narrower, as appeareth by this figure. There was never seen among us so cunning a way to take fish withall, whereof sundry sorts found in their rivers are unlike unto ours, which are also of a very good taste. Doubtless it is a pleasant sight to see the people, sometimes wading and going, sometimes sailing in those rivers, which are shallow and not deep, free from all care of heaping up riches for their posterity, content with their state, and living friendly together of those things which god of his bounty hath given unto them, yet without giving him any thanks according his desert, so savage is this people and deprived of the true knowledge of god. For they have none other than is mentioned before in this work.

Their seething of their meate in earthen pots

THEIR women know how to make earthen vessels with special cunning and that so large and fine that our potters with their wheels can make no better: and they can remove them from place to place as easily as we can do our brassen kettles. After they have set them upon an heap of earth to stay them from falling, they put wood under, which being kindled, one of them taketh great care that the fire burn equally round about. They or their women fill the vessel with water, and then put they in fruit, flesh, and fish, and let all boil together like a galliemaufrye, which the Spaniards call, *olla podrida*. Then they put it out into dishes, and set it before the company, and then they make good cheer together. Yet they are moderate in their eating whereby they avoid sickness. I would to god we would follow their example. For we should be free from many kinds of diseases which we fall into by sumptuous and unseasonable banquets, continually devising new sauces, and provocation of gluttony to satisfy our unsatiable appetite.

Their sitting at meat

THEIR manner of feeding is in this wise. They lay a mat made of bents on the ground and set their meat on the midst thereof, and then sit down round, the men upon one side, and the women on the other. Their meat is maize sodden, in such sort as I described it in the former treatise, of very good taste, deers' flesh, or of some other beast, and fish. They are very sober in their eating, and drinking, and consequently very long lived because they do not oppress nature.

T.B.
17

Their dances which they use at their high feasts

At a certain time of the year they make a great and solemn feast whereunto their neighbours of the towns adjoining repair from all parts, every man attired in the most strange fashion they can devise, having certain marks on the backs to declare of what place they be. The place where they meet is a broad plain, about the which are planted in the ground certain posts carved with heads like to the faces of nuns covered with their veils. Then, being set in order, they dance and sing, and use the strangest gestures that they can possibly devise. Three of the fairest virgins of the company are in the midst, which embracing one another, do as it were turn about in their dancing. All this is done after the sun is set for avoiding the heat. When they are weary of dancing, they go out of the circle, and others come in until their dances be ended, and they go to make merry.

Their manner of praying with rattles about the fire *left*

When they have escaped any great danger by sea or land, or be returned from the war, in token of joy they make a great fire about which the men and women sit together, holding a certain fruit in their hands. This is like unto a round pumpkin or a gourd, which, after they have taken out the fruits and the seeds, they fill with small stones or certain big kernels to make the more noise, and fasten that upon a stick. Thus, and singing after their manner, they make merry: as I myself observed and noted down at my being among them. For it is a strange custom, and worth the observation.

The town of Pomeiooc

THE towns of this country are in a manner like unto those which are in Florida, yet are not so strong nor yet preserved with such great care. They are compassed about with poles stuck fast in the ground, but they are not very strong. The entrance is very narrow as may be seen by this picture, which is made according to the form of the town of Pomeiooc. There are but few houses therein, save those which belong to the king and his nobles. On the one side is their temple, separated from the other

L
F
E
K
G
H
I
E
D
B
C
A
T B
20

houses, and marked with the letter *A*. It is built round, and covered with skin mats, and as it were compassed about with curtains without windows, and hath no light but by the door. On the other side is the king's lodging marked with the letter *B*. Their dwellings are built with certain posts fastened together, and covered with mats which they turn up as high as they think good, and so receive in the light and air. Some are also covered with boughs of trees, as every man lusteth or liketh best. They keep their feasts and make good cheer together in the midst of the town as it is described in the picture of Secota. When the town standeth far from the water they dig a great pond, noted with the letter *C*, whence they fetch as much water as they need.

The town of Secota *see preceding page*

THEIR towns that are not inclosed with poles are commonly fairer than such as are inclosed, as appeareth in this figure which lively expresseth the town of Secota. For the houses are scattered here and there, and they have gardens, expressed by the letter *E*, wherein groweth tobacco which the inhabitants call *uppowoc*. They have also groves wherein they take deer, and fields wherein they sow their corn. In their corn fields they build as it were a scaffold whereon they set a cottage like to a round chair, signified by *F*, wherein they place one to watch, for there are such number of fowls and beasts that unless they keep the better watch they would soon devour all their corn. For which cause the watchman maketh continual cries and noise. They sow their corn with a certain distance, noted by *H*, otherwise one stalk would choke the growth of another and the corn would not come unto his ripeness *G*, for the leaves thereof are large, like unto the leaves of great reeds. They have also a several broad plots *C*, where they meet with their neighbours to celebrate their chief solemn feasts as we have already mentioned above; and a place *D* where after they have ended their feast they make merry together. Over against this place they have a round plot *B* where they assemble themselves to make their solemn prayers. Not far from which place there is a large building *A*, wherein are the tombs of their kings and princes. Likewise they have a garden noted by the letter *I* wherein they use to sow pumpkins. Also a place marked with *K* wherein they make a fire at their solemn feasts, and hard without the town a river *L*, from whence they fetch their water. These people are void of all covetousness and live cheerfully and at their hearts' ease. They solemnize their feasts in the night, and therefore they keep very great fires to avoid darkness and to testify their joy.

Their idol Kiwasa

THE people of this country have an idol, which they call Kiwasa: it is carved of wood in length four foot; its head is like the heads of the people of Florida. The face is of a flesh colour, and the breast white; the rest is all black; the thighs are also spotted with white. He hath a chain about his neck of white beads, between which are other round beads of copper which they esteem more than gold or silver. This idol is placed in the temple of the town of Secota, as the keeper of the kings' dead corpses. Sometime they have two of these idols in their churches, and sometime three, but never above, which they place in a dark corner where they show terrible. These poor souls have none other knowledge of god although I think them very desirous to know the truth. For when we kneeled down on our knees to make our prayers unto god, they went about to imitate us, and when they saw we moved our lips, they also did the like. Wherefore it is very likely they might easily be brought to the knowledge of the gospel. God of his mercy grant them this grace.

The tomb of their weroans or chief lords

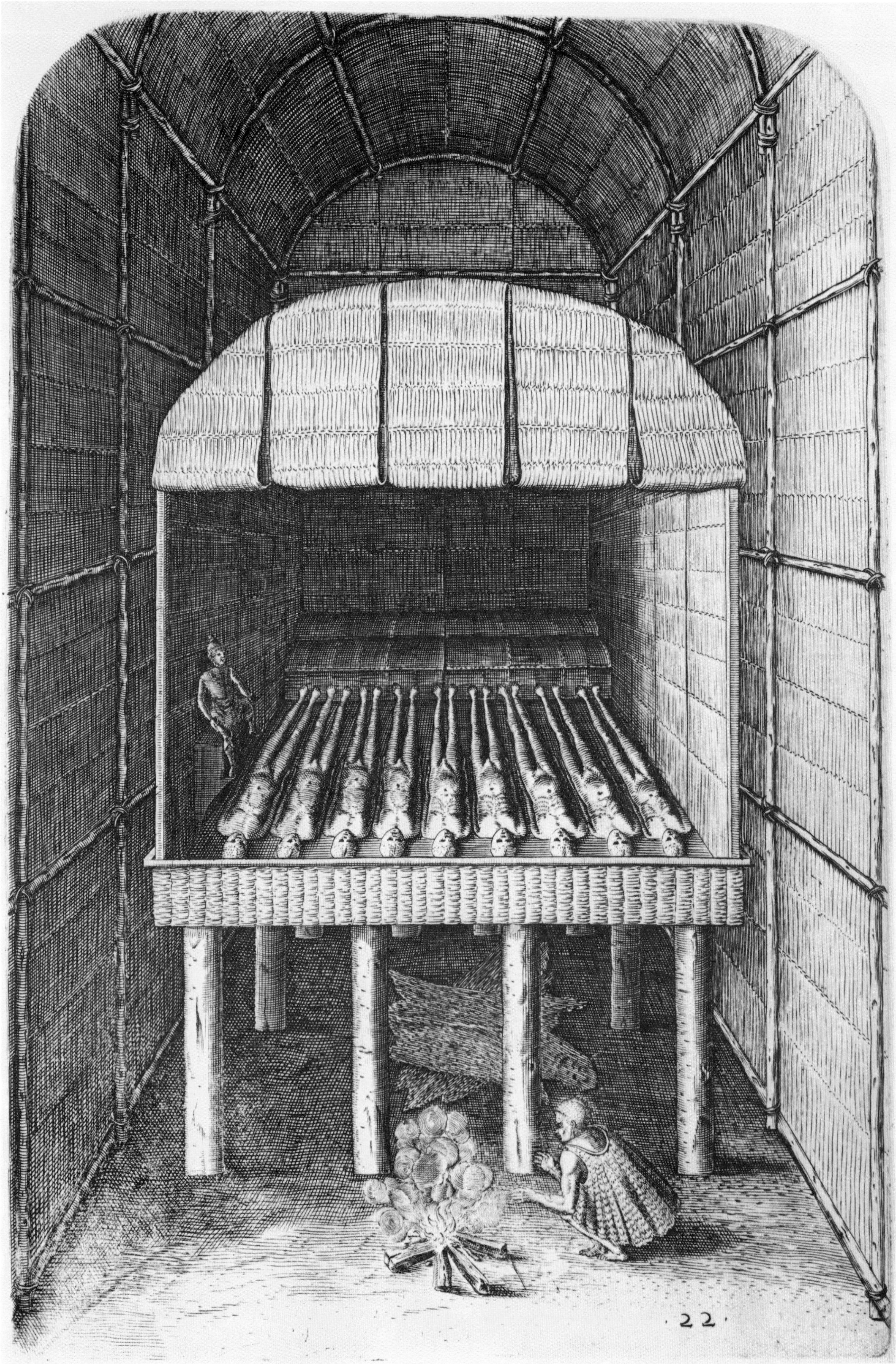

The marks of sundry of the chief men of Virginia

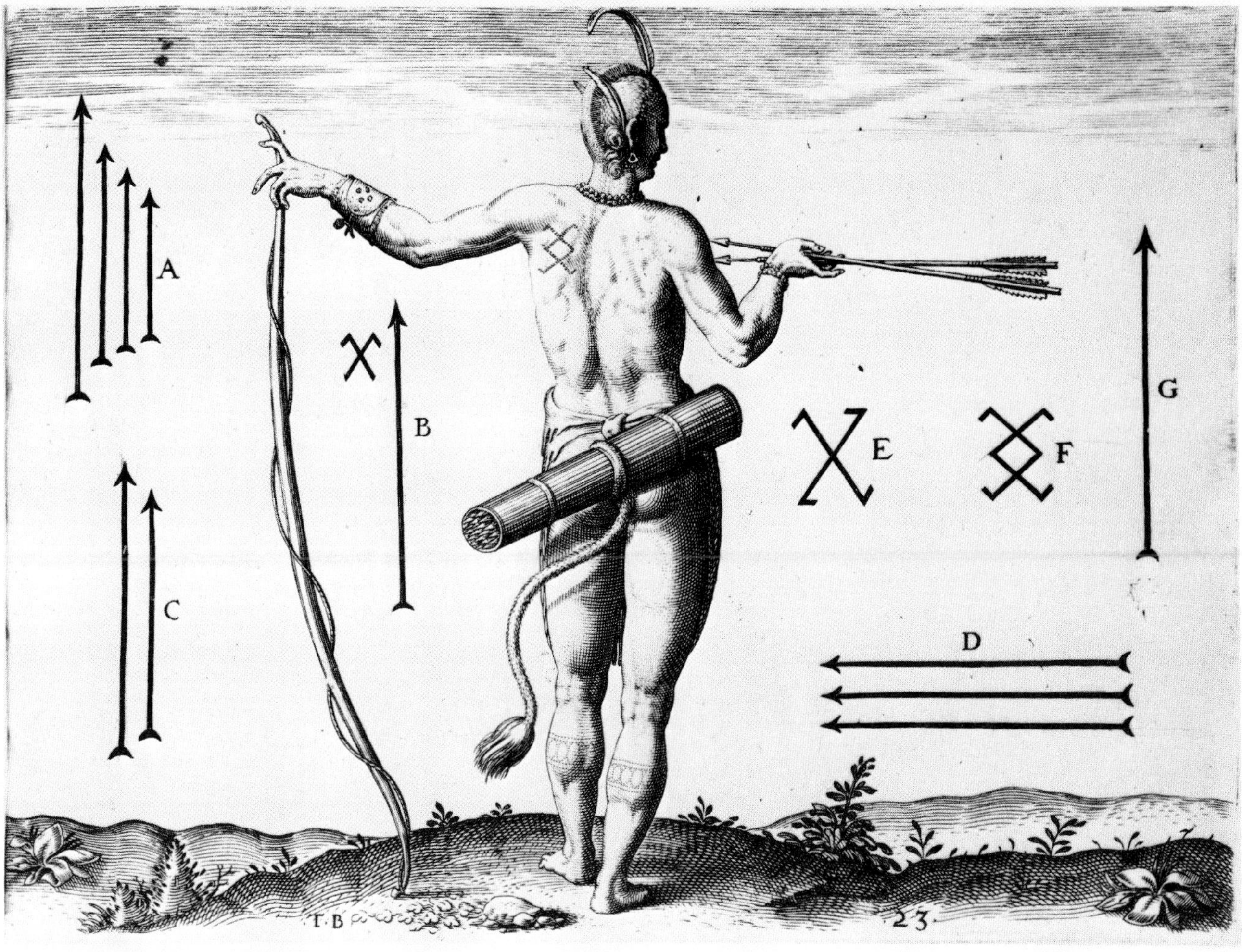

THE inhabitants of all the country for the most part have marks rased on their backs, whereby it may be known what princes' subjects they be, or of what place they have their original. For which cause we have set down those marks in this figure, and have annexed the names of the places that they might more easily be discerned. The marks which I observed among them are here put down in order following: the mark which is expressed by *A* belongeth to Wingina, the chief lord of Roanoke; that which hath *B* is the mark of Wingina, his sister's husband; those which be noted with the letters of *C* and *D* belong unto divers chief lords in Secota; those which have the letters *E*, *F*, and *G* are certain chief men of Pomeiooc, and Aquascogoc.

left

THEY build a scaffold nine or ten foot high, as is expressed in this figure, under the tombs of their *weroans*, or chief lords, which they cover with mats, and lay the dead corpses of their *weroans* thereupon in manner following. First the bowels are taken forth; then, laying down the skin, they cut all the flesh clean from the bones, which they dry in the sun, and, well-dried, enclose in mats, and place at their feet. Then their bones (remaining still fastened together with the ligaments whole and uncorrupted) are covered again with leather, and their carcass fashioned as if their flesh were not taken away. They lapp each corpse in his own skin after the same is thus handled, and lay it in his proper place by the corpses of the other chief lords. By the dead bodies they set their idol Kiwasa, whereof we spake in the former chapter. For they are persuaded that the same doth keep the dead bodies of their chief lords that nothing may hurt them. Moreover under the foresaid scaffold some one of their priests hath his lodging, which mumbleth his prayers night and day, and hath charge of the corpses. For his bed he hath two deers' skins spread on the ground; if the weather be cold he maketh a fire to warm by withall.

At the end of the Virginia volume, de Bry appended five plates after John White, of which two are shown. They show splendidly tattooed Picts and Ancient Britons, men and women, and the legend reads: 'Som pictore of the Pictes which in olde tyme did habite one parte of the great Bretainne. The Painter of whom I have had the first of the Inhabitants of Virginia, give me allso thees 5 figures followinge, fownd as hy did assured me an oolld English cronicle, the which I wold well sett to the ende of thees first Figures, for to showe how that the Inhabitants of the great Bretainne have bin in times past as sauvage as those of Virginia.' In the same spirit, two centuries later, Gibbon reminds us that as late as the fourth century AD 'a valiant tribe of Caledonia, the Attacotti, are accused by an eyewitness of delighting in the taste of human flesh. When they hunted the woods for prey, it is said that they attacked the shepherd rather than his flock and that they curiously selected the most delicious and brawny parts both of the males and females which they prepared for their horrid repast.'

3

Hans Staden among the Cannibals of Brazil

Veritable history and description of a country belonging to the wild, naked, and terrible people, eaters of men's flesh, situated in the New World, America; unknown in Hesse until two years ago when Hans Staden, from Homberg in Hesse, learned about them from his own experience, and now brings them to light in print.

This uncompromising prospectus introduced the first edition of the account by Hans Staden of his adventures among the cannibal Tupinamba Indians of Brazil. Published at Marburg in 1557, it was dedicated to the ruling prince, the Landgrave of Hesse, and backed by a long introduction by the learned Doctor Dryander, Professor of Medicine at the local university, who enthusiastically vouched for its truthfulness. Indeed the facts of the story, even at a time when travellers were apt to be imaginative and their tales difficult to check, were never seriously questioned and many of the author's statements were subsequently confirmed by the account of Jean de Léry, who was with Villegagnon in the same area of Brazil (Rio de Janeiro) even as Staden was writing his book. De Léry, who twenty years later was to publish his own *Histoire d'un Voyage faict en la terre de Brésil*, is said to have remarked that he and the German traveller might have compared notes before writing about the customs of the Indians.

The original Marburg edition was illustrated by fifty-three lively woodcuts. Staden must have supervised their execution and, if naive in drawing, they are highly instructive in content. It was from these, supplemented by material from de Léry and John White, that Theodore de Bry worked up his set of copper-plates which elevate the illustrations into a new technical and artistic dimension. The de Bry edition of Staden's sensational story was published in 1592.

The lank, bearded figure of Hans Staden, sometimes with hands upraised in pious horror, appears throughout the picture-story as he underwent the trials and indignities of his captivity. Not much is known of his early life. In 1547, as a young man, he left Holland for Lisbon where he hoped to join a ship bound for the spicy East. He ended up on a Portuguese vessel carrying convicts and exiles to Brazil and arrived at Pernambuco on 8 January 1548. Brazil had been discovered and claimed for the Spanish crown by Vincent Pinzon in 1500; under the Treaty of Tordesillas, by which the infallible Pope divided the New World vertically into spheres of Spanish or Portuguese ownership, it now fell in the Portuguese zone. But the Portuguese were preoccupied with their more prosperous territories in the East Indies and it was not until 1531 that serious colonization began. The early settlements were frequently engaged in battles with the local Indians and it was as a fighting-man that Hans Staden had his first experiences of the country. After various adventures, duly to be illustrated by de Bry, he returned to Portugal after an absence of sixteen months.

Staden was soon to set out again for the Americas, this time as part of an expedition from Seville bound for the River Plate. After a disastrous voyage, which ended in shipwreck, Hans and a few companions reached San Vincente, a Portuguese sugar plantation near the modern city of Santos. The Indians were aggressive, and martial Europeans were in short supply: Hans was persuaded to take on a job as gunner at one of the newly-constructed forts. While out hunting in the woods he was captured by a party of Tupinamba Indians who had been lying in wait for unwary Europeans. It is with the grisly aftermath that the main portion of the book is concerned.

Not unnaturally the Indians took their prisoner to be a hated Portuguese and as such only good when cooked and eaten. At that time there were a number of French traders in the area; dealing mainly in pepper and parrots, they were regarded as enemies and interlopers by the Portuguese but as friends and allies by the Tupinamba. Hans swore that he was a German, an ally of the French, and referred the matter to the local French trader for confirmation. When the Frenchman found that Hans did not speak his language he immediately told the Indians that he must indeed be Portuguese and the sooner eaten the better! We next see Hans in the Tupi village being fattened-up for his dubious fate. He was held for nine months when, by various ruses and an unshakable reliance on his Lutheran God, he finally persuaded his captors to let him go. He sailed away on a French ship and, after being wounded in a skirmish with the Portuguese in the harbour of Rio de Janeiro, he reached Antwerp in 1555. He must have settled down to write his book almost immediately.

Hans Staden had learned the Tupi language before his capture and it is for this reason, together with an observant eye, that he was able to produce such a comprehensive account of their tribal customs, especially in regard to cannibalism and religious practices. As Robert Southey wrote in his classic *History of Brasil* (1810): 'It is a book of great value, and all subsequent accounts of the Tupi tribes rather repeat than add to the information which it contains.'

AMERICAE TERTIA PARS
Memorabilẽ provinciæ Brasiliæ Historiam continẽs, germanico primum sermone scriptam à Ioãne Stadio Homburgensi Hesso, nunc autem latinitate donatam à Teucrio Annæo Priuato Colchanthe Po: & Med: Addita est Narratio profectionis Ioannis Lerij in eamdem Provinciam, quã ille initio gallicè conscripsit, postea verò Latinam fecit. His accessit Descriptio Morum & Ferocitatis incolarum illius Regionis, atque Colloquium ipsorum idiomate conscriptum.

Omnia recens evulgata, & eiconibus in æs incisis ac ad vivum expressis illustrata, ad normam exemplaris prædictorum Autorum: studio & diligentia Theodori de Bry Leodiensis, atque civis Francofurtensis anno MDXCII.

Venales reperiũtur in officina Sigismundi Feirabendii.

I HANS Stade of Hesse made up my mind, if it should so please God, to see the Indies. Thus I travelled from Bremen to Holland where at Campon I found ships proposing to sail to Portugal to load salt. I went with them and on 29 April 1547, after a voyage of four weeks, we arrived at a city called Sanct Tual. Thence I proceeded to Lisbon, which is five leagues distant. In Lisbon I lodged at an inn, whose keeper was a German called Leuhr the Younger. I spoke with my countryman and asked his advice concerning my journey to the Indies. He told me that I had delayed too long as the King's ships bound for the Indies had already sailed. I begged him to find me another and he took me to a ship where I was signed on as gunner. The captain's name was Pintado. He was bound for Brazil to trade there, but he also had orders to attack certain ships that were trading with the White Moors of Barbary and to take as prizes any French ships trading with the savages of Brazil. He also carried with him to that country some prisoners who had been convicted but had been spared for the purpose of peopling the new countries. Our ship was well founded and armed. We were three Germans on board: Hans von Bruckhausen, Heinrich Brant of Bremen, and I.

We sailed first towards Barbary and captured a merchant vessel of the White Moors which we took to Madeira. Next we sailed back to Cape de Gel to look for more prizes, but the wind was unfavourable and on the night before All Saints' Day we headed away from Barbary towards the Brazils with a strong gale behind us. When we were some four hundred miles out to sea many fishes came about the ship which we caught on hooks and lines. Those which the sailors called *albakors* were large, others called *bonitte* were small, and others were called *durado*. And there were many fish the size of herrings which had wings on either side like a bat. When pursued by larger fish they raised themselves out of the water in great numbers and flew some two fathoms above, sometimes almost as far as one could see. Then they fell again into the water. We often used to find them in the morning lying in the ship where they had fallen while flying in the night. These fish are called *pisce bolador* by the Portuguese.

On 28 January 1548 we sighted Cape de Sanct Augustin. Eight leagues further on we arrived at the haven called Brannenbucke having been eighty-four days at sea without seeing land. There the Portuguese had established a settlement called Marin. The commander was called Artokeslio and to him we handed over the prisoners and landed some of our cargo, intending to sail on and take in other cargo elsewhere.

When we arrived, the formerly friendly inhabitants were rebelling against the Portuguese who were enslaving them, and the Governor begged us to send help to a settlement called Garasu, about five miles from Marin. We therefore sent forty men in a small boat to Garasu, whose defenders consisted of about ninety armed Christians and thirty Moorish and Brazilian slaves, facing about eight thousand savages. At night the savages retired to two fortifications which they had built in the forest. By day they lay in pits which they had dug near the settlement. Indeed our people were so closely invested they could hardly stir. Coming close, the savages would shoot arrows into the air so that they fell among us. Sometimes they would tie cotton or wax to them and ignite them, hoping to set fire to the roofs of the houses! And they would boast how they would eat us as soon as they had got us. Our food soon began to run out, so we sent off two boats to a settlement called Tamaraka for provisions. The savages had cut down two large trees to block the channel but we broke through, only to run aground. They could not harm us in the boats, but they threw tinder between us and the shore and burned pepper plants to smoke us out. However, the tide turned and we sailed on. On our return we found they had again put trees across the channel, and had also partly felled two trees and tied them at the top with *sippo*, a plant which grows like a hop, but thicker. They had tied the other ends in their forts, and intended to pull the trees down on us as we passed. One tree fell towards their fort and the other went in the water behind us. We had called to our friends in the settlement but the savages shouted us down. We successfully brought in the supplies and the savages, realizing that they could accomplish nothing, made peace overtures and withdrew. The siege had lasted almost a month, with several savages dead, but not one Christian. When we saw the natives were peaceable we left for our great ship which lay at Marin.

We now sailed to a harbour named Buttugaris, about forty miles away, where we intended to load up with Brazil wood and raid the savages for food. Here we found a French vessel loading Brazil wood and we attacked it intending to capture it. But with one shot they knocked down our mainmast and escaped us. Several of our crew were shot dead and others wounded. After this we agreed to return to Portugal, arriving after many adventures at Lisbon about 8 October 1548.

I rested some time at Lisbon determined to sail with the Spaniards to the new countries they occupy. I left Lisbon in an English ship to a Castilian city called Porta Santa Maria, where they intended to load up with wine. Thence I travelled to Civilien where I found three ships fitting out for a voyage to a country called Rio de Platta in America. This region, with the rich gold country of Pirau, was discovered some years ago and is on the same continent as Brazil. I joined one of the ships and in the month of September we directed our course towards America.

After many tempestuous days at sea I came again to the continent of America. As we approached the coast we could not find the harbour we sought. From two Portuguese who arrived in a canoe filled with savages we learned that we were some thirty miles north of the island of Sancta Catherina, whither we were bound, and that there was in that region a nation of savages called Carios against whom we should be well on our guard, unlike the savages in our present place who were called Tuppin Ikins, who were their friends and whom we need not fear.

It was on St Catherine's Day, 1549 that we lowered anchor and put off a boat to reconnoitre the harbour. It seemed that we were in the river called Rio de San Francisco which is in this province and the further we went up it the longer it appeared to be. We could see no sign of smoke though we came upon some huts in a clearing, but they were old and deserted. Towards evening we came to a small island in the river and decided to spend the night there. It was already dark when we reached it and we dared not land until we had sent some of us ashore to see if it was inhabited. Finding it empty we lit a fire and felled a palm tree and ate the pith. We spent the night there and when day broke we sailed on as we wanted to know if the country was inhabited since, having found the huts, we did not think it could be wholly deserted. While exploring the neighbourhood we sighted in the distance a piece of wood which looked like a cross standing on a rock and we asked ourselves who could have placed it there? We came up to it and found a crucifix secured with stones to the rock and to it was tied a piece from the bottom of a barrel upon which letters had been cut. We could not easily read these letters but took the piece of barrel with us. As we sailed along one of us sat down and studied the letters until he understood them. The following was carved in the Spanish language: 'If by chance any of his Majesty's ships should come here they should fire a gun to have an answer.' And so we sailed back to the cross and fired off a falconet. Then we saw five canoes full of savages who approached rapidly so that we prepared to defend ourselves. When they drew near we saw a bearded man who wore no clothes. He stood up in the front of the canoe and we saw that he was a Christian. When he came near we enquired where we were and he replied 'You are in the harbour called Schirmirein in the savage tongue, but which is also called St Catherine's Harbour.'

This Christian had been sent by the Spaniards of La Soncion in the province of Rio de Plata to persuade the Carios to plant *mandioca* roots so that ships arriving there might obtain provisions.

How I was sent out to our ship with a boat full of savages

OUR captain asked the man we had found among the savages to send one of us in a canoe out to our great ship so that it might follow us into harbour and I was selected to go with them. We had been absent for three nights and they did not know what had become of us, so that when we arrived within gunshot they made a great noise and prepared for defence, nor would they let me approach nearer but called out asking what had become of the others and how I came to be alone in a boatload of savages. I gave no answer, for our captain had ordered me to say nothing and to look sorrowful to see what they would do.

As I did not reply they thought something must be amiss, that the others must be dead, and that other savages would come to seize the vessel in the rear. They made ready to fire, whereupon I called out to them: 'Be comforted! I have good news! Let me approach to tell it.' I told them how matters stood and they were exceedingly glad. We then brought up the ship to where the savages dwelt and lay there at anchor awaiting the arrival of the other two ships we had earlier lost in a storm. Their village is called Acuttia and the man we found there was called Johann Ferdinando, a Buschkeyner from the town of Bilka. The savages were called Carios and they brought us much game and fish, for which we gave them fish-hooks.

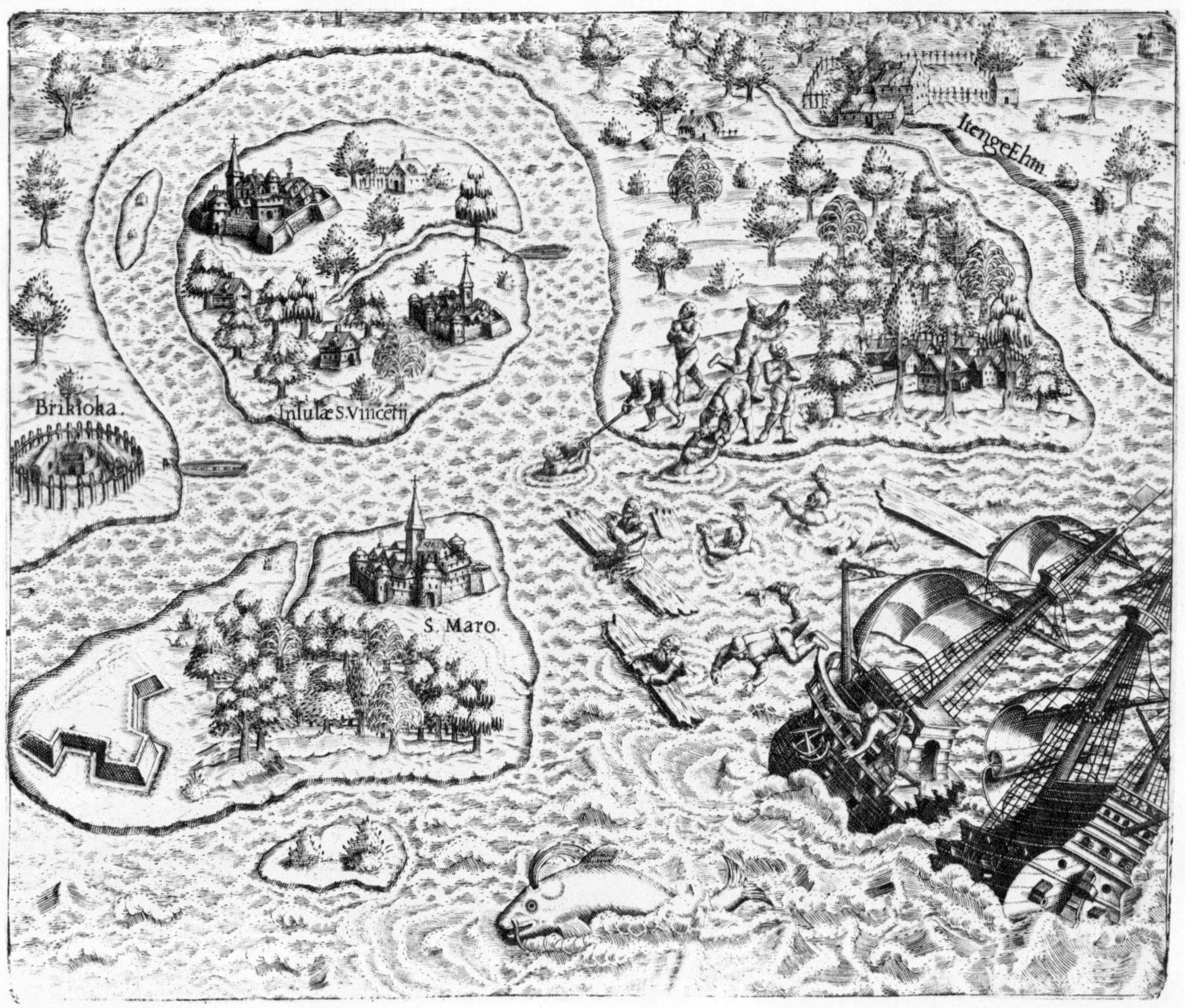

AFTER we had been in this place for about three weeks one ship, in which our head pilot was, arrived, but the third vessel was lost and we heard nothing more of it. Having collected six months' provisions we prepared to sail on, but when everything was ready we lost our great ship in the harbour, thus preventing our departure. We lay for two years in that wild place suffering great hunger and having to eat lizards, field-rats and other strange creatures as well as shell-fish hanging from the rocks. Most of the savages, having obtained sufficient goods from us, departed for other villages.

At last it was decided that one party should proceed overland some three hundred miles while the others sailed in the remaining ship for the island of San Vincente, occupied by the Portuguese, which a man called Roman assured us he could find. In about two days we arrived at an island known as Insula de Alkatrases which abounds in sea birds, called *alkatrases*, which were easy to catch as it was nesting time. We killed a number which we cooked and ate.

Fogs and clouds obscured the coast and the waves were so great that we had to throw everything weighty overboard to lighten the ship. When we could see land again Roman was persuaded that the harbour lay ahead and that we should find it behind a certain rock. This we steered for and as we drew near to land the waves swept us so high that we seemed to be looking down from a wall. Since there was no harbour we were driving straight for the shore and at the first shock with which the ship went aground she broke into pieces. Some leapt into the sea and made for the shore while others clung to planks from the broken ship, and so by the grace of God we all came ashore alive.

At length we reached San Vincente, where I became a gunner at the fort of Brikioka which lies five miles from there. I contracted to stay for four months, but consented to stay there for two years, being much commended by the King's officer, Tome de Susse, for my service.

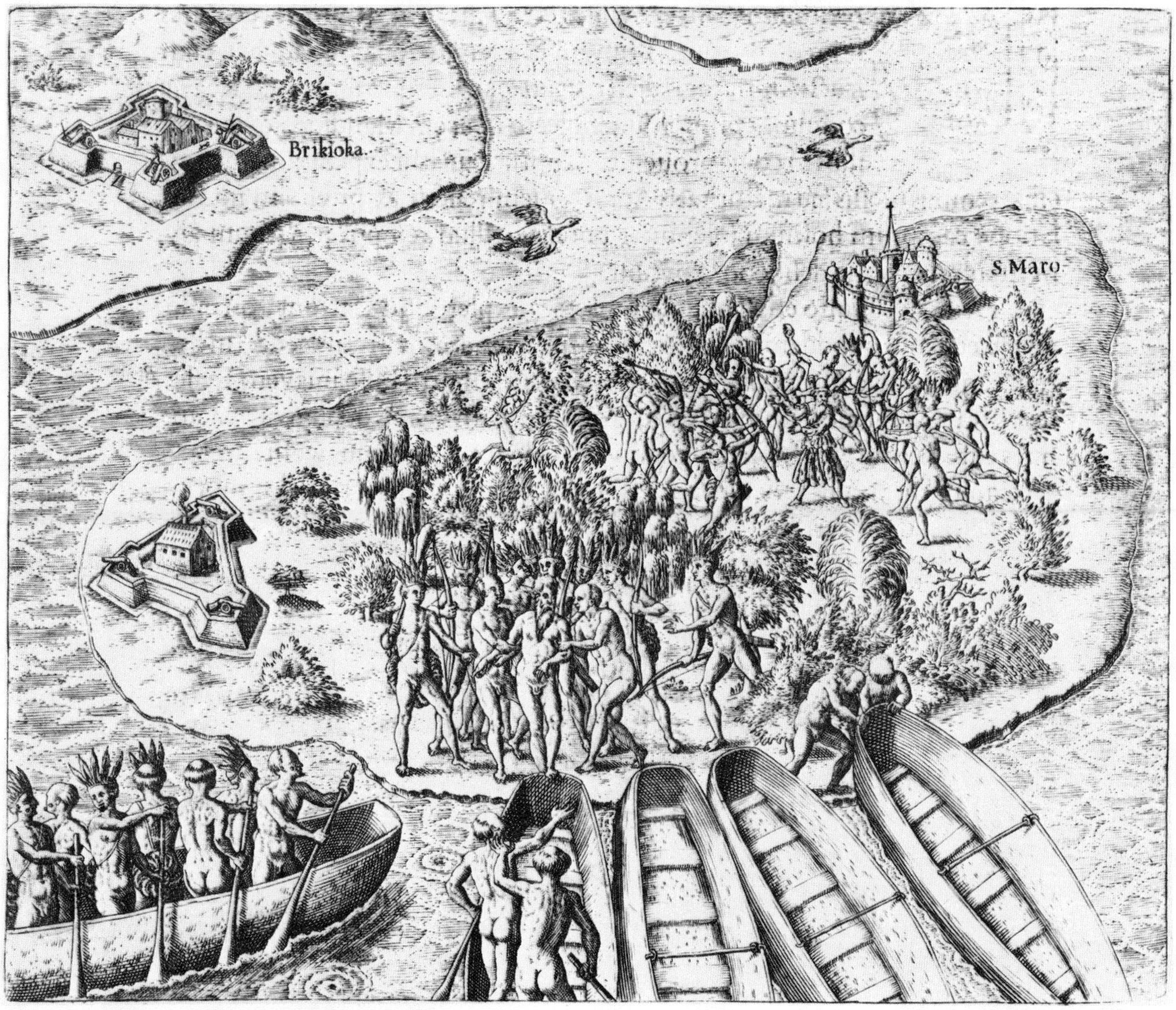

ONE day I was walking through the woods hunting game, when I heard loud yells such as the savages make and at once a company of them came running towards me and surrounded me, shooting at me with their bows and arrows. I cried out 'May God now preserve my soul' and they struck me to the ground and shot and stabbed me. They had only wounded my leg, God be Praised! They tore the clothes off my body, one taking the jerkin, another my hat, a third my shirt and so on. Then two of them took me by the arms and ran with me and the others to their canoes which were drawn up on land under a hedge. When the feathered savages who had remained there saw me they pretended to bite their arms as if it was me they were eating. A chief then approached me with the club with which they despatch their prisoners and said that now they had captured me from the *Perot* (their name for the Portuguese) I was their slave and they would revenge on me the death of their friends.

When they had brought me to their canoes they began to argue as some wanted to kill me on the spot and make a division, but at last the chief, who wanted to keep me, ordered that I should be taken home so that their wives might also see me and feast upon me. He proposed that I should be killed *Kawewi Pepicke*, that is to say they would assemble together and brew drink and have a feast and share me. At these words they stopped quarreling and, binding four ropes around my neck, made me climb into the canoe and set off home. They make their canoes from a tree, *Yga Ywera*, the bark of which they remove from top to bottom, building a platform round the tree so that they can remove it in one piece. This they carry down to the sea where they heat it at the fire, bending it upwards, before and behind, but first lashing two pieces of wood to it so that it does not stretch. The bark is the thickness of a thumb, about four feet wide and forty long. They paddle very fast and though they do not go more than two miles from land, they travel long distances along the coast.

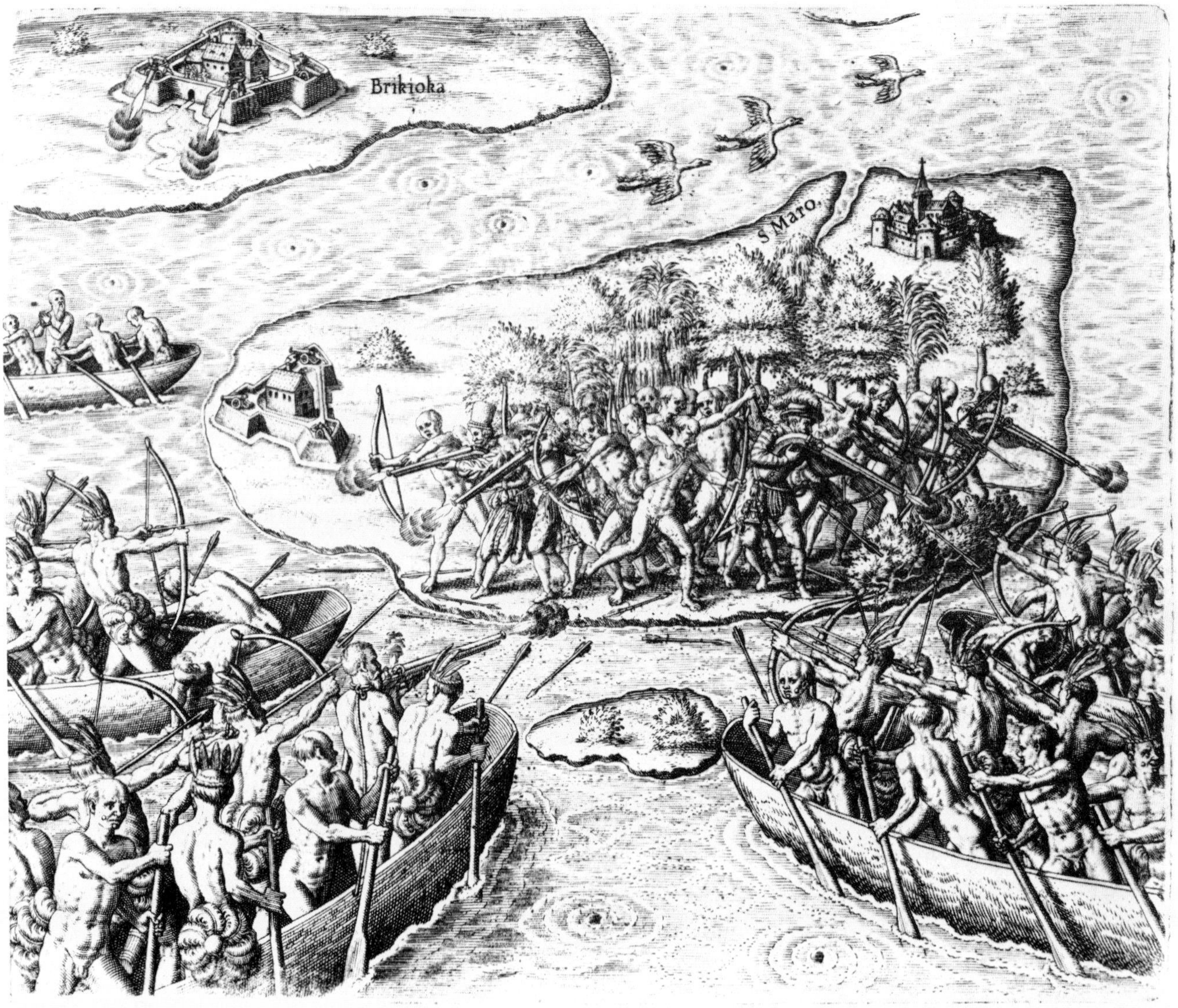

NEAR where I was captured is another small island on which certain water birds called *uwara* are to be found nesting. They asked me if the Tuppin Ikins had been there that year and caught the birds and their young. I answered 'Yes', but they determined to see for themselves for they greatly value their feathers, from which many of their ornaments are made. A peculiarity of these birds is that the first feathers they grow are whitish grey; the next however, when they are fledged, are blackish grey; with these they fly for about a year after which they become as red as any red paint. Expecting to find these birds they made for the islands, but when they were two musket shots away from where they had left their canoes they looked back to see the beach crowded with Tuppin Ikins and some Portuguese. They had come to rescue me, for a slave who was following me when I was captured had escaped to raise the alarm. They shouted to my captors that they were cowards if they would not return and fight; my captors accepted this challenge by turning about. Those on shore fired blowpipes and arrows at us, to which those in the boats replied. My hands were untied, though the rope remained round my neck, and I was forced by the chief, who had a gun and some powder bartered by a Frenchman for Brazil wood, to fire on my friends.

After fighting for some time my captors feared reinforcements might arrive in boats, and after three of them had been shot they withdrew. They passed within a falconet shot of Brikioka where I had been stationed and made me stand up in the boat so that my companions there might see me. They fired two large guns at us from the fort, but their shot fell short. Several canoes set out to pursue us but my captors paddled too fast and they had to return to Brikioka.

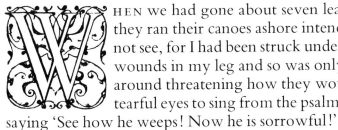

WHEN we had gone about seven leagues from Brikioka we reached an island where they ran their canoes ashore intending to stay the night. When I was landed I could not see, for I had been struck under the eyes, nor could I walk well on account of the wounds in my leg and so was only able to lie down on the sand. The savages stood around threatening how they would eat me. In my terror and misery I began with tearful eyes to sing from the psalm: *De profundis clamavi*. This caused them to rejoice saying 'See how he weeps! Now he is sorrowful!'

Finding no good place for encampment they moved on to the mainland where there were some deserted huts. It was night when we arrived and they made a fire and led me to it. There I had to sleep in a net which they call *inni*, which are their beds, and are tied to two posts or made fast to two trees! They lashed the rope which I had around my neck to the tree above me and all night they lay around mocking and calling out in their language '*Schere inbau ende*' – 'Thou art my bound beast'.

They set off again before dawn and paddled the whole day. At evening a great black cloud arose behind us and as we were yet two miles from the place where they intended passing the night they rowed quickly. But when they saw they could not escape the storm they said to me, '*Ne mungitta dee. Tuppan do Quabe, amanasu y an dee Immi Ranni me sis se!*' which means 'Speak with thy God so that the great rain and wind may do us no harm.' I kept silent and prayed to God as they had demanded.

I lay bound in the canoe so could not turn to see the weather but they looked constantly behind them, beginning to say, '*Oqua moa, amanasu*', or 'The great storm is passing away.' Then I raised myself a little and saw that the great cloud had passed off, upon which I gave thanks to God.

When we came to land they tied me to a tree as they had previously done. They said that we were now near their country and should arrive the following evening, which caused me little regret.

THE following evening we reached their village, some thirty leagues from Brikioka. It consisted of seven huts and was called Uwattibi. Their women were in a mandioca plantation and I was made to call: *'A junesche been ermi vramme'*, or 'I, your food, have come.'

When we landed they all ran from their huts to look at me, then the warriors entered the huts leaving me to the women who danced around me singing the songs they sing to their own people when they are about to eat them. Next they brought me into their fort and the women struck me with their fists and plucked at my beard crying *'Sche innamme pepicke a e'* or 'By this blow I avenge my friend, who those you have been among have killed.' Meanwhile the men were in a hut drinking praises to their gods for having prophesied my capture.

I thought I was to be killed and eaten then, but my captors had presented me as an act of friendship to their father's brother, Ipperu Wasu, who was to keep me until I was ready to be eaten. He would then kill me and so gain a new name for himself.

Then my captors led me to an *aprasse* or dancing. Several of the women led me along by the arms and several by the ropes that were tied round my neck, so roughly that I could barely breathe. I consoled myself with thoughts of the sufferings of Our Lord Jesus Christ at the hands of the vile Jews. Then they brought me to their chief, who was called Vratinge Wasu, or Great White Bird. They sat me down on some newly dug earth before his huts and I looked round for the *Iwara Pemme*, which they use to club men, and asked if they were going to kill me. They answered 'Not yet' and a woman came towards me from the crowd holding a fragment of crystal, set in a thing like a bent ring, with which she shaved off my eyebrows. She would also have cut off my beard but this I would not suffer and said that I would die with my beard. Then they answered that they were not yet ready to kill me, and left me my beard. But later they cut it off with scissors the French had given them.

How they danced with me before their idols

THEN they led me to the huts where they kept their idols, Tammeraka. They made a circle round me and tied objects which rattled to my legs. At my neck they fastened a square of tail-feathers so that they rose above my head; this they call *Arasoya*. Then the women began to sing and I had to keep time with my leg rattle though my leg wound was now so painful that I could hardly stand upright.

When the dance was ended I was handed to Ipperu Wasu. The people told me their idols had prophesied they would capture a Portuguese but I told them I was a friend and ally of the French and came from Allemanien. The French were their friends and came every year bringing knives, axes, mirrors, combs and scissors in exchange for Brazil wood, cotton, feathers and pepper. But the Portuguese had many times captured them and handed them to their enemies to be eaten. Eventually a young Frenchman whom they called Karwattuware came and I was brought to him. When he addressed me in French I was unable to reply and he told the savages 'Kill him and eat him, the worthless one, for he is indeed a Portuguese, your enemy and mine.' I begged him for mercy but he was adamant. And so the savages resolved to prepare for the day of my killing. Meanwhile they kept me in close confinement, mocking me continuously, both young and old.

Troubles, men say, never come singly. At that time one of my teeth began to ache so violently that because of the pain I could not eat and I began to lose flesh. My master discovered why I ate so little and came with an instrument made of wood and wanted to pull out the tooth. I told him that it no longer troubled me. Nevertheless he tried to draw it by force, but I resisted so vigorously that he desisted. Then he said that if I did not eat and grow fat again he would kill me before the appointed day. God knows how much I wanted to die in peace if it was His will, before the savages could have their way with me.

I SHALL now give a brief and truthful account of the manners and customs of the Tuppin Imbas, whose prisoner I was. They make war at two particular seasons of the year. The first is the month of November when a certain fruit they call *abbàti* ripens from which the Tuppin Imba make a drink called *kawaway*, which is the fruit mixed with the root mandioca. They prepare this drink against their return from war to enjoy along with the eating of any enemy they may have captured. The second season when they might be expected is in August, when they go after a fish which runs up certain rivers from the sea in order to deposit spawn in the fresh water. They called these fish *bratti*, but the Spaniards call them *lysses*. They catch them in small nets or shoot them with arrows. They roast them and take them home or make a flour which they call *pira kui*. They are accustomed to make war at this season as they can be sure of their supplies.

They are a well-made race, like the people of this country, only they are brown from the sun, for they all, young and old, go naked; they wear nothing over their sexual parts and they disguise themselves with painting. They have no beards, for they pull the hair whenever it grows, and they pierce holes in the mouth and ears, from which they hang stones that are their jewels, and they deck themselves with feathers. They often fall upon their enemies when they want to capture them, and they will sit down behind dry wood, which stands near hostile huts to await their enemy who comes to fetch it. They behave more cruelly to their enemies than others; for example to show their great hatred they often cut off their legs and arms when they are still alive. They hold in honour the man who has captured and slain many enemies. It is their custom that for each man slain the slayer may take another name. And those who have many names are the noblest among them. They kindle fire with two pieces of wood, usually roasting the flesh they eat. They travel, taking with them wife and children. When they make camp near enemy country they make thickets around their huts so that they cannot be surprised, also as protection from wild animals. They place sharp thorns round their huts as we do foot-hooks. They attack with loud yells, stamp hard on the ground, and blow trumpets made of pumpkins. They shoot rapidly and will cast on their enemy's huts fiery arrows. When one is wounded they have their specific herbal remedies.

Their huts are about fourteen feet wide and at least a hundred and fifty feet long. They are about twelve feet high and vaulted at the top, which they roof with branches of palm to keep out the rain. Inside the hut all is open and no one has a chamber to himself. Each couple, man and woman, has a space measuring about twelve feet and their own fire. The chief of the hut lives in the centre. The huts generally have three doors, so low that people have to stoop to get in or out. Few villages have more than seven huts. Between the huts is a space where they kill their prisoners. The savages fortify their huts by making a stockade of split palm trees to a height of about nine feet, built so thick that no arrow can pierce it. Small holes are cut out in it through which they shoot arrows. Outside the stockade they make another of high stakes, set so that the space between them is too narrow for a man to crawl through. Certain of them have the custom of setting up at the entrance to the outer stockade the heads of men they have eaten. They prefer to erect their dwellings near wood and water, game and fish. After they have destroyed everything in one district they migrate to another, and when they want to build their huts a chief among them assembles a party of men and women, about forty couples, or as many as he can, and these live together as friends and relations. Most of them have only one wife, but some of them more, several of their chiefs having as many as thirteen or fourteen, the first wife being the principal. Each has her own lodging in the huts and her own root plantation. The one with whom he cohabits gives him food. The men also have the custom of giving away a wife if they are tired of her and they also make presents of their daughters and sisters.

They betroth their daughters at an early age and when they reach puberty they cut the hair from their heads and scratch strange marks on their backs and tie the teeth of wild beasts around their necks. The hair grows again but the cuts are treated with a black substance so that the scars remain black, which is held to be a great honour. After these ceremonies the girls are delivered to their betrothed. The men and women conduct themselves decently and do their business secretly. There is no common ownership of goods among them and they know nothing of money. Their treasure is the feathers of birds; he that has many is rich and he that has a stone in his lip is also counted among the rich. Each couple has its own plantation of roots which supplies them both with food. The men

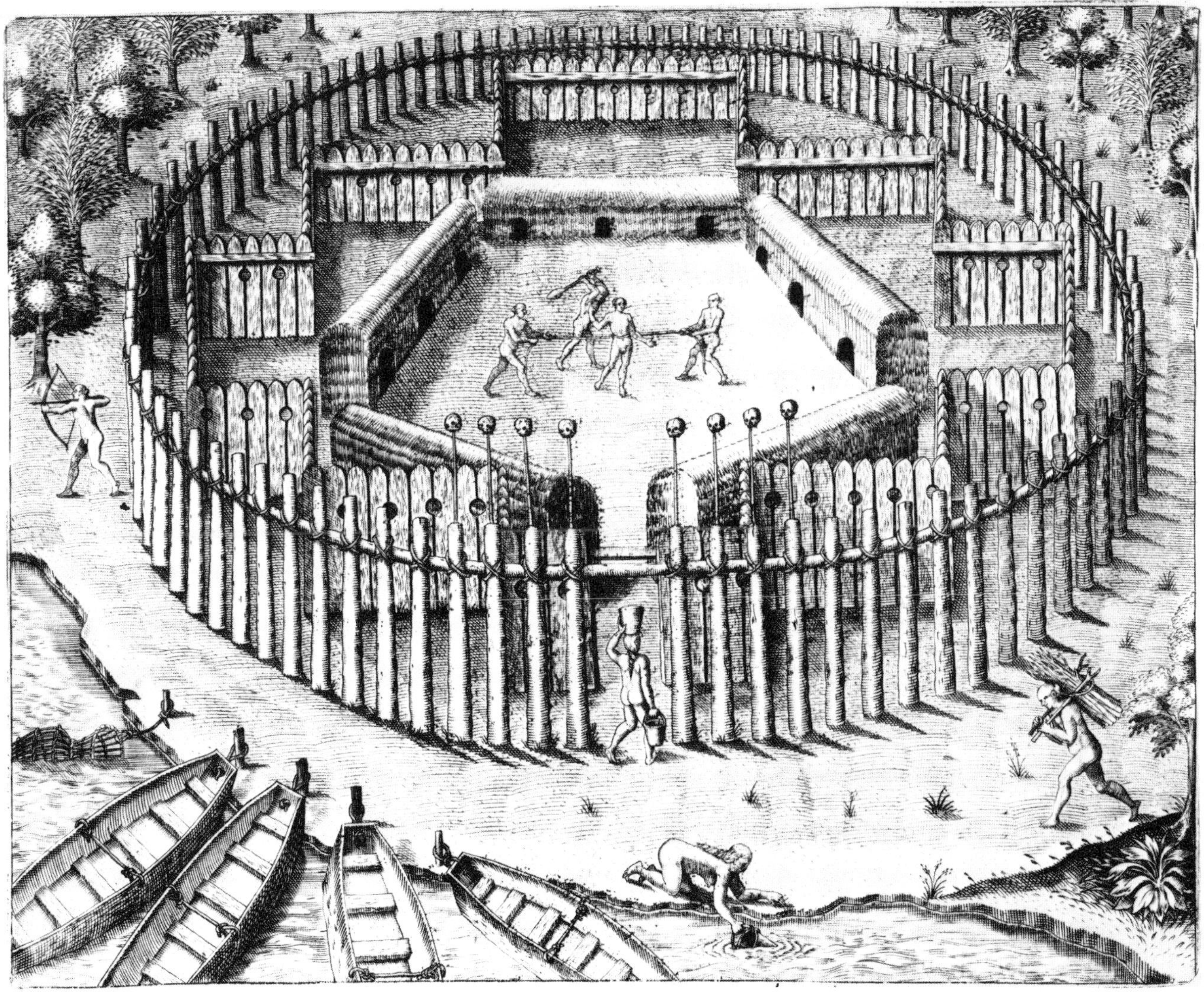

have a bare space on the top of the hair with a circle of hair like a monk. I have often asked them where this fashion originated and they said that their forefathers had seen it on a man called Meire Humane who had worked many miracles among them and was supposed to be a prophet or an apostle. They also have a thing made of feathers which they bind round their head, which they call *kannittare*.

Some have a large hole in the lower lip. When they are still young a little hole is pricked with a sharpened deer-horn in which they stick a small stone or piece of wood and apply salve to it. Thus the hole remains open. When they are big enough to bear arms they enlarge the hole and insert a large green stone, so shaped that the narrow end is inside the lip and the wider outside. They have another small stone on both sides of the mouth and in either cheek. Some, of crystal, are narrow and long. They also wear ornaments made from large snail-shells called *mattepue*. This ornament is snow-white and crescent shaped and is called *bogesso*. They paint themselves black and decorate themselves with gaily mixed red and white plumes. Sometimes they feather their entire bodies, first smearing themselves with a sticky substance from trees. They also paint one arm black and the other red, and decorate legs and body in the same manner. They also make an ornament of ostrich plumes which they tie to their posteriors when they go to war or make a feast. It is called *enduap*. They call themselves by the names of wild beasts.

The women paint themselves under the eyes and in the manner of the men and allow their hair to grow long. They have no particular ornaments except in the ears where they drill holes and hang round objects about a span long and the thickness of a thumb. When they pick lice from their hair they eat them. I asked them why they did this and they told me that the lice were their enemy who ate up their heads, and thus they took vengeance on them. They have no special midwives; when a woman is in labour the nearest person, man or woman, runs to help her. I have seen them going about on the fourth day after giving birth.

To make a plantation, they cut down the trees and three months later they burn them. Then they plant *mandioca* roots between the trunks. To prepare the roots they rub them into crumbs then press off the juice with an object made of hollow palm tree so that it becomes dry. Then they sieve it and bake it into thin cakes. They also put fresh roots in water till they rot, then dry them. To use it, they pound it with a wooden mortar when it becomes white like corn flour, from which they bake cakes. They also pound dried fish and flesh into a powder which they eat with root meal. This keeps for a long time. They do not use salt, but when they boil anything they generally add green pepper. They make a thin broth called *mingau*. If they wish to keep food they smoke it above a fire and when they wish to eat it they boil it up again.

Drinks are also made by the women. They boil *mandioca*, then when it has cooled they chew the boiled roots. After all has been chewed it is put back in the pot, mixed with water, and reheated. They pour the liquid into special vessels which are half buried in the ground, and leave it for two days to ferment. It is thick but pleasant flavoured. Each hut makes its own drink and when a village desires to make merry, which generally happens once a month, the men go first to one hut and drink there until the drink is finished; then they go round the other huts drinking their fill until there is nothing left. When they drink they gather round the pots sitting, some on fire sticks, others on the ground. The women help them to the liquor in an orderly manner. The drinkers sing and dance round the pots and on the spot where they drink they void themselves of their wine. The drinking lasts the whole night, with dancing between the fires and the blowing of trumpets. They make a terrible noise and they get drunk, but they rarely quarrel. They also behave generously to each other and if one man has more food than his neighbour he will share it with him.

THEY believe in a thing shaped like a pumpkin. It is hollow and they pass a stick through it and cut a mouth-shaped hole, filling it with stones so that they may rattle. Each man has his own.

There are certain men, called *paygix*, who are esteemed as soothsayers, and every year they travel throughout the country saying that a spirit from afar has visited them and given them the power to make *Tammeraka* speak and grant wishes. Then they prepare a feast with dancing, prophesying and many strange ceremonies. The soothsayers ordain a day and a hut is cleared of women and children. Each man paints his *Tammeraka* red and decorates it with feathers. They all go to the hut and each man places his *Tammeraka* on the ground before him and offers gifts to the soothsayers. Then one of the soothsayers picks each rattle up in turn and fumigates it with a herb called *bittin*. Then he seizes it and shakes it saying *'Nee kora'* 'Now speak! Let us hear you! Are you within?' And he whispers so the people imagine the rattle has spoken. Each man thinks great virtue has entered his rattle, and the soothsayers command them to make war since the *Tammeraka* desire flesh.

Then each man builds a little hut for his rattle and sets food before it and worships it as a true god. They believe heaven and earth have always existed, though they say there was once a great flood and all were drowned save those who escaped in canoes. This I imagine must have been the Deluge.

This is how they make soothsayers of women: they first go to a hut and take all the women in turn and fumigate them. Then the women are made to jump and yell and run about until they are exhausted and fall to the ground as if dead. Then the soothsayer says: 'See now, she is dead. Soon I will bring her back to life!' When she comes to herself again the soothsayer tells her that she is now able to foretell the future.

 see also following pages

WHEN one enemy eats another they do it not from hunger but from great hatred and jealousy, and when they are fighting one will call out to his adversary, filled with hate, *'Dete Immeraya, Schermiuramme, heiwoe'* – 'Cursed be you, my meat!'; *'De kange Jueve eupota kurine'* – 'Today I will cut your head off'; *'Sche Innamme pepicke Reseagu'* – 'Now I am come to avenge the death of my friends'; *'Yande soo, sche mocken Sera Auora Ossorime Rire'* – 'This day before sunset your flesh shall be my roast meat.'

When they first bring home a captive enemy the women and children set upon him. Then they decorate him with grey feathers and shave off his eyebrows and dance around him, having first bound him. They give him a woman who attends him and has intercourse with him. If the woman conceives they bring up the child until it is fully grown and then they may kill it and eat it whenever the fancy takes them.

They feed the prisoner well, keeping him for a time while they prepare things, making many pots for their drinks and special pots in which they mix the ingredients of the paint with which they daub him; and they make feather tassels which they tie to the club with which they will kill him, and prepare a long cord, called *mussurana*, to bind him when the time comes for him to die. When all is ready they fix the day of his death and invite the savages from other villages. Then they fill the vessels and a day or two before the women make the drink the prisoner is brought out once or twice and they dance round him on the spot he is to die.

When the visitors are assembled the chief of the huts welcomes them saying: 'Now come and help eat the enemy!' The day before they begin drinking they tie the cord *mussurana* about the victim's neck. The same day they paint the spade-shaped club called *Iwera Pemme*, with which they intend to

despatch him. This club is about a fathom long and they spread over it a sticky mess, then they take the grey-coloured egg shells of a bird called *mackukawa* which they crush to powder and spread over the club. Then a woman sits and traces lines in the powder while other women dance and sing around her. When the club *Iwera Pemme* is suitably decked with tassels and other objects, they hang it on a pole in an empty hut and sing before it all night.

In like manner a woman paints the face of the prisoner while the others sing, and when they begin to drink they take him with them and chat with him while he drinks with them. When the drinking is over they rest and the following day build a hut on the place where he is to die in which he spends the night closely guarded. A good while before dawn on the following day they dance and sing before the club and continue until day breaks. Then they lead the prisoner from his hut, which they break up and clear away. Having thus cleared a space they take the *mussurana* from the prisoner's neck and tie it round his body, drawing it tight at both ends while numbers of them hold the two ends of the cord. They leave him thus for a time, having placed stones beside him which he can throw at the women who run around him boasting that they will eat him. These women are painted and ready to take his four quarters when he is cut up and run with them round the huts, in which the others find entertainment. Then they make a fire about two feet from the prisoner which he has to tend. After this a woman comes running up with the club *Iwera Pemme*, waving the tassels in the air, shrieking with joy, and showing it to the victim. Then a man also shows him the club. When this is done he who is going to do the deed retires with fourteen or fifteen others to paint their bodies grey with ashes. Then the slayer returns with his companions and the man who has been holding the club before the prisoner hands it to him. The chief of the huts now intervenes and, taking the club, thrusts it between the slayer's legs. This is considered a great honour. The slayer then takes the club and says

'Yes! Here I am! I will kill thee, for thy people have also killed and eaten many of my friends.' To which the victim replies: 'When I am dead I shall have many friends who will revenge me well.' Then the slayer strikes him on the head from behind, so that his brains are dashed out. The women immediately seize the body and drag him to the fire. They scrape off his skin, making him quite white and stop up his fundament with a piece of wood so that nothing of him may be lost. Then a man takes the body and cuts off the arms and the legs above the knee. Then the four women carry away the four pieces and run with them round the huts with cries of joy. Then the posterior is separated from the forepart and they divide it among themselves; but the entrails are kept by the women, who boil them and make a thick broth or *mingau*. This they and the children drink. They devour the bowels and the flesh from the head; the brains, the tongue and whatever else is eatable is given to the young. When this is done all go home, taking their share with them.

The slayer takes an additional name and the chief scratches his arm with a wild beast's tooth. When it is properly healed the scars can be seen and this is a great honour. He must lie all that day quietly in a hammock but is given a small bow and arrow for him to pass the time shooting into wax, to exercise his arm so that his aim may not become uncertain from having struck the death-blow. I was there and have seen all this with my own eyes.

After I had been there for some days, they took me to another village, called Arirab, to see their great chief, Konyan Bebe. The chief was sitting drunk on *kawaway* with his companions, who looked at me savagely saying: 'O our enemy art thou come?' I said: 'I am come but I am not your enemy.' Now I had heard of Konyan Bebe, what a great man he was and a great eater of human flesh, and this I told him. Then he arose and began to strut about with vast conceit. He had a large stone through his lips and some six fathoms of sea-shells hanging round his neck and thus I perceived he was of the noblest. I told him I had been forced to fire on them at Brikioka, but he replied that I

was certainly a Portuguese as the Frenchman, whom he called his son, had informed him. He told me he had eaten five Portuguese who had all said they were Frenchmen and yet had lied, and I gave up hope, thinking I must surely die.

Then he began to ask what the Portuguese thought about him and that they must surely be in terrible fear of him. I replied: 'They speak much of you and how you like to wage war against them. But now they have fortified Brikioka more strongly.' He replied that therefore he would catch them now and then in the woods as they had caught me. I then told him that his real enemies were the Tuppin Ikins, and that they were even then equipping twenty-five canoes to invade his country, as indeed occurred. Then, as the liquor was now finished, the chief and his friends moved to another hut. There they began to mock me, and the chief's son bound my legs in three places and I was made to hop thus through the huts at which they laughed and said: 'Here comes our dinner hopping towards us!' Then I asked my master if he had taken me there to be killed, and he said no, it was the custom to treat enemy slaves thus. They now unbound my legs and walked around me grabbing at my flesh, one saying that the skin of my head belonged to him and another claiming the fleshy part of my legs. Then I was made to sing to them and I sang hymns and when they asked me what I sang I told them I was singing of my God. They made me translate the hymns into their language and they said my God was *teuire* which is to say 'filth'. These words wounded me much and I thought 'Dear God, Thou art indeed long-suffering!'

The following day I was carried back to Uwattibi, where I was to be killed; but my master always comforted me saying I was not to be killed just yet.

How the Tuppin Ikins came as I had predicted

MEANWHILE it so happened that the savages who were friendly to the Portuguese came in twenty-five canoes and one morning attacked the village. When they began shooting at us there was distress in the huts and the women prepared to flee. Then I said: 'You take me for a Portuguese, your enemy; now give me a bow and arrows and free me and I will help to defend the huts.' They gave me bow and arrows and as I shot them I exhorted them to be of good heart and no harm would befall them. All the time it was my intention to break through the stockade surrounding the huts and run to the others. But they watched me too well and when the Tuppin Ikins saw that there was nothing to be done, they went back to their canoes and departed. After that I was guarded closer.

That evening, when it was moonlight, the people assembled between the huts, and placing me in their midst, they mocked me, deliberating when to kill me. I was sad and looking at the moon, said to myself, 'O my Lord God, help me through this peril to a peaceful end.' They asked me why I looked so constantly at the moon and I replied: 'I see that she is angry!' Then Jeppipo Wasu, who was to have me killed, asked with whom the moon was angry. I said: 'She looks towards your huts.' Whereupon he began to rage at me and in order to appease him I took back those words and said: 'It will not be your huts. She is angry with the Carios slaves.' 'Yes,' he said, 'Let misfortune fall on them.' Next we heard that the Tuppin Ikins had burned down a village and captured a small boy. A group of our men went to help the people there. In the meantime a Portuguese ship from Brikioka arrived and fired a gun so the savages would come to parley with them. The Portuguese asked after me and they replied that they might cease their enquiries. Whereupon the ship sailed away. God knows what my feelings were! As for the savages, they said among themselves: 'We have the right man. They are already sending ships after him!'

SOON after this I heard weeping and thought the war party had returned, but I found instead that many of the savages had fallen sick and their chief, Jeppipo Wasu, told me how the sickness had come and that I had been well aware of it, for he still remembered how I had said that the moon looked angrily on the huts. When I heard these words I thought: 'Surely it must have been God's Providence that I spoke thus about the moon that night.'

Then I told him that this had happened because he wanted to eat me, so he promised I should not be harmed if he recovered. I went among them laying my hands on their heads, but they began to die; first one of the children, then the chief's old mother, then more of his family. The chief begged me to tell my God to withdraw his wrath. I told him that he would recover his health if he gave up all thoughts of killing me. He ordered all those in his huts to stop mocking me and threatening to eat me. He finally recovered as did one of his wives who had been stricken, but eight of his friends died, as well as others who had treated me with great cruelty.

Another chief dreamed about me, which greatly terrified him. Having called me to his huts and given me food he told me how on one of his expeditions he had captured a Portuguese whom he had killed, after which he had eaten so much of him that his stomach had ever since been delicate, and he vowed he would never eat a Portuguese again. Now that he had dreamed of me he was afraid he was about to die. I told him not to worry, but that he must never again eat human flesh.

Several of the old women also said 'We have eaten several Portuguese, but their God was not as angry as yours. By this we now see that you cannot be a Portuguese.' And so they left me alone for a while not knowing whether I was a Portuguese or a Frenchman. They said I had a red beard like a Frenchman, while most Portuguese had black beards.

The return of the Frenchman who had told the natives to eat me

MEANWHILE the Frenchman, Karwattuware, returned and this time he tried to help me, but the savages replied that they would only exchange me for a ship load of gifts. When he had left they became angry because he had given me nothing to pass on to them, and they started to murmur that a Frenchman was no better than a Portuguese. So I began to fear harm again.

Then another ship arrived from San Vincente. On board were some of my friends including a Frenchman. The savages allowed me to approach the ship and speak to him. Then spake one Johann Senches, a Biscayan: 'My dear brother, it is for your sake that we are come in this ship, not knowing if you were dead or alive, for the first ship brought no news of you. Now Captain Brascupas at Sanctus has ordered us to find out if you are alive and if so to learn if they will sell you, and if not we must see if we can capture several of them for whom to exchange you.'

Then I said: 'They will not sell me to you, therefore think not of it. But do not let them think otherwise of me than that I am a Frenchman and give me, for the love of God, some fish-hooks.' This they did at once. When I saw that the savages would not allow me to talk longer I said to the Portuguese: 'Look well, they are planning to attack Brikioka.' They replied that the savages, their allies, were also preparing for war and would attack the village where I was.

I gave the knives and fish-hooks to the savages saying: 'All these my brother, the Frenchman, gave me.' They asked me what we had said together and I replied that I had told my brother to escape from the Portuguese and return to our home and bring back a ship well-stocked with goods. 'For', I said, 'you are good people and treat me well enough and I am anxious to reward you when the ship comes.' Thus I had at all times humoured them and they were mightily pleased. Afterwards they said to each other: 'He must surely be a Frenchman. Let us treat him more kindly in future.' They took me into the forest from time to time and I was obliged to help them in their work.

How the slave who had spoken ill of me was himself eaten

The savages had a slave from the Carios, which people were also enemies of the tribes allied to the Portuguese. This man had been a slave of the Portuguese at San Vincente but had escaped. The savages do not kill people who have escaped unless they have committed some crime, but they hold them as slaves. This man had now been three years among the Tuppin Imbas and had told them that he had seen me among the Portuguese and that I had shot one of their chiefs when they had come on a raid, and he had urged them constantly to kill me. This was false for only a year had passed since I had reached San Vincente. And I prayed to God to protect me from his lies.

It happened in the year 1554, in the sixth month of my captivity, that the Cario had been ill for nine or ten days, and his master begged me to help make him well again so that he could catch game for us to eat. Now the savages keep for several purposes the teeth of a wild beast called *backe* which they sharpen and use to cut through the skin when the blood is sluggish, in the manner that we let blood. I took one of these teeth, intending to open the middle vein, but I could not cut it as the tooth was too blunt. The savages asked me if he would recover. I told them that I had not succeeded and that as they had seen no blood had flowed. Then they said: 'Yes. He will die. So let us strike him dead at once.' I answered: 'Do not kill him for he may possibly recover.' But I could not restrain them and they dragged him away and two of them held him. Then the Cario's master came up and struck him on the head so that his brains spilled out intending to eat him. But I warned them that as he had been sick they might also become ill if they ate him. Nevertheless one of them cut him up and divided him equally with the others, as is their custom, and they devoured everything except the head and bowels, which they held in great distaste as he had been sick. I saw them roasting here the feet, there the hands, and elsewhere a piece of the trunk and I told the savages that this Cario had always spoken ill of me and it was on this account that my God had been angry with him.

THE time now approached when the savages were ready to go to war. I hoped that when they went off they would leave me with the women, so that I might make my escape. Some eight days before they were due to set off a French ship had arrived about eight leagues off at a harbour called Rio de Jenero. There the French used to load Brazil wood and they now came in a boat near Uwattibi to trade pepper, monkeys and parrots. One of them called Jacob, who understood the savage tongue, came ashore. I begged him to take me with him to the boat, but my masters refused to let me go in such a manner saying they would require many goods for me; I told them they should take me to the ship where they would be given all they might require by my friends. But they would not, saying: 'These are not your real friends or they would have given you a shirt when they saw you were naked. Clearly they take no account of you.' (Which was indeed true.) When I saw that the boat was making to depart I thought: 'O God, if the ship sails without me I shall certainly perish, for this is a people whom no man can trust.' With this I left the huts and ran towards the water, but the savages saw me and rushed after me. The first who caught up with me I struck aside, and soon the whole village was at my heels, yet I escaped them and swam to the boat. But when I tried to climb into it the Frenchmen thrust me away saying that if they took me away against the will of the savages they would rise against them and become enemies. So I sadly swam back to the shore for I saw it was God's will that I remain there longer in misery. But if I had not tried to escape I should have blamed myself afterwards.

When the savages saw me come back they were joyful and said: 'Now he comes back to us'. Then I reproached them saying: 'Do you think I would leave you in such a manner? I went to the boat to tell my countrymen to send again for me after your return from the war and to bring many goods to give you.' This pleased them and they were once more content.

How the savages went to war taking me with them

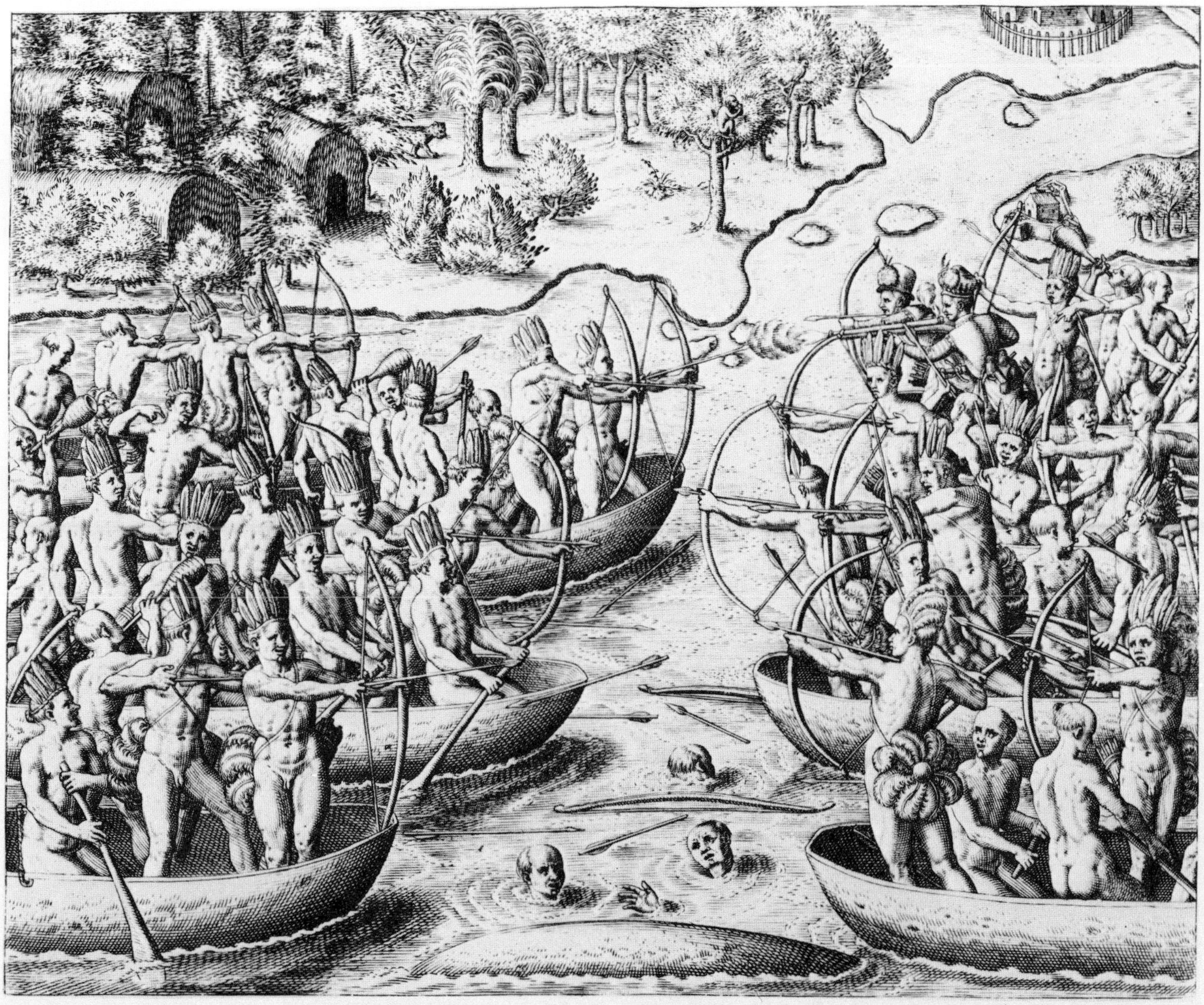

On the 14 August 1554 the savages set off in a war party of thirty-eight canoes to attack their enemies, the Tuppin Ikins, taking me with them. This was the season for going to war, for then a type of fish which they call *bratti* and which are as large as a good-sized pike, came up-river to spawn, so they could be sure of supplies on the way.

When we were within a few days' journey of our objective we camped on an island and at daybreak the chiefs gathered round a cauldron filled with stewed fish. As they ate they recounted their dreams, for if they were good ones they had decided to set forth into enemy country to a place called Boywassu Kange, where they would rest until evening. They asked me what my presentiments were and, for want of something to say, I told them 'The enemy will meet us by Boywassu Kange. Have courage!' It was at this place I intended to escape, for we were only six miles from where they had captured me.

As we were proceeding along the coast, we saw other canoes coming towards us from behind an island. 'Here come our enemies, the Tuppin Ikins!' they called out and we tried to hide ourselves and our canoes behind a rock, so that the others might pass them unawares. But they saw us and began to make for home. We rowed after them as fast as possible and caught up with them after four hours. There were five canoes-full of them and they all came from Brikioka. I knew them all. In one of the canoes there was six Mamelukes who had been baptized including the two brothers Diego and Domingo de Praga. These two defended themselves stoutly and almost between them kept our thirty canoes at bay for two hours. But when their arrows were exhausted the Tuppin Imba fell upon them and captured them, being clubbed or shot. The two brothers were unhurt, but two of the six Mamelukes were badly wounded and several of the Tuppin Ikins, among whom was a woman.

The enemy had been captured two full miles out to sea and we hastened back as quickly as possible to the place we had camped at the previous night. It was evening when we arrived and each man took his prisoner to his hut. The badly wounded were carried to land where they were at once despatched and cut up and broiled according to their custom. Among those who were roasted that night were two of the Christian Mamelukes; one was a Portuguese named George Ferrero, son of a captain by a native woman; the other was called Hieronymous, who had been captured by a savage from my hut who spent the whole night roasting Hieronymous scarcely a yard from where I slept.

That evening, after they had lain down, I went to the huts where they kept the two brothers to speak with them, for they had been my good friends at Brikioka. They asked me whether they also would be eaten. I said that they must leave that to the will of God. They also asked me how it fared with their cousin Hieronymous. I told them that he lay before the fire and was roasting, and that I had seen a piece of Ferrero's son eaten. Then they wept. I comforted them again saying that as they knew well I had been among the savages for eight months and that God had yet preserved me.

While I was thus conversing with them the savages ordered me to return to my hut and asked me what I had been saying to the prisoners for so long. Commending them to God I went out of their hut. I could have escaped from this place but I refrained on account of the Christian prisoners, of whom four were still alive. For I thought: 'If I run away from them they will be angry and immediately kill them. Meanwhile, perhaps, God will preserve us all.' And I determined to remain there and comfort them. But the savages were very well disposed towards me, for I had told them that we would encounter the enemy and as this had in truth happened they said that I was a better prophet than their *Tammeraka*.

WHEN we reached the home of the chief, Konyan Bebe, I begged him to spare the Mamelukes, but he replied they should certainly be eaten. Later, at Uwattibi, when all was ready to feast on Hieronymous, they brought out the Christians and we were all forced to drink with the savages, but before we would drink we made our prayers to God that he would be merciful to Hieronymous and to us when our hour had come. After this I was taken to be given away. I heard later that the two brothers escaped but to this day I do not know if they were recaptured. I was taken to a place called Tackwara Sutibi and given to a chief called Abbati Bossange who treated me well, for he had been warned that my God was terrible towards those who did me harm.

After a fortnight a ship arrived and the captain agreed to help me to escape at last. We made a plan that about ten sailors, who looked something like me, should gather round and state that they were my brothers and wanted to carry me home with them. They said that they would not suffer me to go on shore but that I must return with them as our father wished to see me once more before he died. Then the captain said that although he was captain of the ship and desired I should go on shore yet he could do nothing as he was only one and my brothers were many. These were all pretexts so that we might part from the savages on good terms. I told my master that I should be very glad to return with him but that my brothers would not permit it. Thereupon he began to weep and cry about the ship and said that if they really wanted to take me with them I must return with the first ship, for he had considered me as his son and was very angry with the people of Uwattibi for having threatened to eat me. After this the captain gave him various articles worth no more than five ducats, knives, hatchets, looking-glasses and combs. With these they came on land and made their way home. Thus did Almighty God save me from the hands of these tyrants.

4

Benzoni in the New World

In 1541, at the age of twenty-two, Girolamo Benzoni set out from his birthplace, Milan, to seek adventure and fortune in the New World. He was to spend fifteen years in the territories conquered and being exploited by the Spaniards, travelling widely through the South American continent – the Caribbean, Venezuela, Guatemala, Mexico, Peru, Panama and Nicaragua. He had a good ear for gossip and a good eye for local colour. Exactly what he was doing in the New World is not clear: he attached himself to various military expeditions though he was not by nature a fighting man; he reveals a good knowledge of political intrigue but does not apparently become involved in politics; he is informed about economics but does not discuss the commodities he traded in. Was he perhaps a spy? Whatever his purpose he failed to make a fortune, for we learn that the 'few thousand ducats' he had accumulated was partially lost in a shipwreck on his way home.

An Italian in a Spanish arena, Benzoni maintained an individualistic outlook and though occasionally befriended by influential people seems to have been treated as an outsider by the conquerors. When he was in Peru the Governor, della Gasca, ordered all foreigners out of the country because, according to Benzoni, 'it had been represented to him by some Spaniards that the Levantines, that is *we*, were false and cruel and had caused the death of several of them.' This questionable situation is not enlarged on: Benzoni simply states that in any case he 'was quite tired of remaining in those countries'. On 13 September 1556 he arrived back at his port of embarkation, San Lucar de Barrameda, with nothing much more than wealth of experience.

The tale of his experiences was not to be made public for ten years. By this time the nations of Europe, jealous of Spain's material advantages in the New World, were leaguing against her influence. Benzoni had strong views about Spanish imperialism, and in 1565 *La Historia del Mondo Nuovo* came out at an appropriate moment. Published in Venice and dedicated to Pope Pius IV, it was translated into Latin, German and Flemish and in abbreviated form by Purchas into English. The de Bry version, which was spread over three volumes of *America*, was issued between 1594 and 1596. A number of the plates were based on the crude woodcuts of the Venice edition.

Benzoni was not an intellectual but, as a fellow-countryman wrote, he had 'a clear intelligence and tenacious memory'. He is at his best when he is recounting his own adventures or writing from personal knowledge of political intrigues. It cannot be claimed that the work is more than a hearsay source for the stories of Columbus and of the Conquistadors which are tangled up with his text. But the descriptions of the cruelties of the Spaniards towards the Indians, though often echoing stories from Las Casas, cannot be dismissed as mere anti-Spanish propaganda. Benzoni was *there*. He witnessed endless reciprocal atrocities and the partial extinction of the Indians who interested him and whom he admired and pitied.

Pages 124–5 Map of the New World from de Bry's *America*, Part VI

AMERICAE
PARS SEXTA.
SIVE
HISTORIÆ AB HIERONYMO BĒTONO
Mediolanēse scriptæ, sectio tertia, res nō
minus nobiles & admiratione plenas con
tinens, quàm præcedentes duæ. In hac
enim reperies, qua ratione Hispani opulē
tissimas illas Peruani regni provincias oc
cuparint, capto Rege Atabaliba: deīde orta
inter ipsos Hispanos in eo regno civilia bella.
Additus est brevis de Fortunatis insulis Cōmenta
riolus in duo capita distinctus.
Item additiones ad singula Capita Histo=
riam illustrantes.
Accessit Peruäni regni chorographica Tabula.
AD
INVICTIS: RUDOLPH: II: ROM: IM: AVG:
Omnia elegantibus figuris in æs incisis expressa
à Theodoro de Bry Leod: cive autem Frācofurtēse.
A° M D XCVI.
Cum privilegio S. C. Ma tis.

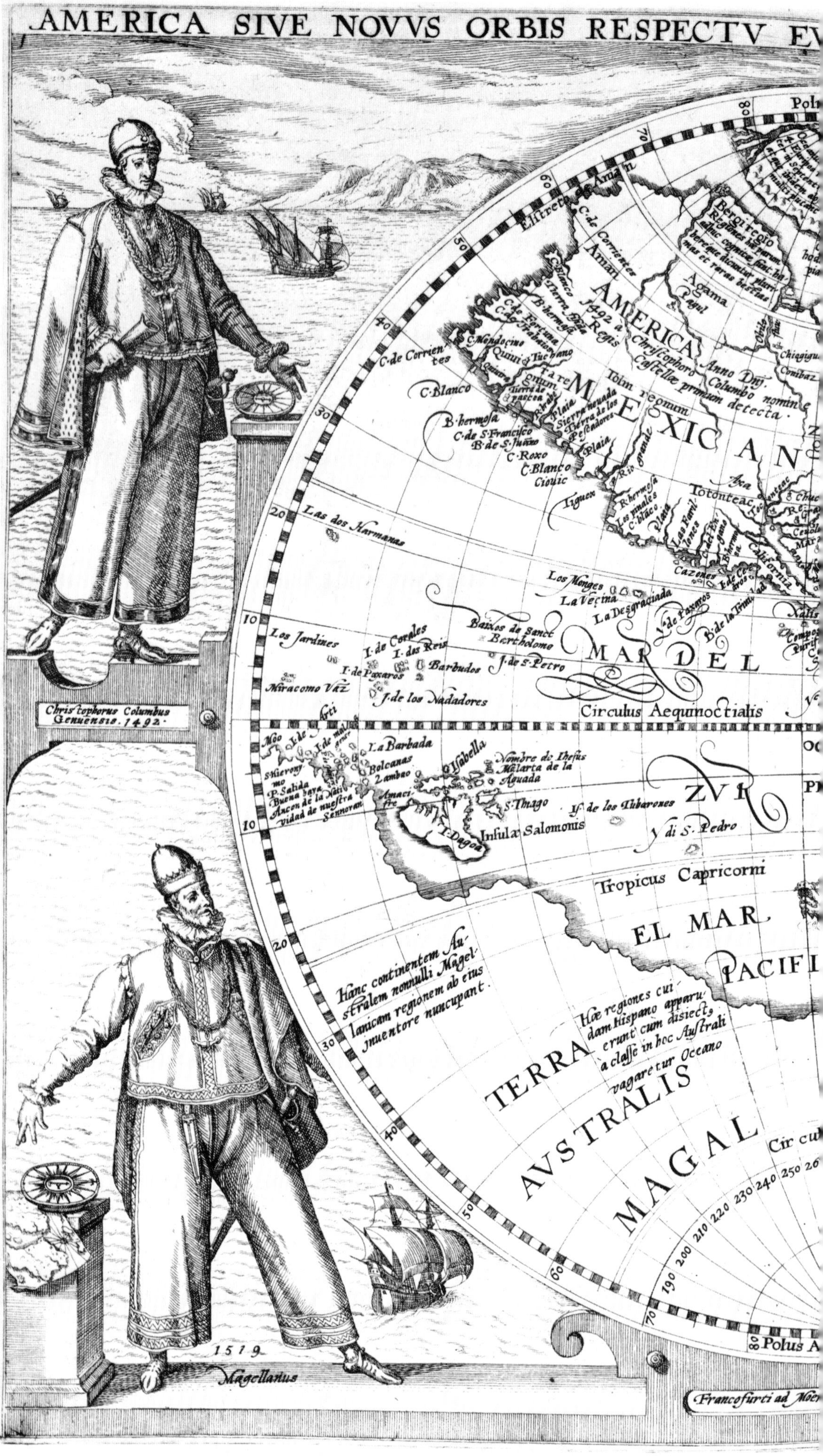
AMERICA SIVE NOVVS ORBIS RESPECTV EV
Christophorus Columbus Genuensis. 1492.
1519
Magellanus
AMERICA 1492 a Christophoro Columbo nomine Regis Castellæ primum detecta.
MEXICANA
MAR DEL
Circulus Aequinoctialis
Tropicus Capricorni
EL MAR PACIFI
TERRA AVSTRALIS MAGAL
Hanc continentem Australem nonnulli Magellanicam regionem ab eius inuentore nuncupant.
Hæ regiones cuidam Hispano apparuerunt cum disiecta a classe in hoc Australi vagaretur Oceano
Insulæ Salomonis
Francofurti ad Moen

PAEORVM INFERIOR GLOBI TERRESTRIS PARS · 1596
Groenlandt
Arcticus
NOVA FRANCIA
Norombega
La Bermuda
Asores Insulæ al. Flandricæ
Tercera
Tropicus Canceri
Hesperides insulæ
Cabo Verde
Florida
Golfo Mexi
Hispaniola
Cuba
MAR DEL NORT
Panama
Quito
Peru
PERUANA
Brasil
Pernambuco
C. de S. Augustino
Fretum Magellanicum
Terra del fogo
Antarcticus
Americus Vesputius Florentinus · 1497 ·
Theod. de Bry
1526.

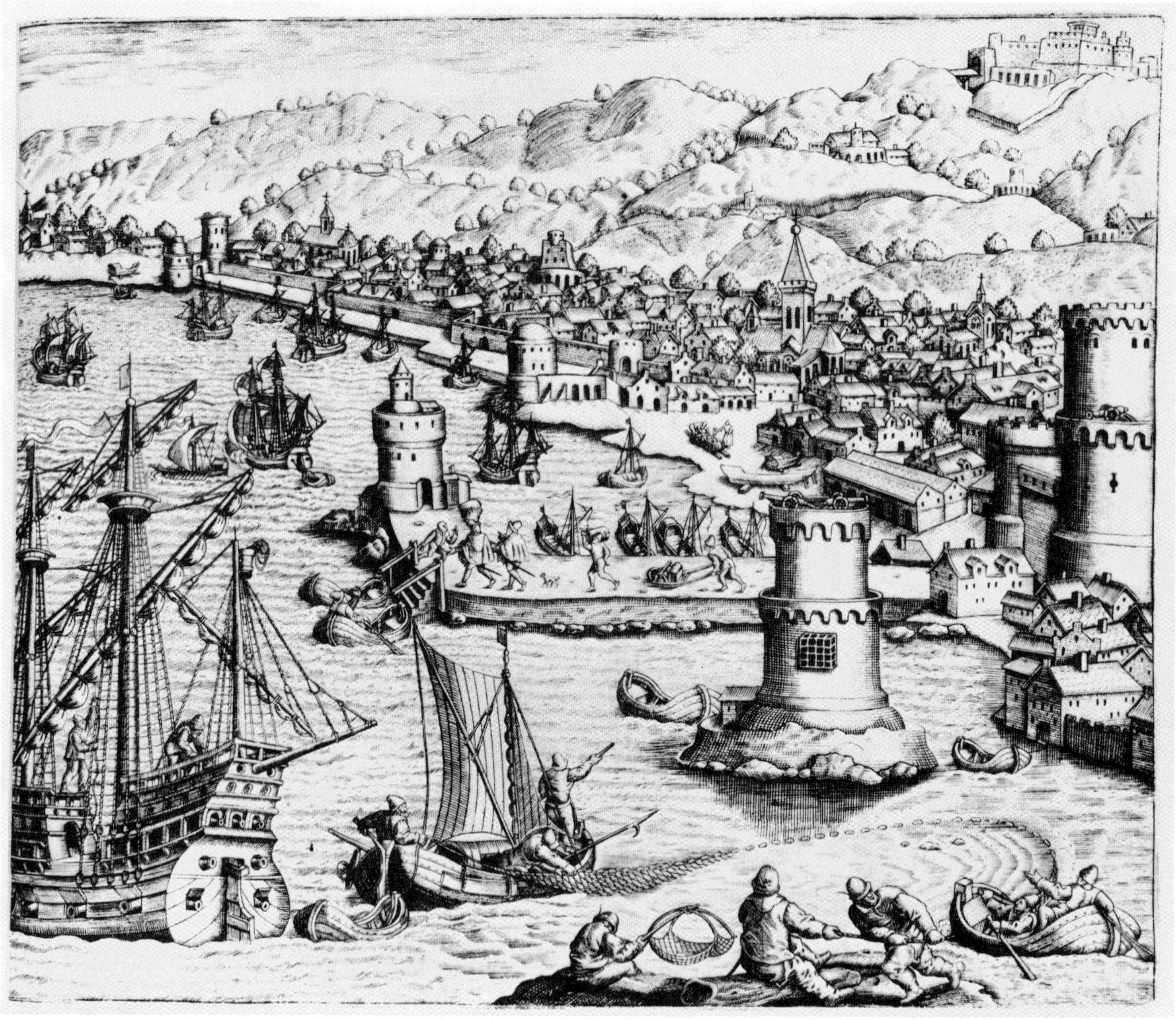

When I was a young man of twenty-two I was, like many others, anxious to see the world and hearing of those lands of the Indians, lately found, and called by everybody the New World, I determined to go there.

In the year 1541 I started from Milan going by land to Medina del Campo. From thence I went to Seville and thence by the river Guadalquivir to San Lucar de Barrameda, this being the port generally frequented by ships going to or coming from the Indies. Being unable to find a ship going direct, I embarked on a ship about to sail for the island of Great Canary, for I had heard that in the Canary islands, which are seven in number, there are constantly ships going to the Indies laden with wine, flour, apples, cheese and other things that might be required in those countries. There I learned that a caravel in the island of Palma was loading wine, wherefore I went there to join it.

Having sailed for fourteen days with a favorable wind, we saw a great quantity of seabirds, from which, to our joy, we judged we were close to land. Often in the night certain fishes about a palm in length flew on board, having what were almost the same as the wings of a bird. On a Sunday morning, at about sun-rise, we saw land.

There are many islands but the largest is called Guadeloupe. They are mostly full of Indian Caribs who eat their enemies. Then we reached Cubagua, where I met the governor.

At his urgent request I remained with him, for he offered me many inducements, telling me that he wished to assemble a large number of Spaniards and go to that part of his government now called by the Spaniards El Dorado, and that soon we should all become very rich. And thus, on the strength of these vain promises, and others he made me, I remained, being equally as desirous to see men and countries as to become rich.

Benzoni meets an ugly old woman

When we were at Cumana we were visited by an Indian woman, the wife of one of the principal chiefs of the province, bringing a basket of fruit. She was such a woman as I have never before or since seen the like of; so that my eyes could not be satisfied with looking at her for wonder. Having entered Governor Pedro Herrera's house and placed the basket of fruit before him she sat down on a bench without speaking a word. This is how she looked: she was quite naked except where modesty forbids, such being customary throughout all this country; she was old, and painted black, with long hair down to her waist; her ear-rings had so weighed down her ears that they reached her shoulders – a thing wonderful to see. She had her ears split down the middle and filled with rings of a certain carved wood, very light, they call *cacoma*. Her nails were immoderately long, her teeth were black, her mouth large, and there was a ring in her nostrils. Altogether she appeared to us like a monster rather than a human being.

The island of pearls *see following page*

On his third voyage to the Indies Columbus reached Cubagua which they called the Island of Pearls. The reason for this was as follows: cruising about the gulf in his caravels the almirante saw some Indians in a boat fishing. In order to learn what sort of people they were and where they came from he sent some sailors after them in a boat. The natives were fishing for oysters, and supposing they were good to eat they turned to open them, but were still better pleased to find them full of pearls. The Indian women were adorned with beautiful pearls yet these did not seem to be prized by their possessors. Merely for a broken earthenware plate that a sailor gave to an Indian woman she gave him four rows of her pearls. The almirante said: 'We have reached the richest country in the world!'

WHILE we were at Cumana, Captain Pedro de Calice arrived with upwards of four thousand slaves. He had captured many more, but from want of food, from labour and fatigue, and from grief at leaving their country, their fathers, their mothers or their children, they had died on the journey. And when some of them were unable to walk the Spaniards, to prevent their remaining behind where they might make war, killed them by burying their swords into their sides or breasts. It was a most distressing thing to see how these wretched creatures, naked, tired and lame, were treated. The unfortunate mothers bound with cords or chains, with two or three children on their shoulders or clinging around their necks, appeared overwhelmed with tears and grief. Nor was there a girl that had not been violated by the depredators; as a result, from too much indulgence, many Spaniards entirely lost their health. This captain had gone seven hundred miles into the interior of the country which, before the Spaniards arrived, was full of people, but was nearly depopulated by the time I went there. All the slaves the Spaniards catch in these provinces are sent to Cubagua. They are all marked with a hot iron in the face and on the arms with a *C*. The governors and captains do what they like with them. Some are given to the soldiers, who afterwards sell them or gamble them away among each other. When ships arrive from Spain they barter these Indians for goods. And even when some of the Indians are pregnant by these same Spaniards, they sell them without any conscience. Then the merchants carry them away and sell them again. They place them below the deck and, being inland people, the Indians suffer severely from the horrors of the sea. They are not allowed to move out of those sinks, and what with their sickness and other wants, and having to stand in filth like animals, and the sea often being calm and provisions failing, the poor wretches miserably expire there below.

Spanish cruelties cause the Indians to despair

After the death of Columbus, other governors were sent to Hispaniola, both clerical and secular, till the natives, finding themselves intolerably oppressed and overworked, with no chance of regaining their liberty, with sighs and tears longed for death. Many went into the woods and having killed their children, hanged themselves, saying it was far better to die than to live so miserably serving such ferocious tyrants and villainous thieves. The women terminated their pregnancies with the juice of a certain herb in order not to produce children, and then following the example of their husbands, hanged themselves. Some threw themselves from high cliffs down precipices; others jumped into the sea and rivers; others starved themselves to death. Sometimes they killed themselves with their flint knives; others pierced their bosoms or sides with pointed stakes. Finally, out of two million inhabitants, through suicides and other deaths occasioned by the excessive labour and cruelties imposed by the Spaniards, there are not a hundred and fifty now to be found.

THE Spaniards taught their hounds, fierce dogs, to attack and devour the Indians as if they had been swine in the space of time that one might say a Credo. These dogs wrought great destruction and slaughter, and forasmuch as sometimes, although seldom, when the Indians put to death some Spaniards upon good right and law of justice; they made a law between them that for one Spaniard they had to slay a hundred Indians.

A certain Spaniard went one day to hunt deer or rabbits but found none and, worried lest his dogs should go hungry, he took a sweet little baby which he bereaved the mother of, and cut off its arms and legs. These he chopped into small gobbets and fed them to the dogs, and when all these morsels were thus dispatched, he cast the rest of the body or carcass into the kennel.

It is also said that when Balboa was crossing the isthmus of Panama he had forty hermaphrodites killed by dogs.

FERNANDO de Soto, with five hundred Spaniards, was appointed governor of Florida, which province was discovered by Ponce de Leon. Soto went scouring about through many districts in the hope of finding some great treasure. Having seen several Indians wearing gold trinkets, he enquired where they got them and they said from a very distant country. The governor, thinking they said this only to be rid of him, began to torture some of them in order to make them confess the whereabouts of the gold. Amongst other cruelties he inflicted on these people, he seized fifteen *caciques* and threatened to burn them if they did not show him whence they obtained the gold. These miserable men, surprised and frightened, and hardly knowing what they were saying, promised to lead him within eight days to a place where he would find it in great abundance. But after marching upwards of twelve days without seeing any signs of gold, the governor, becoming bitterly enraged, had their hands cut off and set them loose. Then the governor proceeded, sometimes in one direction, sometimes in another, hoping to find very rich mines, without caring about building a town. After five years he died of a flux of blood, thus losing his life and his thirst for gold at the same time, as well as the treasure he had obtained from Peru.

THE Indian chiefs of the province of Cumana, seeing that the Spanish captain d'Ocampo had gone off with most of the soldiery, agreed to rise in arms. There only remained the Christians whom the doctor had left together in a group, besides those who were wandering about rapacious for pearls, licentious to the women, and doing many other wanton violences. On a Sunday morning the natives assailed the Spaniards, so that all who were in Amaracapanna and along the seashore to the west were killed. The monks were killed while saying mass, and in Cumana they attacked the doctor's house and took it, and nearly all the horsemen were most cruelly killed with poison darts. The rest escaped in a boat with some monks who fled to Cubagua carrying the sacrament with them. The houses, churches and monasteries were all burned, the huts pulled down, the images broken, as well as the crucifixes, and strewn about the place in contempt. They destroyed even the dogs and fowls, nor would they forgive the Indians themselves who were in the service of the Spaniards and their priests. Such was their violence that even the Spaniards who lived in Cubagua were afraid for their lives. Nor is there any doubt but that had the Indians sufficient boats they would have gone over to the island, which is only twenty-two miles distant in the gulf, and made an end to all the Spaniards there.

A proof of Spanish mortality

When the Spaniards first went to conquer the island they call San Juan de Porto-rico on account of the abundance of gold and silver found there, the Indians believed that they were immortal. A certain chief decided to put the matter to the test and ordered his men to seize a Spaniard who was lodging in his house, carry him to the river, and then hold him under water so long that if he was mortal he would be drowned. Having thus drowned him, they carried him back on their shoulders to their master, who, seeing that he was dead, considered that all the others must also be mortal. Thus he concerted a revolt with the other chiefs who had suffered ill-treatment from the Spaniards. They killed about a hundred and fifty who were dispersed about the island seeking gold and had not Diego Salazar arrived with reinforcements the Spaniards would have been cut to pieces to a man.

SUCH was the cruelty of the Spaniards to the Indians at the pearl fisheries that one morning, at dawn, the Indians assailed the Spaniards, made a bloody slaughter of them and with dancing and leaping, ate them, both monks and laymen. Some few escaped in a caravel that was lying in the Cumana river and sent to San Domenico to inform the governor of the rebellion. He immediately raised three hundred soldiers under command of Diego d'Ocampo. Approaching the scene of the rebellion, he ordered that all except the sailors should hide below decks so that the Indians, seeing few Spaniards, would be tempted to come on board supposing that they had come direct from Spain and were ignorant of the massacre. Accordingly, when the Indians asked from whence they came they replied from Castile and invited them on board the ship. The Indians were suspicious, but seeing so few Christians on board, were persuaded they were from Spain. The captain, pretending not to know anything, received them kindly and bartered for pearls, and entreated them by signs to go and fetch more pearls as well as provisions for the ship. The Indians informed their *cacique* that the Christians were few and they could easily kill them all, upon which he ordered a great many of his men to return to the ship and to tempt the sailors to come ashore with promises of a great store of pearls for barter. When sufficient Indians were on board the captain made his soldiers rush up from their hiding place. Some they took prisoners, others they killed and the rest jumped overboard. Those that were captured, the captain hanged from the yard-arms to strike terror into the survivors; and thus he returned to Cubagua, leaving the islanders astounded and confused at such a spectacle.

The Indians pour molten gold into the mouths of the Christians

ALONG most of the coast of Darien they are accustomed to eat human flesh, though some were afraid to eat the flesh of Spaniards, thinking that even in their bodies it might do them harm. Those they caught alive, in particular the captains, they used to tie up by their hands and feet. Then they would throw them to the ground and pour molten gold into their mouths saying 'Eat, eat gold, Christian', and to further ill-treat and humiliate them, with flint knives some cut off an arm, some a shoulder, some a leg, and then roasting the meat on embers they would eat it, dancing and singing. They would hang up the bones in their temples or in the chiefs' houses, as trophies of victory.

 see also following pages

WHEN the natives of Hispaniola began to be extirpated, the Spaniards provided themselves with blacks from Guinea, which was a conquest of the king of Portugal, and they have brought great numbers from there. When there were mines they made them work at extracting gold and silver; but since those came to an end they have increased the sugar works and it is in this industry and in tending the flocks and in the general service of their masters that they are chiefly occupied. Some of the Spaniards were not only cruel, but very cruel. If a slave had committed some crime, or had not done a good day's work, or had failed to extract the usual quantity of gold or silver from the mine, he might be severely punished. When the negro came home at night his master, instead of giving him supper, might make him undress, if he happened to have a shirt on, and being thrown on the ground have his hands and feet tied to a piece of wood laid across (which was permitted by the Spaniards under the law of Baiona, a law suggested, I consider, by some great demon). He was then beaten with a thong or rope until his body streamed with blood, after which they took a pound of pitch or a pipkin of boiling oil and poured it gradually over the unfortunate victim; then he was washed with some country pepper mixed with salt and water. He was thus left on a plank covered over with a cloth until his master thought he was able to work again. Others dug a hole in the ground and put the man in upright, with only his head out, and left him there all night, the Spaniards saying that they have recourse to this cure because the earth absorbs the blood and preserves the flesh from forming any wound, and so they get well sooner. And if any die (as sometimes happens) through great pain, there is no heavier punishment by law than that the master shall pay another slave to the king.

Thus, on account of these very great cruelties, some of them escaped from their masters and wandered about the island in a desperate state. They have gradually multiplied to such a degree that they have caused, and still cause, the Spanish population a great deal of trouble. The presidents and

auditors of the island, finally seeing how these blacks multiplied, and that all the Spaniards who fell into their hands were made to die under every form of torment, began to collect men together and send them into all parts of the island where the negroes hid themselves. At first it turned out well for the Spaniards, for taking with them some blacks who knew the locality and promising them liberty, they would attack the runaways in the night, and finding them asleep like a herd of animals, they would capture and kill a great many of them. But in the end the negroes learned to keep watch and be very vigilant whereby the Spaniards often got the worst of it. Thus the blacks have become so fierce and numerous that when I was residing on the island it was asserted that there were upwards of seven thousand. And in the year '45, while I was there, it was reported that the *Cimaroni* (for so the Spaniards in those countries call the outlaws) had joined a general rebellion and were rampaging all over the island and doing all the mischief they could. Many Spaniards prophesy for certain that the island in a short time will fall entirely into the hands of these blacks.

How they make objects of gold in Quito

SINCE the province of Quito has a temperate climate the kings of Cusco lived there much of the time and had goldsmiths shops in many parts of the town. These craftsmen still manufacture wonderful objects even without the use of any tools of iron. They work in the following manner: in the first place, when they want to melt the metal, they put it into either a long or round *grisolo* made of cloth daubed with a mixture of earth and pounded charcoal. When dry it is put into the fire and filled with metal. Then several men, each with a reed, blow the fire until the metal is fused. It is now taken out and the goldsmiths, with some black stones of the proper shape, make, or rather used to make during the days of their prosperity, whatever they were commissioned to do: hollow statues, vases, sheep, ornaments and, in short, any animal they saw. (Their kings used to have private gardens where all the trees, flowers and plants were made out of gold.)

How the Indians defended their hill against the Spaniards

On his way to Sibolla with seven hundred soldiers and horses Alvarado received news that the Indians of Salisco had rebelled against the Spaniards. He therefore went to the assistance of his countrymen with the greater part of his force. They went to a large hill, the summit of which the Indians had fortified with tree-trunks which were holding back large boulders. When the Spaniards, with great ferocity, began to run up the hill, the Indians, yelling frightfully, cut the trees asunder so that everything fell headlong down to the bottom in such a way as to kill a great number of the assailants. Alvarado was thrown from his horse and died in the course of two days. When he was asked what pained him, he said his *soul* afflicted him sorely. He was of moderate stature, a great talker, but false, and so ungrateful of any benefits received that it is said of him that he never kept his word to any friend. He married two sisters, and cohabited with both of them.

The Spaniards burn an Indian village *see following page*

While the governor Hodeida was fighting with the Indians at Carthagena, Diego de Niquesa arrived there with a fleet carrying about seven hundred men. He found Hodeida much afflicted because a few days earlier he had gone to a tribe twelve miles inland hoping to capture gold. But he found the Indians in arms and returned to the sea shore with the loss of seventy-five soldiers. With Diego di Niquesa he resolved to avenge the death of those killed.

They set off one evening and surprised the Indians at dawn. The Indians endeavoured to escape but they were nearly all killed. Some threw themselves on the flames, preferring a voluntary death in the fire to a forced one on a Spanish sword. This tribe had about a hundred huts made of reeds and roofed with palm. When the ashes had cooled they searched for gold, but found little.

OWING to complaints lodged against Balboa with the Council of the Indies, a rigorous sentence was pronounced against him though it was not afterwards carried out because he discovered the Southern Sea.

When his accuser had left Darien, Balboa started inland in search of gold. He made friends with some chiefs, one of whom was called Panciaco, who gave him full information and led him to the Southern Sea. This man was then baptized with the name of Don Carlos. He gave the Spaniards a certain quantity of gold, but seeing how they quarreled in the sharing of it, he tossed it all out of the scales onto the ground saying: 'I am not a little surprised that you Christians make so many difficulties about so vile a thing, as if it were good for eating or drinking. But since you have such a desire for this metal, I will lead you to a place where you may all satisfy ourselves with it.' He then conducted them to the Southern Sea. Balboa, on account of the great riches he found in this province, named it the Golden Castille; and there the city of Panama is now established.

MEANWHILE we caught a great many turtles of immense size, for during four months they flock to the beach to lay their eggs which are consequently found there in great numbers. Like crocodiles they lay them in the sand and there the intense heat of the sun hatches the young turtles. We took off the shells and collecting the fat, reduced it down and filled large earthen jars. We also salted some of the flesh, but it soon spoiled, though when fresh it was very wholesome and excellent eating. The first day we entered port the Governor graciously placed me at his table and took pleasure in conversing with me. The greater part of his conversation was about gold and silver and the wars, and the cruelties inflicted on wretched Italy, especially Milan. But when he saw that such subjects were disagreeable to me he took a dislike to me and never could stand the sight of me after.

AFTER spending eleven months in Hispaniola I sailed from San Domingo in a ship bound for Terra Firma and in six days we saw the snowy mountains of Santa Martha. We shortly entered the port of Carthagena, so called because it has an islet at the entrance like Carthagena in Spain. In these parts the people have plenty of fruit, fish, and all the other necessities of life. Their only clothing is a decent bandage round their loins. When they go to war, the women fight as well as the men. Their arms are poisoned arrows. They eat their enemies and have eaten many Spaniards and would do the same by the rest if they could. On feast days they would adorn themselves with ornaments of gold, pearls and emeralds, putting some on their arms, on their legs, on their faces, and other parts of the body. Their principal products are salt, fish, and pepper; and they barter these inland where there is a deficiency. In prosperous times they held fine large markets of grain, fruits, cotton, feathers, ornaments, gold, pearls, slaves and other goods.

right

IN Nicaragua I lodged in the house of one of the principal chiefs of the province called Don Gonzalo, who was seventy years old, and understood Spanish perfectly. Whilst seated at his side one morning he looked me in the face and said: 'What is a Christian? The Christians? They ask for maize, for honey, for cotton, for mantles, for women, for gold, for silver; Christians will not work, they are liars, gamblers, perverse, and they swear. When they go to church to hear the mass they discourse on those who are absent; they wound each other.' Finally, he concluded that the Christians are not good; and when I told him that it was the wicked among them who behaved thus, he enquired: 'Then where are the good ones? for I have known none but the wicked.' Then I asked him why and how it was that they had allowed the Christians to enter their country? He replied: 'Sir, thou shalt

Benzoni discourses with his Indian hosts

know that, hearing the Christians were coming to our countries, killing, burning and robbing, we took council with all our friends and allies and decided that rather than allow ourselves to be subjugated we would all die, fighting valorously. So we prepared lances and stone darts and other arms, and when the Christians reached our people we assaulted them, and fought a great part of the day. But at last most of us were so frightened by the impetus of the horses that we fled. We then sent two ambassadors to the captain of the Christians to ask for peace, only with a view to reconstituting our forces, and thus he accepted us as friends. Then a considerable number of us paid them a dissimulating visit, dancing and singing, and carrying many presents of gold and other things. In three days we were ready to assault them, but again our people ran away; and again we sued for peace. . . . Having obtained it, we assembled and decided in council that we would rather die than serve the invaders and that if any of our nation ran away they should be put to death. Thus resolved, we prepared to attack, but our wives came and entreated us to serve the Christians rather than die. If not, we should first kill them and their little children, so that they should not remain alone in the hands of those cruel men. Thus we submitted to the rapacious rule of the Spaniards. But in a short time some of our tribes rose against them, for which they were punished and even their infants were put to the sword. The Spaniards seized other tribes, claiming that they were going to rebel; these they tormented and sold into slavery. We were no longer masters of our wives, or our children, or anything that we possessed. Many men killed their children, others hanged themselves, others starved themselves to death; so that after innumerable and unbearable sufferings, tyrannies and miseries, the King of Castile sent a decree that we should be restored to liberty.'

Hoping to obtain food and shelter for the night from the Indians, we stealthily approached a dwelling that we saw to be occupied, so they would not run away under the impression that we had come to take them as slaves. As soon as the Indians awoke and saw us they set up a cry of 'Guacci, Guacci', which is the name of a small quadruped that prowls about at night, living on prey, and this is a name they have given to all the Christians! Having seized them I may say that I have never heard so much crying, especially from the women, as I did that night, for they thought they were going to be taken as slaves. They threw their heads about disconsolately, talked grievously together, knocked their heads on the ground, tore our clothes with their hands and teeth like wild beasts and spat in our faces. Truly, if we had not prevented them, some of them would have killed themselves. We sought to appease them by signs that we had only come to their houses for food, and that for the future they need have no fear, for the King of Castile had commanded that there should be no more slaves. Thus they were somewhat pacified and provided us with bread, fish, fruits, and the flesh of wild pigs, which in India always have bristles along the back. In payment we gave them some knives and a little salt.

FRENCH ships sacked many places on the coast. To put an end to their depredations the Spaniards took certain actions off the island of Cubagua, during the time of the flourishing pearl fishing. Detecting the arrival of a French ship they sent two local boats with fifty Indians armed with bows and arrows. They told the Indians that the French were all pederasts and if they did not kill them they would leap on shore and seizing the Indians would make infamous use of them. The Indians did not wait to hear more but went immediately towards the ship. The French stared at the new naked people, perhaps thinking they were only going to look at them or barter for pearls; but when the Indians got close to the ship they began to throw their darts and wounded some of the French. The French had greater knowledge of the pearls in those parts than of the poisonous herbs the Indians used on their arrows. As soon as they were wounded and found that those darts were mortal, they immediately hoisted sail and went away. Nor, as far as I have heard, has any French ship ever again ventured to the island. It was in this cunning manner that the greatly alarmed Spaniards freed themselves of the French.

5

Customs of the Indians in Mexico and Peru

José de Acosta, whose account de Bry used for the following plates, was born in 1540 at Medina del Campo, near Valladolid, Spain. He became a member of the Society of Jesus at the age of fourteen and for the next eighteen years seems to have devoted himself to sacred and classical studies. Little information is available about his life save that which can be extracted from his writing, in particular from his greatest work *Historia natural y moral de las Indias (The Natural and Moral History of the Indies)*.

Acosta went to the New World with some brother Jesuits in 1570 at the age of thirty. He landed at Carthagena and again at Nombre de Dios from whence he journeyed overland to Panama. His work as a missionary took him to Lima, Peru, where he was ordered to join the viceroy, Francisco de Toledo, the other side of the Andes. At about the time of Acosta's arrival nineteen years after the downfall of the Inca, Atahualpa, in Peru, de Toledo had ordered the beheading of the young Inca, Tupac Amaru. Acosta accompanied the energetic Viceroy on an administrative tour of the provinces and then settled down at Julli, near Lake Titicaca, where the Jesuits had established a college for the study of native languages and where they had set up a printing press.

Acosta was appointed historian to the Third Council of Lima, which discussed among other things the customs and superstitions of the Indians which the Church might wish to suppress. From material collected for the consideration of the council together with information gathered from the leading Spanish savants in the New World, he assembled a mass of miscellaneous data which was to form the basis of his history. Like Pliny, who was to some extent his inspiration, Acosta had an enquiring mind and covered a wide variety of subjects from religious philosophy and social customs to physical geography and natural history. He returned to Spain in 1587 and prepared his material for publication. The complete work, published in Seville in 1590, was entitled:

> *Historia natural y moral de las Indias. . . .* In which are discussed the notable things of the heavens, the elements, metals, plants, animals; and the rites, ceremonies, laws, governments, and wars of the Indians.

It contains much interesting information, and in 1601 the de Bry family (Theodore had by now died) issued part of the text in Part IX of the *America* series under the title *De novi orbis natura . . . (Concerning the nature of the New World)*. There was no mention of the author, nor is there any evidence as to the source of the illustrations which, though lively, must in many cases be considered works of the imagination.

Acosta went to Rome in 1589 and published a number of learned theological works. He became head of the Jesuit College at Salamanca where he died in 1600.

AMERICAE
PARS QVARTA.
Sive,
Insignis & Admiranda Historia de reperta
primùm Occidentali India à Christophoro
Columbo Anno M. CCCCXCII
Scripta ab Hieronymo Bezono Mediolanense,
qui istic ānis XIIII. versatus, diligēter omnia observa=
vit.
Addita ad singula ferè capita, non contemnenda scholia,
in quibus agitur de earum etiam gentium idololatria.
Accessit præterea illarum Regionum Tabula
chorographica.
Omnia elegantibus figuris in aes incisis expre=
ssa à Theodoro de Bry Leodiense, cive
Francofurtensi Anno cIↃ Iↄ XCIIII.
Cum previlegio S. C. Maiestat.

How they crossed rivers without bridges

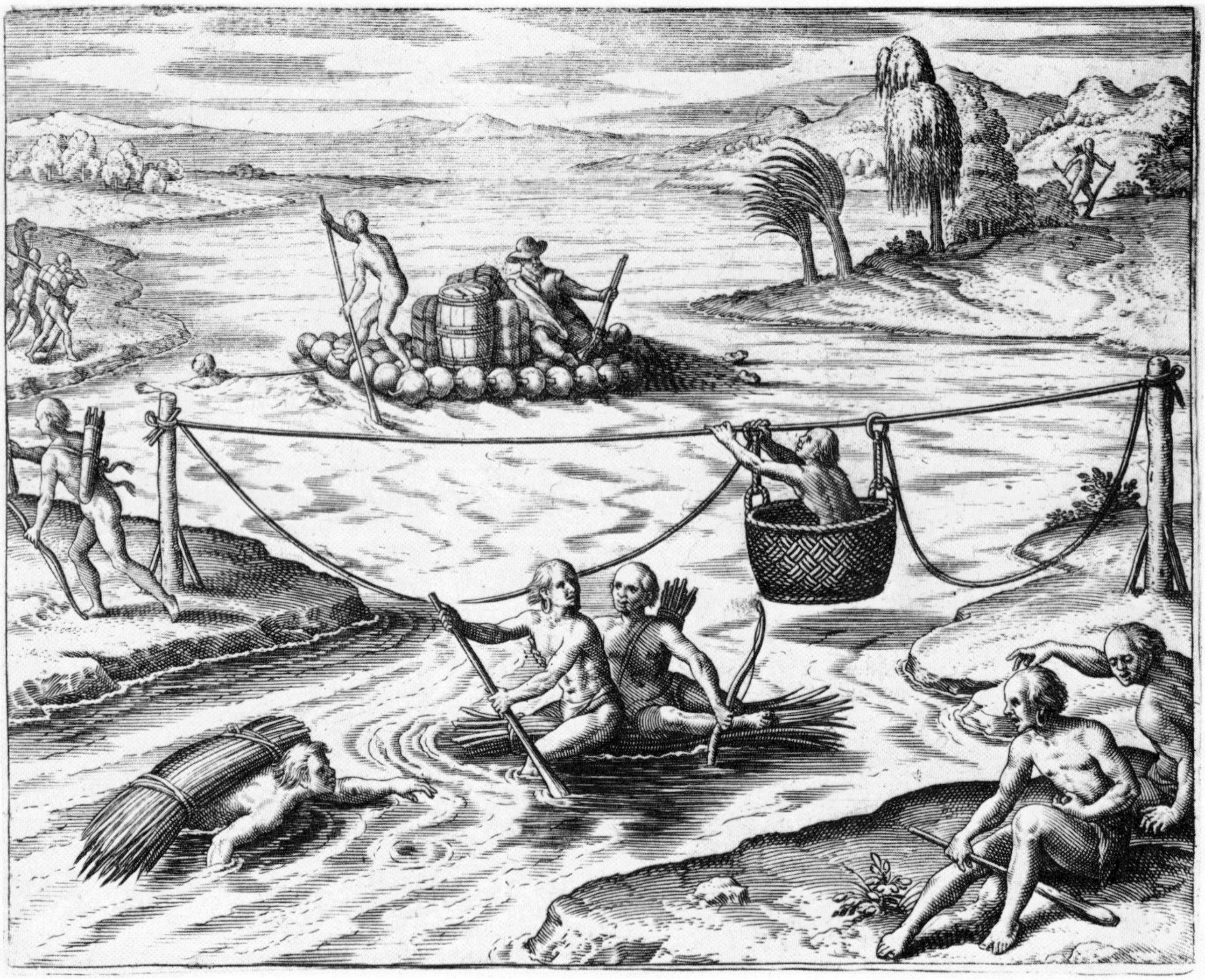

In America the rivers are many and large, larger than any in Europe. As the Indians had no bridges, they stretched a rope over the water, attaching it at both ends to two poles. From this rope they hung a basket. Sitting in the basket it was possible to either be pulled or pull oneself across the river, using the rope. Others, again, had bundles of reeds on which they could sit and row themselves over. They also constructed large rafts made of dried pumpkins and thus rowed to one shore and back, transporting passengers and merchandise.

THE Mexicans were told by their god, Vitzliputzli, that they would know when they had reached the land they were looking for by watching out for the Tunal Tree which grew on its shore. They found the tree and in it was sitting the most beautiful eagle they had ever seen. Seeing this beautiful eagle they fell on their knees and prayed. Then they honoured their god by building an altar and later the city of Mexico. The Mexicans had to bring a yearly tribute to the king of that region whose name was Azcapuzalco. They brought him a beautiful garden with plenty of fruit, also some storks and geese. The garden was supposed to grow on the water and was not allowed to be transported anywhere else except where there was water.

BOTH in New Spain and in Mexico, the Indians had many different dances. For amusement, many dances were performed on a rope and in others they danced or jumped on each others' shoulders. They also had a special dance to assemble all the dancers. The instruments used are a collection of drums accompanied by singers. The dancers, drummers and singers all keep in time by stamping their feet. The most usual dance, commonly made in spacious places, was the *mittotte*, a dance they held so brave and honourable that the king himself danced. The people, wearing their finest clothes, made great circles round the noblemen and ancients, who danced slowly and softly, while the people danced more noisily together.

A VERY particular sort of sheep exists in Peru, which the Indians called *llamas.* They used these animals to transport goods and silver from the mines, they ate their meat and used their wool for making blankets. These sheep were not expensive to keep because saddles were not necessary and they ate whatever they found in the fields. However, the llamas were supposed to be very stubborn. If they did not want to advance, nothing could be done save lie next to them for two or three hours until they were prepared to continue. If sometimes they refused to come down a mountain, and it was necessary to regain the merchandise they were transporting, they were shot so that they would fall down the mountain.

How the Indians mine silver from the rock

THE Indians work in the mountain range called Potosi, known to be the richest in Mexico for the amount of silver to be found there.

The silver has to be mined out of the rock and the workers are separated into two shifts; one group works during the day, the other during the night. Neither see much daylight because they work deep below the surface and so always need candles in order to see. They have constructed a long ladder made of ox-hides by which they bring the silver out of the mountain. As they need both hands to hold on to the ladder, they always attach a candle to their thumb and carry the heavy loads on their backs up to the daylight. So they may rest occasionally, they have carved stone-benches into the rock.

How the Mexicans were provoked into battle

THE Indians of Cuyoacan saw that the Mexicans were becoming stronger in number and more powerful so they decided to try and provoke them into a battle and hopefully defeat them. As annoying the Mexican women in the markets did not seem to affect them, they planned to invite the Mexicans to a large feast. When they arrived, they apparently were forced to wear women's clothes. Having been totally ridiculed by the Indians, the Mexicans fled, only to return later, reinforced by their troops, finally to defeat the Indians of Cuyoacan.

Their methods of hunting game *see following page*

THE Indians in Mexico have a strange way of hunting. In the morning, at the sound of a trumpet, the hunters assemble. The procession starts to ascend a hill where the hunt is to take place. They are equipped with a statue of their god, bows and arrows and other attire. On the top of the hill they build an altar of green twigs where they place the statue. Then they go to the bottom of the hill again and make a few fires around it to chase the game out and up to the top where they finally kill it by shooting or hitting it to death. After which, they take their god down and proceed back to their village. To honour and thank the god, the hearts of all the dead game are sacrificed to him.

It is said of the Mexican superstition concerning their dead, that when a nobleman died, he was stretched out in a private chamber with his armour placed next to him. Then friends and relatives arrived to honour and greet him and offer him presents as if he were still alive. After this he was left alone. When the time of the funeral approached he was carried by a priest and followed by a procession to the place where he was to be buried. Instruments were played and ritual songs performed. Then came the priests carrying incense containers, followed by the dead man with his servants carrying his armour and all his presents. The servants were burned and buried with their master in order to continue serving him in his other life. When the procession arrived at the burial place, the deceased and all his servants were burned under the supervision of a priest in devil's dress. The ashes were collected, put into a container and buried with all the presents and the armour.

How the priests atone for the sins of ordinary people

THE priests in Mexico have particular fasting days to honour their god, Vitzliputzli. They meet and play their instruments. The high priest arrives with incense for the god and then, with a special wooden device, he pierces his leg or foot and smears the blood on his forehead. The wooden device is then put back in its special place in the temple so that everyone can see the extent of their atonement. Also, during particular times of the year, the ordinary people castigate themselves with ropes and stones and even, on certain occasions, with stinging nettles.

Concerning human sacrifices in Mexico *see following page*

ONCE a year the Indians of Mexico had a ceremony in which all their prisoners were led up to the Mexican Temple where the 'Mountain of the Round Skulls' is and were seated side by side there.

Shortly afterwards, a priest descended from the highest square mountain, wearing his ceremonial robe and holding a statue of their god in one hand. With this he went from one prisoner to the next, saying, 'Look! This is your god.' After which a prisoner was taken to the top of this mountain where the sacrifice took place. Six priests stood there awaiting him. Four held the man over a stone and put a wooden band round his neck. Then the fifth, who was the high-priest, cut open his breast and took the heart, still warm and pulsating, showed it to the people, and cast it on the image of their god. The body was rolled down the steps.

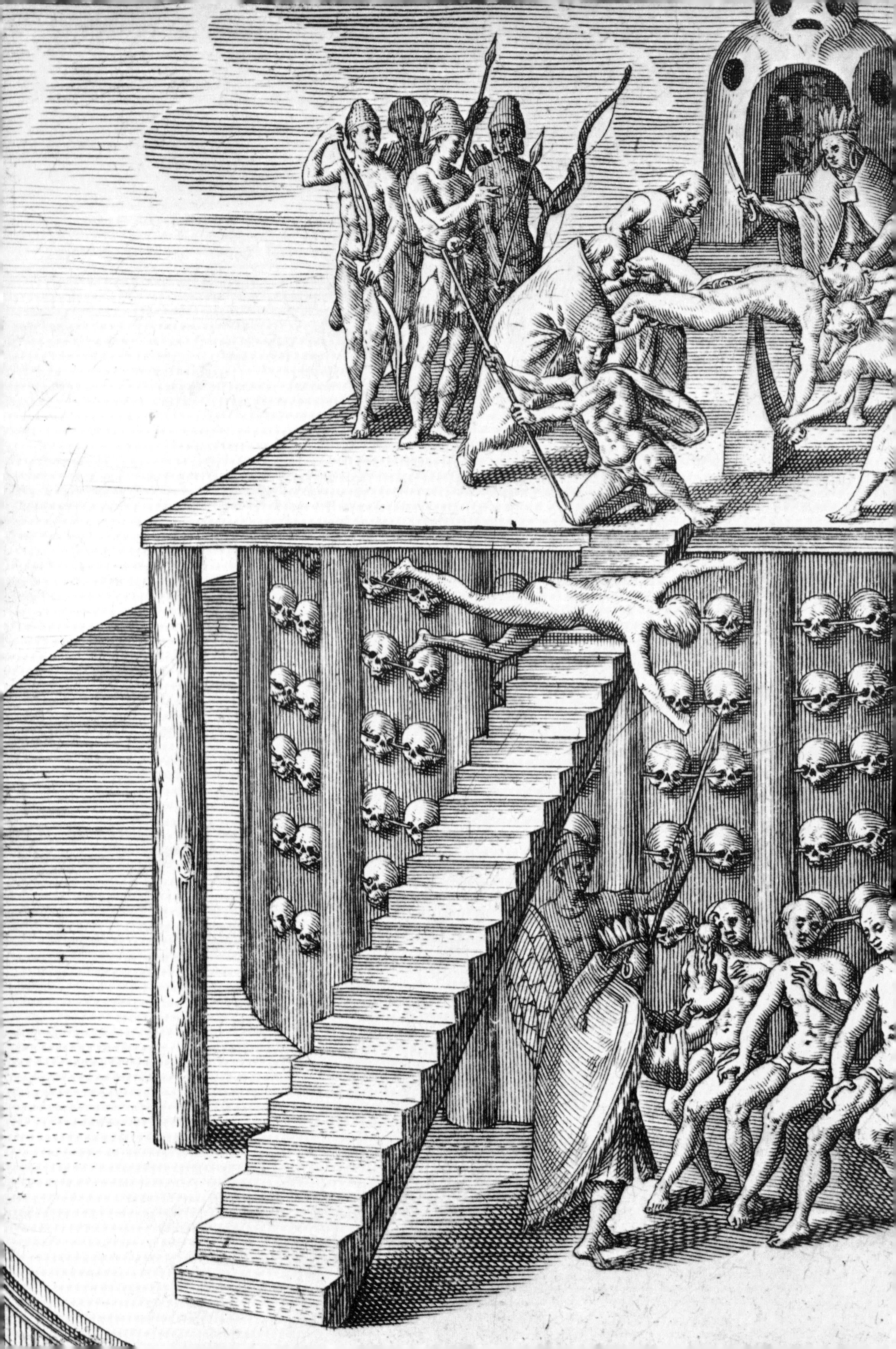

THE Mexicans also had another kind of human sacrifice. A prisoner was chosen and given the most beautiful apartment in the temple. He was dressed with the god's jewels and was served the most exquisite food while wives with noblemen kept him company at table. During the night he was imprisoned in a large birdcage, but during the day he could go wherever he chose, although, of course, he was always accompanied by the guards who also served him. Wherever he went the people would clear the way to let him pass and would fall on their knees to worship and honour him. So for one year he could do as he pleased. At the end of this year, at a certain feast, he was bound by one foot to a stone, and given a sword and shield to fight against a priest who challenged him. If the priest was slain, the prisoner was freed and greatly honoured. However if the prisoner was defeated he was immediately skinned alive. Then his skin was taken from house to house and finally offered to the god.

THE Indians of Florida fished whales in the following manner. When after large whales, every Indian went in a canoe. As soon as a whale appeared, the fisherman drove towards it and stepped from the canoe onto the animal's back, he then drove two wooden pegs into its air-holes. When the whale became tired through lack of air, the Indians pulled him ashore by means of a rope which they attached to the pegs. Then they could cut him to pieces. The Indians of Peru fished in another way, with nets. First, they built themselves small rafts, made of long reeds and held together by string. These could be sat upon like a horse. Then they rowed themselves out on the rafts to where they wanted to throw their nets. After they had fished enough they returned, untied their rafts and left the reeds to dry on the land.

6

Sir Walter Raleigh searches for El Dorado

His Virginia project a failure, out of favour with Queen Elizabeth, Sir Walter Raleigh concentrated his energies in pursuit of a legend – El Dorado, or Manoa, golden city of the expropriated Inca that travellers' tales located in the jungles of Guiana. A half-crazed priest, a Spanish governor captured at sea, and the man on the spot, Don Antonio Berreo, indicated the Orinoco as the way thither. In May 1595 Raleigh was at its mouth ready to row up the muddy estuarine branches. After a week of hard work along the main watercourse they reached the junction of the Caroni and had reports of 'a nation of people whose heads appear not above their shoulders' and Amazon ladies who brought up their daughters to be warriors. As for the gold, that again was legend. The mythical city failed to materialize up the Caroni and Raleigh returned home with no more than plans to establish a great British empire in Guiana. In 1617 he persuaded James I to release him from the Tower of London to search again for El Dorado. It was elusive as ever. His men had killed Spaniards on the expedition: Raleigh, on the insistence of Spain, was beheaded in 1618.

His description of the expedition, published in 1596, was entitled:

> THE DISCOVERIE OF THE LARGE RICH AND BEWTIFUL EMPYRE OF GUIANA, WITH a relation of the Great and Golden City of Manoa (which the Spaniards call El Dorado), and the provinces of Emeria, Arromaia, Amapaia and other Countries, with their rivers, adioyning.

Its text was issued by the de Brys in 1599 with a few imaginative illustrations and a map. It is regrettable that Raleigh did not take along with him an artist of the calibre of John White.

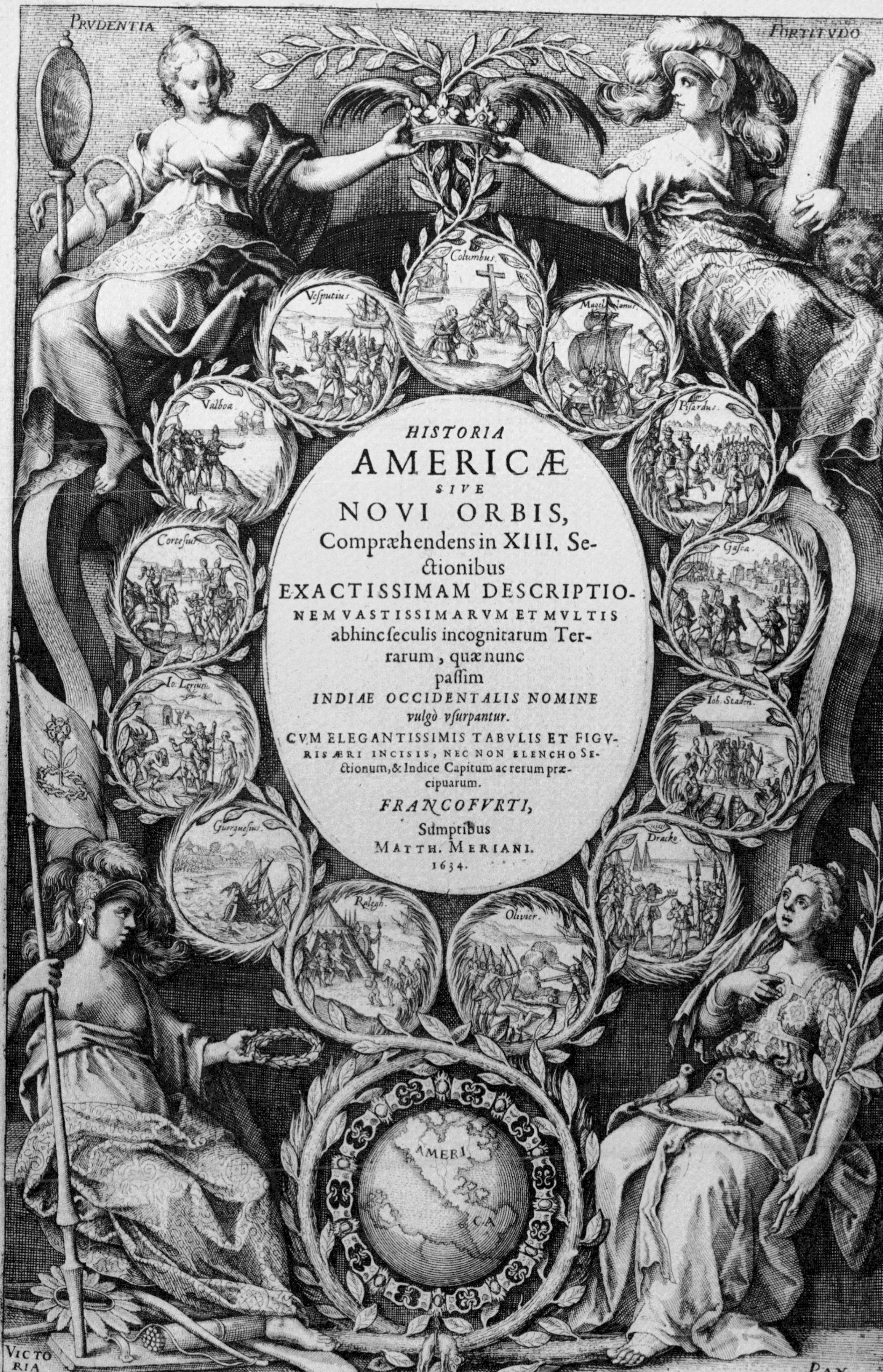
PRVDENTIA
FORTITVDO
Columbus.
Vesputius.
Magellanus.
Valboa.
Pisardus.
HISTORIA
AMERICÆ
SIVE
NOVI ORBIS,
Compræhendens in XIII. Sectionibus
EXACTISSIMAM DESCRIPTIONEM VASTISSIMARVM ET MVLTIS abhinc seculis incognitarum Terrarum, quæ nunc passim
INDIAE OCCIDENTALIS NOMINE vulgò vsurpantur.
CVM ELEGANTISSIMIS TABVLIS ET FIGVRIS ÆRI INCISIS, NEC NON ELENCHO Sectionum, & Indice Capitum ac rerum præcipuarum.
FRANCOFVRTI,
Sumptibus
MATTH. MERIANI.
1634.
Cortesius.
Gasta.
Io. Lerius.
Ioh. Staden.
Gurguesius.
Dracke.
Relegh.
Olivier.
AMERI
CA
VICTORIA
PAX.

How Sir Walter Raleigh conquers a city and takes as prisoner a Spanish Governor

WHEN Sir Walter Raleigh arrived at the island of Trinidad with his ships, he had only kind words and friendly gestures for the Spanish at Puerto de los Espanioles, thus enabling him to obtain all information concerning the general situation on the island and their fighting capabilities. Having investigated the information he had acquired, he summoned 100 soldiers under Captain Caulfield's command and one evening attacked the city of St Joseph, where the Spanish Governor, Don Antonio de Berreo, resided. The Spaniards put up little resistance and abandoned their city after only a few shots had been fired. Raleigh freed all the soldiers but took Berreo and his companions to his ship as prisoners.

DON Antonio de Berreo had acquired a patent to conquer Guiana, having seen that much gold was to be found there from presents brought by a chief called Morequito. One Vides, governor of Cumana, later acquired a patent himself and disputed the precedence of de Berreo by making an alliance with Morequito by which Berreo's men were to be frustrated in their efforts to explore the country. Morequito pretended to help them and gave them a guide. Berreo claimed that he had reached Manoa, great city of the Inca. It was said that they had in fact obtained this gold in other towns this side of Manoa, of which there were many, very great and rich, built like the towns of Christians, with many rooms.

As Berreo's men were returning laden with gold the people of Morequito set upon them and took all of it and killed nine soldiers and a friar. Only one lived to bring the news to Berreo, having escaped by swimming a river. Morequito took refuge in the care of Vides, but he was betrayed and delivered to Berreo's campmaster and was hanged.

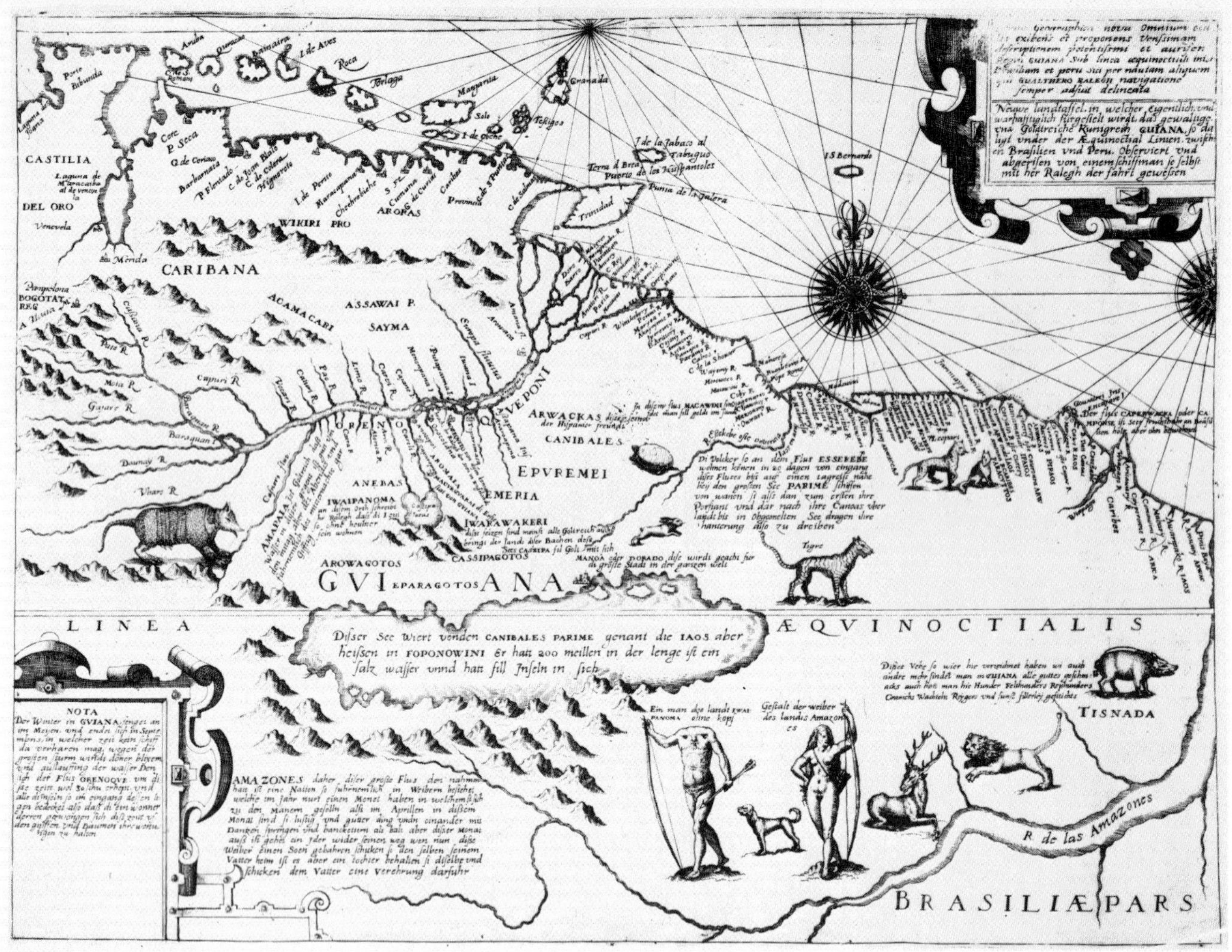

ONCE a year all the kings of the borders and the queens of the *Amazons* assemble, and after the queens have chosen, the rest cast lots for their Valentines. For one month they feast, dance and drink. If they bear a son they return it to the father, if a daughter they nourish it and retain it. But that they cut off the right dug of the breast was not found to be true.

The *Ewaiponoma* are reported to have eyes in their shoulders and their mouths in the middle of their breasts and a long train of hair growing backwards between their shoulders. They are said to be the most mighty men in the land and use bows, arrows and clubs thrice as big as any in Guiana.

How Guianan noblemen would dress in gold

LIKE their neighbours, the people of Guiana loved to drink, but they surpassed any other nation at gambling.

When a Guianan nobleman gave a feast, he first had his servants paint his entire body white, then with a small tube they blew very fine gold sand over it. The gold sand stuck to the paint and so gave the impression that their master's body was made of gold. After this, from fifty to a hundred people sat together and gambled for many days until they had enough.

Once, when the English came to a village, they saw a *cacique* called Toparimaca, who was entertaining as his guest a foreign *cacique*. They were both sitting in a brasil *hamoca* or bed, with two women serving them. Their drink was made of different herb juices and tasted very spicey. It was kept in large earthen containers.

Sir Walter Raleigh is visited by a very old king *see following page*

AT the port of Morequito a pilot was sent to look for the king of Aromaia. The king came before noon on the following day having travelled on foot fourteen English miles, and was to return the same day, and this at the age of 110. Many women and children came with him to wonder at the English and to bring victuals, which they did in plenty, such as venison, pork, chickens, fowl, fish, with divers sorts of excellent fruits and roots and great abundance of *pinas*, the princess of fruits that grow under the sun, especially those of Guiana. They also brought bread and wine and a sort of *paraquitos* no bigger than wrens. One of them gave Raleigh a beast the Spaniards call *armadillo*, which they call *cassacam*, which seems to be barred all over with small plates somewhat like a *renocero*, with a white horn growing in his hinder parts; this was as big as a great hunting horn and they would blow it instead of a trumpet. Monardus writes that a little powdered horn put in the ear will cure deafness.

How the Guianans used to make gold castings

THE inhabitants of the country of Guiana often used to mould their images and plate from gold grains, sometimes as big as small stones, which they found in the large lake of Manoa and also in different rivers leading into the sea. This is how it was used: the gold was mixed with a little copper to make it smoother and put in a large container. This container had little holes all round the bottom and in them, on one side, small tubes were placed. On the other side forms were placed and that part was put to the fire to heat up. Then they blew through the tubes to increase the fire until the gold melted and ran into the forms of stone or clay.

How during winter people lived on trees and large rocks. Their ceremonies for the dead

DURING the winter in America, the Tiuitiuas had to live in trees and large rocks because of the river Orenogue, which would, from May until September, rise thirty feet, making it twenty feet above sea level. They fed on fish and all edible things found in the river at this time.

Their neighbours, the Capuri and the Macuri, have a particular ceremony for their dead. When their elders died and were buried they had performances with songs and dances to show their pain. After a while, when the flesh had decayed, they dug up the skeletons, which were only held together by nerves and tendons, and hung them in their houses, in memory of these dead people. They decorated their heads with beautiful feathers, their arms and legs with golden plates and all sorts of objects which the deceased had collected during their lifetimes. And so these skeletons would hang.

7

Dutch voyages via the Straits of Magellan 1599–1624

At the end of the sixteenth century the Dutch, late starters in maritime expansion, were taking advantage of Portuguese and Spanish weakness by stepping up their infiltration of the East India trade. The usual route to the Moluccas, or 'Spice Islands', favoured source of cloves, nutmeg and mace, was round the Cape of Good Hope. But Magellan, Drake and Cavendish had shown in their circumnavigations that there was a shorter, if more difficult, way in an opposite direction. In 1598 a large fleet left Holland to sail to the East via Africa, but in the same year two smaller fleets set off independently to attempt the passage through the Straits of Magellan. The first to leave was a group of five ships; though the expedition was commanded by Simon de Cordes, it has come to be associated with the name of one of its captains, Sebald de Weert. The other fleet, of four ships, sailed three months later under the command of Oliver van Noort.

The first fleet entered the Straits of Magellan on 6 April 1599. There was no longer any likelihood of Spanish opposition: after Drake's passage and his deadly raids on Spanish shipping off Chile and Peru, Sarmiento had brought four thousand men to build a fort to defend the Straits, but they had all perished in their inhospitable outpost. The Dutch passed several months holed up in a sheltered bay, much to the annoyance of William Adams, the English pilot: 'Many times in the winter we had the wind good to go through the Strait, but our General would not', he complained. De Cordes finally entered the Pacific, or the South Sea as it was generally called, and having harassed the Spaniards on the Peruvian coast and lost a ship to them, sailed for the Moluccas. De Cordes was killed by Indians on the way there, and Adams ended up in the employment of the Emperor of Japan.

Meanwhile Sebald de Weert, accidently left behind in the Straits, was expecting to meet up with de Cordes when he encountered van Noort instead. He finally returned to Holland by the way he had come, in the only ship of the expedition to reach home. Van Noort managed to complete a circumnavigation, but with only one ship and little in the way of goods to satisfy his sponsors.

After these unsatisfactory attempts to establish an alternative route, the Dutch ships continued to sail via the Cape of Good Hope until Portuguese and Spanish harassment made them again attempt to establish the viability of the south western route. The Dutch East India Company, established in 1602 with a monopoly on Dutch oriental trade, sent out six ships under the command of Admiral Joris Spilbergen. They sailed in August 1614 and had passed through the Straits of Magellan by May of the following year. Orders, as in the case of their predecessors, included attacking the rich but vulnerable Spanish settlements up the coast of Chile and Peru. Having worsted a Spanish fleet and looted and burned as far as Santiago, Spilbergen returned to Holland via the Moluccas.

The Dutch East India Company's monopoly prevented other Dutch ships from sailing to the East either by the Straits of Magellan or the Cape of Good Hope. In order to evade this restriction a group of independent Dutch merchants decided to open a route south of Tierra del Fuego through the gap they thought must surely exist between South America and the putative continent to the south. William Schouten was in command, accompanied by Joseph le Maire as the representative of the merchants. They reached the Straits in December 1615, where they lost one of their two ships in a fire. Le Maire and Schouten sailed southwards along the coast of Tierra del Fuego. On 25 January 1616 they passed through the channel which became known as the Le Maire Straits, between the mainland and the land mass they named Staten Land, which in fact turned out to be an island. Despite winds and currents they soon rounded the 'high hilly land covered with snow, ending with a sharp point'. This they named Cape Horn, in honour of Schouten's home town. Le Maire died on the way back, but Schouten reached Holland on 1 July 1617. Ship and cargo were impounded by the East India Company.

The next Dutch expedition to the West was the so-called 'Nassau Fleet' commanded by Admiral Jacob l'Hermite. Sailing in 1624 under the auspices of the East India Company, it was composed of eleven heavily armed ships, and its bold intention was to destroy Spanish power in South America. Owing to contrary winds they had enormous difficulty rounding Cape Horn, anchoring on the mainland at a bay they named Schapenham, after their Vice Admiral. Shortly after, l'Hermite died of an illness and without its leader the great fleet wandered up and down the American coast killing Spaniards and looting cities with ineffectual and undisciplined enthusiasm. Having bullied their way up to Mexico, and failed to catch the Spanish Treasure Fleet en route for Panama, the Dutch headed for home via the Moluccas with little to show for so formidable an expedition. Twenty years later Captain Hendrick Brouwer sailed with five ships and the same purpose in mind. His failure ended Dutch plans to wrest the New World from Spanish domination.

This brief summary of Dutch passages through the Pacific gives the background to the de Bry illustrations which relate to happenings on the various voyages while in the area of Tierra del Fuego and Patagonia. The voyages were treated separately in various volumes of the *America* series but here, owing to the infrequency of the plates, they are collected in a single sequence. The de Brys used contemporary accounts of the expeditions, several of which contained illustrations on which their plates are based.

Neundter vnd letzter Theil
AMERICÆ,
Dariñ gehandelt wird/ von gelegen-
heit der Elementen/ Natur/ Art vnd eigenschafft
der Newen Welt: Item von derselben Völcker/ Abergläu-
bischen Götzendienst/ Policey vnd Regiments Ordnung: Beneben
einem feinen Register oder Catalogo, aller Könige/ von anfang ihrer
Königreich an/ biß auff den letzten König der Mexicaner, Moteçu-
ma genannt/ den andern deß Nahmens/ Sampt eygentlicher Beschreibung der Wahl/ Krönung/ vnd Todt derselben/ vnd letz-
lich was diese Indianer für Krieg wider einander geführet haben.

Alles auffs trewlichste aus Niederländischer Beschreibung
Iohan. Hugen von Lintschotten/ in vnser Hochteutsche Sprache
versetzet/ durch Iohannem Humberger VVetteravium.

Ferner auch von der Reise der fünff Schiffe/ so im Junio deß 1598.
Jahrs/ in Hollandt außgefahren/ der meynung/ durch das Fretum Magelanum, zu den
Moluckischen Inseln zu schiffen/ wie sie nemlich von einander kommen vnd zerstrewet wor-
den/ also daß nur allein der Hauptmann Sebald de VVeert, sampt noch einem Schiff bey-
sammen blieben/ vnd auff die vier Monat lang/ mit grosser gefahr in dem Freto sich auff-
gehalten/ Welcher auch endlich/ als er vber die 2. Jahr auff solcher Reise elen-
diglich zugebracht/ mit einem Schiffe/ Anno 1600. vnverrichter
Sache wider anheim kommen.

Zu nutz vnd ergetzlichkeit Teutscher Nation/ aus Niederländischer Sprach beschrieben/ durch
M. Gothardt Artus von Dantzig.

Alles mit schönen Kupfferstücken gezieret/ vnd an
Tag geben/ durch
Dietrichs de Bry seligen Wittib/ vnd
zween Söhne.

Gedruckt zu Franckfurt am Mayn/ Bey Wolffgang Richter.

Spilbergen in the Straits of Magellan

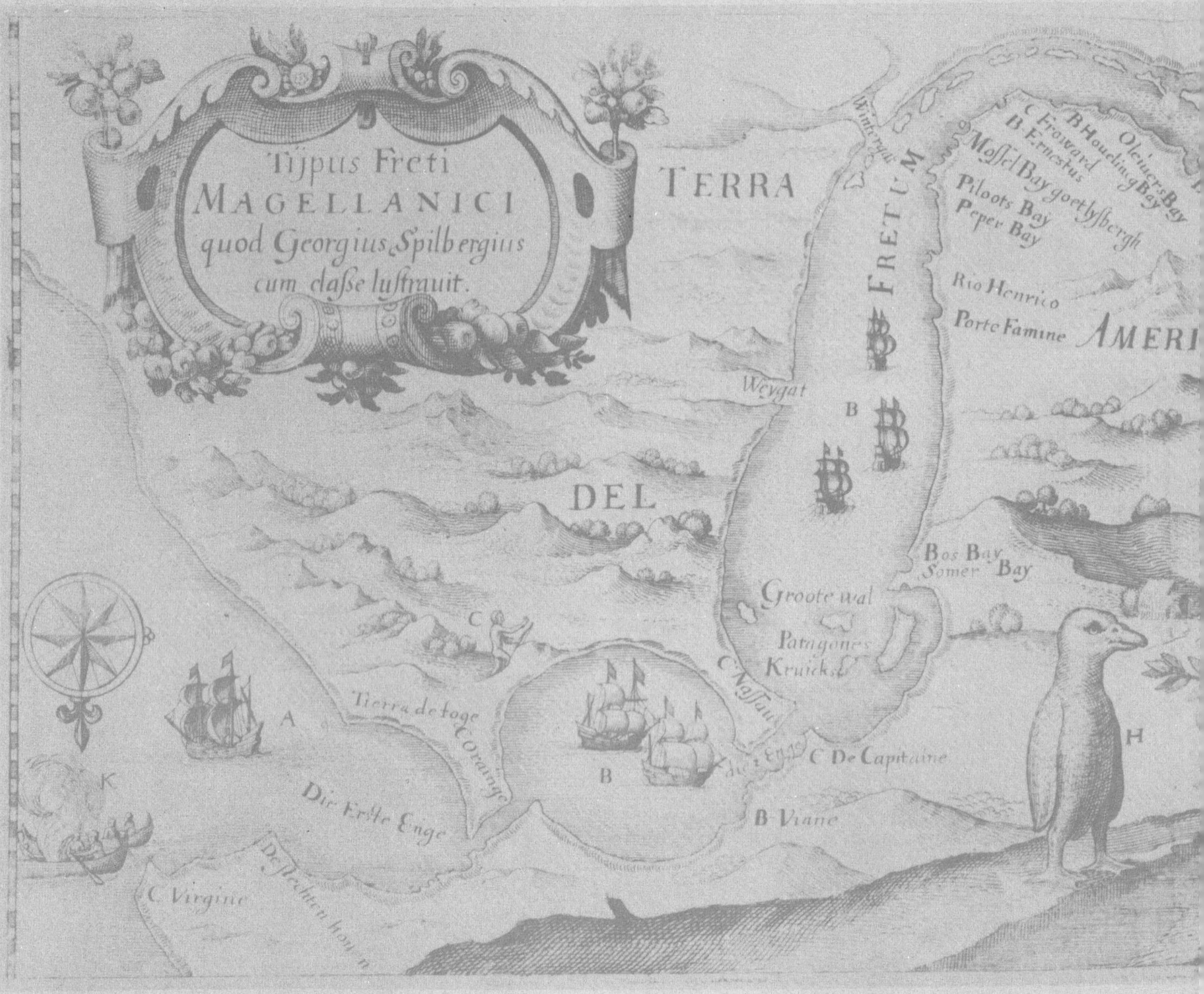

Here is shown Magellan's route, as it was re-discovered by George von Spilbergen. *A* stands for the boat that was removed by the sailors, and *B* for the five other boats as they were entering the route. *C* stands for the man whom we often observed standing on the shore. *D* shows the savages killing the Dutch with their clubs, and *E* stands for some savages, standing on the shore, who addressed the Dutch in a foreign tongue. *F* was where the Dutch gave the savages some Spanish wine, which they seemed to like very much. *G* stands for some red berries, with a delicious taste, that seemed to grow there a lot. *H* stands for a bird called *pinguin*, of which there were many there. *I* stands for the Dutch shooting birds. *K* was a particular form of boat belonging to the savages.

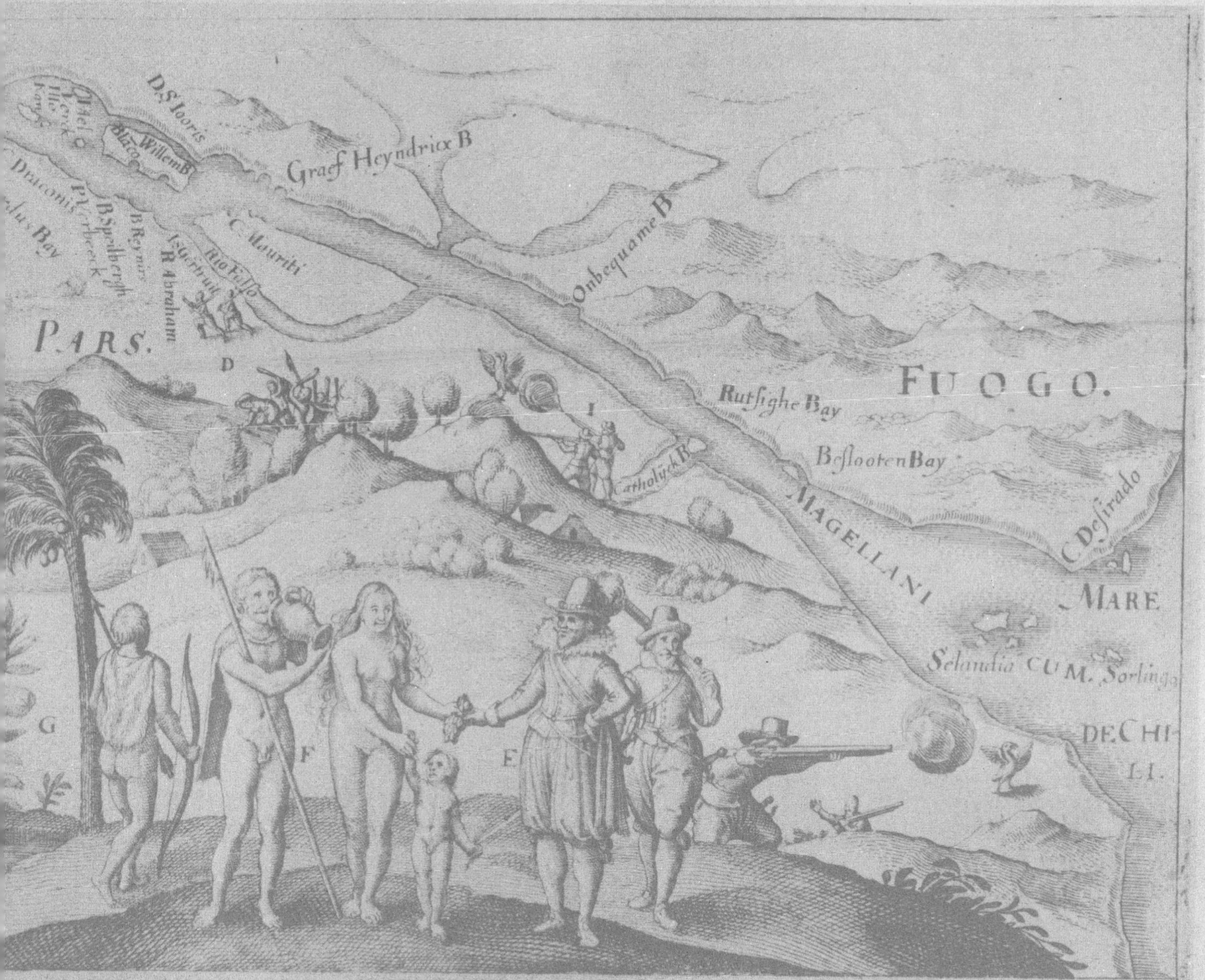

D.S. Ioris
Graef Heyndricx B
Onbequame B
C. Mauriti
R Abraham
PARS.
D
I
Rutsighe Bay
FUOGO.
BesslootenBay
MAGELLANI
C Desirado
MARE
Selandia CUM. Sorlingo
DE CHI LI.
G
F
E

WHEN the Dutch came to collect penguins, the Indians tried to prevent their landing, though they threw several penguins into their boat. But the Dutch landed and chased the natives into a cave, and slew them all, except for some mothers who had thrown themselves on the ground to protect their children from the fatal thunder of the Dutch muskets. They took four boys and two girls away with them. From one of them, whom they taught to speak Dutch, they learned that they dwelt in caves under the earth. They lived on penguins and ostrich flesh and clothed themselves in penguin skins which they sewed most cunningly. The men tied their private parts with a string, the women hiding theirs with a penguin skin. The men wore their hair long and the women were shaven. There was another tribe of giants ten or twelve feet high who often went to war with the lesser men, who they called 'Penguin Eaters', whereby it may be assumed that they themselves used other meat, no doubt man's flesh.

The Dutch catch nine hundred penguins

WHEN they were in the Straits of Magellan, the Dutch went to the island they named Penguin Island because of the great numbers of that bird to be found there. These were so numerous that twenty-five ships could have been filled with them. They themselves caught nine hundred but were unable to stay longer because of the bad weather. These birds are handsome to look at, about the size of a goose, quite plump and weighing eight to sixteen pounds. Their back is black and their stomach white, their feet black almost like a goose. They have no wings but can swim and walk rapidly.

Schouten's fleet at Port Desire *see following page*

ON this map, *A* marks the port which they reached by mistake when they exposed themselves to danger of losing the ships. *B* is the place where they landed and walked with sore feet. *C* is Bird Island, where they found many young birds, and *D* is Lion Island. *E* is the right island behind which the ships anchored. *F* is where one of the ships burned. *G* is the place where they got fresh water and carried it in small casks to the ship. *H* shows the graves of the dead: big people with skeletons ten to twelve feet long, the heads so large that the Dutch could wear them as helmets. *I* and *K* are sea lions and lionesses, a number of which were caught and eaten. *L* is an animal like a stag, with a neck longer than its whole body. These animals can run fast and great multitudes of them were seen in the mountains. *M* shows peacocks in great masses. *N* is a sort of fort made of stone, as if created by humans with great effort.

A
N
M
F
H
I

L
B
E
F
C
D
G
K

On one occasion the Dutch went to Penguin Island in their boat. They had filled it with about four hundred and fifty birds when they were overtaken by a storm. Their boat was destroyed and they began to think they must perish. But after having assembled to say prayers they dragged their boat out of the water and set about repairing it. In a penguin hole they found a woman surrounded by wild animals and set her free. There were no living men on the island, only the dead who were decorated with feathers.

WHEN Captain de Weert went ashore in the Straits of Magellan he saw three boats with Indians. These fled into the mountains, leaving behind them a woman with two little children. She was naked except for a fur covering her shoulders and wore a necklace of shells. Her hair was very short, unlike that of the men. The Dutch offered her their food, but she would not accept it. Instead she took a bird from the boat, plucked the coarsest feathers, and ate it raw so that the blood spurted out of her mouth onto her breast. The woman during her meal never made the least smile, notwithstanding that the seamen burst into frequent shouts of laughter.

THE people of Tierra del Fuego decorate themselves with a string of shells. Some of them cover their shoulders with fur or skin. Their huts are made from trees, round at the bottom and joined at the top. Inside they are dug two to three feet into the earth. There is nothing to be found in them other than strange baskets which contain their fishing equipment, which consists of fish-hooks made out of stone after our fashion. They bait them with mussels and can catch as many fish as they desire. As for their weapons, some have bows and arrows, some a sharp stave, sharp stone knives, and also a rope which they can throw with great power. They carry their weapons with them because they are always at war with another tribe. Their canoes or little boats are worth looking at as they are decoratively painted in the following fashion: they take the whole bark of the thickest tree and cut out sections which they sew together so that it takes the form of a gondola. This they can do very industriously. These boats can be ten, fourteen, sixteen or twenty feet long and can seat seven or eight people comfortably.

WHEN the Dutch were in the Straits of Magellan and wanted to row over to the island they noticed seven canoes filled with naked, horrible men. They were ten feet tall and of a reddish brown colour; they were completely naked and had long hair. When the Dutch realised they were going to be attacked they shot at them and killed some, which caused them to flee to the shore. The savages pulled up trees for their protection, awaiting the Dutch with arrows and stones. But the Dutch did not want to fight these cruel people and did not follow them. Whereupon they caught up with the Dutch and tore them into pieces.

8

Virginia – The Jamestown Settlement

It was not until 1606, sixteen years after John White's fruitless return to Virginia in search of his lost colonists, that another serious project to establish an English settlement in North America matured. Captains Gosnold, Waymouth, Pring and others had made reconnaissance and trading trips along the eastern seaboard and brought back optimistic reports and charming descriptions. Sir Walter Raleigh was languishing in the Tower of London on a charge of High Treason, his patents to Virginia lapsed; but his friend Richard Hakluyt, encouraged by Gosnold, activated a new petition to Elizabeth's successor James I to grant patents for the settlement of two 'plantations' – the word implied people rather than produce – up to fifty miles inland between latitudes 34 and 45 degrees, that is roughly between Bath, Maine and Wilmington, N. Carolina. They were to be operated by merchant organizations known as the London Company and the Plymouth Company, with the Hudson River as the approximate dividing line between their territories.

The London Company was the first to move, sending out 104 settlers in three ships under the command of Captain Christopher Newport. In April 1607 the *Susan Constant*, the *Discovery* and the *Godspeed* arrived off Chesapeake Bay and sailed up the river running north west from its entrance. They named it the James, in honour of the king, selecting a muddy and malarial spot about thirty miles upstream for the construction of their base, Jamestown.

The occupant of the territory in question was a small confederation of Indian tribes ruled over by a locally powerful chief called Powhatan, who had met would-be settlers before and was by no means anxious to have them in his midst except to extract the interesting goods they brought to trade. Though he and his men showed wary friendship, especially when placed in a position of weakness, his avowed object seems to have been to await the moment when his visitors would lapse into carelessness and he could destroy them to a man.

This proud and in some ways admirable Indian met a worthy opponent in a leading settler, John Smith, who at twenty-six had led an adventurous life as a mercenary and had had various misadventures in Turkey and Russia. His arrogance at first caused him to be rejected by the settlers' council, to which he had been appointed on instructions from London, but he was soon reinstated when, having failed to take his advice to build a wooden fort such as he had seen in Russia, the settlement was overrun by 400 Powhatan Indians, who would have massacred everyone had they not been frightened off by cannon shot.

Three months after its establishment forty-six members of the colony had died from disease, starvation and Indian action. As they seemed incapable of growing their own food or catching their own game, Smith was sent out to try to obtain food from the reluctant Indians. On this excursion up the James River he was captured by Powhatan's men and only the production of his 'magic' compass saved him from immediate death. He was hustled into the presence of Powhatan and the extraordinary confrontation took place as pictured by the de Brys on page 195. Having been symbolically saved by Pocohontas, the chief's twelve-year-old daughter, the two men established a personal friendship and Smith was allowed to return to Jamestown. The enchanting Pocohontas, whom Smith described as 'the non-pareil of Virginia', became a frequent visitor to the English settlement and several times warned them of impending treachery.

Despite Indian aid the colony did not prosper in its early years. Even with new inflows of immigrants the settlers seemed incapable of serious labour and it was only through the exhortations of Smith, who was 'president' between 1608–9, that some discipline was instilled into the many 'unruly gallants packed hither to escape their destinies'. Smith was badly wounded by the explosion of his powder-bag and returned to England. He was the only man the Indians respected and after his departure they cut off their supplies of food. Within six months only 60 settlers remained of the 500 he had left. This was the period they called the 'starving time', when all they had to eat was roots, berries and even an exhumed Indian.

The colony was saved from total extinction by the arrival of Lord De la Warr, who was to give his name to the neighbouring state, with a 150 new settlers and a store of provisions. Under his rule, and that of his deputy, Thomas Dale, the colony gradually established itself. The planting of tobacco, inaugurated in 1612, was to have a considerable effect on its commercial viability. The settler John Rolfe is credited with improving curing methods to produce a sweet-tasting leaf that became a European favourite. Rolfe married Pocohontas in 1614 and two years later took her back to England where she died of small-pox.

Immigrants were now allowed fifty acres of land and, with the success of the tobacco business, new fields were established up the river on some of Powhatan's most fertile lands. This and other aggravations led to an Indian attack in 1622 and the massacre of 347 settlers. But by this time there were over 3,000 of them and the Indians were soon totally subdued; the Powhatan confederacy was broken up and its remnants began to move out of the area.

In 1614 John Smith had been sent out again to form a colony in the northern sector. He made maps of the coast from Penobscot to Cape Cod and from them the name 'New England' was established. He also made several unsuccessful attempts to plant settlers, but it was not until 1620 that the project became a going concern with the arrival of the *Mayflower* and a 102 passengers from Plymouth, England, half of whom were Protestant separatists who had emigrated to the Netherlands. These 'Puritans' landed on December 26 at the spot marked 'Plimouth harbour' on John Smith's map.

Pages 192–3 Map of Virginia from de Bry's *America*, Part XIII

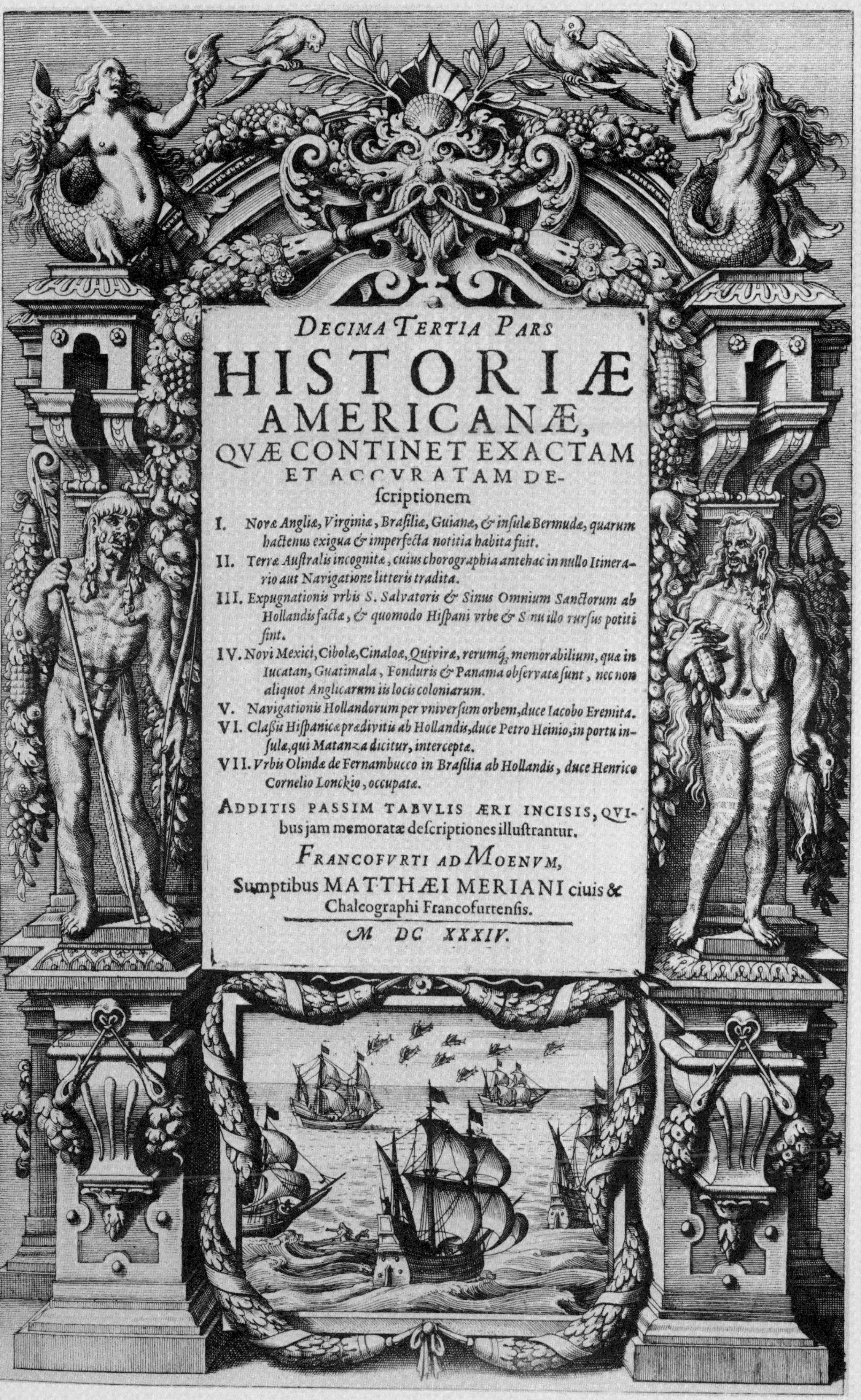

Decima Tertia Pars

HISTORIÆ AMERICANÆ,

QVÆ CONTINET EXACTAM ET ACCVRATAM DEſcriptionem

I. *Novæ Angliæ, Virginiæ, Braſiliæ, Guianæ, & inſulæ Bermudæ, quarum hactenus exigua & imperfecta notitia habita fuit.*

II. *Terræ Auſtralis incognitæ, cuius chorographia antehac in nullo Itinerario aut Navigatione litteris tradita.*

III. *Expugnationis vrbis S. Salvatoris & Sinus Omnium Sanctorum ab Hollandis factæ, & quomodo Hiſpani vrbe & Sinu illo rurſus potiti ſint.*

IV. *Novi Mexici, Cibolæ, Cinaloæ, Quiviræ, rerumq; memorabilium, quæ in Iucatan, Guatimala, Fonduris & Panama obſervatæ ſunt, nec non aliquot Anglicarum iis locis coloniarum.*

V. *Navigationis Hollandorum per vniverſum orbem, duce Iacobo Eremita.*

VI. *Claßis Hiſpanicæ prædivitis ab Hollandis, duce Petro Heinio, in portu inſulæ, qui Matanza dicitur, interceptæ.*

VII. *Vrbis Olindæ de Fernambucco in Braſilia ab Hollandis, duce Henrico Cornelio Lonckio, occupatæ.*

ADDITIS PASSIM TABVLIS ÆRI INCISIS, QVIbus jam memoratæ deſcriptiones illuſtrantur.

Francofvrti ad Moenvm,
Sumptibus MATTHÆI MERIANI ciuis & Chalcographi Francofurtenſis.
M DC XXXIV.

POWHATAN
In solcher Maiestät hat sich der
König für dem gefangenen Capitain
Schmidt erzeigt und sehen lassen.
VIR
MONACANS
Monahassanugh
Rassawek
Monasukapanough
Massinacack
Mowhemcho
Powhatan flu:
The Fales
Powhatan
P
O
W
H
A
T
Arrohateck
Orapaks
Cattachiptico
Passaunkock
Appamatuck
Chickahamania flu:
Appocant
Nechanicock
Quackcohowaon
Mattapanient flu:
Utenstank
Accoqueck
Secobeck
Martughquaunk
Anaskenoans
Muttamussinsack
Checopissowo
Nandtanghtacund
Anrenapeugh
Toppahanock flu:
Kerahocak
Pissaseck
Nawacaten
Mangoraca
Wecuppom
Matchopick
Pissacoack
Cawwontoll
Acquack
Onawmanient
Vitamussamacoma
Parankatanck flu:
Matchutt
Cinquoteck
Mamanassy
Pasaughtacock
Poruptanck
Mattacock
Werowocomo
Opiscopank
Kiskiack
Cantaunkack
Capahawasick
Tindals poynt
Wiffins poynt
Poynt Werde
Pamaunk flu:
Iames towne
Mathomauk
Warraskoyack
Mokete
Nandsamund
Mattanock
Teracosick
Sharpes Isl
Mantoughquemed
Chesapeack
Mortons baye
Cape Henry
Cape Charle
Poynt comfort
Powhatan flu:
Poynt hope
Gosnolds baye
Cader Insul
Paspahegh
Chawopo
Quiyougheobanock
MAN-
GOAG
CHA-
WONS
CHE
SA
Russels Isles
Accowmack
Accohanock
Kealesbill
Smydts Insul
Wighcocomoco
Cuttata women
Cekakawwon
Cinquack
Stingray Ile
Readers poynt
Watkins poynt
Stegar
Shackaconia
MAN
KU
VIRGINISCHE

GINIA
Massawomecks
Massawomeck
Die Bedeutung der Merckzeichen wo ein ✠ bey stehet, ist es
durch sie selber erkundiget worden: was weiter ist, hat man
auss der Einwohner Relation und Bericht.
Königliche heüser
gemeine heüser
HONI SOIT QVI MAL Y PENSE
Tanxnitania
Hassinuga
AHOACKS
Mahaskahod
Sparkes
Content
Demacrites tree
Quiyough flu:
Quiyoug
Burtons Mont
Patawomeck
Pamacocack
N
Nussamek
Matoughquament
Pamacocack
Nushemuck
Tauxenent
Cinquaoteck
Namassingakent
Potaphaco
A
Moyaons
Assaomeck
Namo raughquend
Pocatamough
Quotough
Tessamatuck
Wolameus
Nacotchtanck
Mattpament
Wascocup
Onuatuck
Pawtuxunt
Quactataugh
Opament
Richards cliffes
Tauerners roade
Bolus flu:
Smals poynt
Willowbyes flu:
PEACK BAY
Powels Iles
Winstons Isle
Bornes poynt
Broo kes Forest
Ozinies
Point Pesiuge
Nantaquack
Tockwogh flu:
Kuskarawack
ARA WAOKS
TOCK WOGHS
Gunters Harbaur
Peregrins mont
Sasquesahanougs
Die Giganten sein also bekleydet.
Cepowig
SASQVE SAHANOVGH
Utchowig
Attaock
Tesinigh
Quadroque
Sasquesahanough
Smits fales
Sasqusahanough flu:
ATQVANACHV

Captain Gosnold trades with the Indians

HAVING come from the islands we named Marthaes Vineyard and Elizabeth Isle, we stood awhile, ravished at the beauty and delicacy of the mainland, with its clear lakes and large meadows of green grass. We espied seven savages who at first expressed fear but later followed us. The next day we decided to fortify ourselves on the island in the lake. Eleven canoes with some fifty savages came towards us and, not wishing them to see our building, we went towards them and exchanged with them knives, hatchets, beads, bells and suchlike trifles for skins of beavers, lynx, martens, foxes, and wild cats. We saw that they had much red copper with which they made chains, collars and drinking cups which they so little esteemed that they would give them to us for small toys. They stayed with us for three days, retiring every night two or three miles from us. When they departed with many signs of love and friendship, they left seven behind who helped us with digging and carrying sassafras. They were comely proportioned and the best condition of any savages we had yet encountered. They had no beards but counterfeited them to look like ours, and tried to exchange them with our great-bearded men. Some of the baser sort would steal, but the better sort we found very civil and just. We saw but three of their women, and they were but of mean stature, attired in skins like the men, but fat and well favoured. The wholesomeness and temperature of this climate rather increased our health than otherwise and for all our toil, bad diet and lodging, not one of us was sick.

Captain Smith is saved by Pocohontas

BEING captured by the savages Captain Smith showed them his compass at which they stood dazed with admiration, and rather than kill him there, took him to Powhatan, their emperor. Here, more than two hundred grim courtiers stood wondering at him as if he was a monster. Powhatan sat before the fire on a bedstead covered with a great robe of raccoon skins with the tails hanging down. On either side of him sat a young wench of sixteen or eighteen years, and along each side of the house, two rows of men with as many women behind them. At Captain Smith's entrance, all the people gave a great shout. The Queen of Appamatuck brought him water to wash his hands and another a bunch of feathers instead of a towel. Later, they held a consultation. Then two great stones were placed before Powhatan, and Captain Smith was dragged to them and made to place his head upon them, while the men stood by with their clubs to beat out his brains. Then, when no entreaty could prevail, Pocohontas, the King's dearest daughter, got his head in her arms, and laid her own upon his. Whereat the King was contented that he should live.

The abduction of Pocohontas *see following page*

CAPTAIN Argall, having learned that the Great Powhatan's delight and darling, his daughter Pocohontas, was staying nearby, resolved to possess himself of her by stratagem in order to ransom the Englishmen who were prisoners of her father. A ship was in harbour and Captain Argall offered a copper kettle to Japazaws to persuade her to come aboard the ship, promising that no harm should come to her. Japazaws, an old friend of Captain Smith, caused his wife to pretend she was

continued on p. 198

This answer, it seemed, much displeased him, for we heard no more of him for a long time until Captain Argall took Pocohontas together with several ships and a hundred and fifty men to up the river to Powhatan's principal village. The savages affronted us with many scornful bravados, proudly demanding why we came thither. We made answer that we had brought Pocohontas to receive the ransom, or perforce to take it. They, nothing dismayed, told us that we were welcome if we came to fight, for they were ready for us, but advised us, if we loved our lives, to retire. We told them we would presently have a better answer, but we were no sooner within shot of the shore than they let fly with their arrows among us in the ship.

Being thus justly provoked we presently manned our boats, went on shore, burned all their houses and spoiled all we could find. Then they answered that our swords and weapons would be brought next day but that our men had run away in fear that we should hang them. After we had made peace two of Powhatan's sons came to us to see their sister. When they saw her well, despite what they had heard to the contrary, they much rejoiced promising that they would persuade their father to redeem them and for ever be friends with us. We sent them back to Powhatan accompanied by Master John Rolfe and Master Sparkes.

continued from p. 195

desirous to see the ship and then said that he would only let her go if Pocohontas would go with her. Thus they betrayed the poor innocent Pocohontas aboard, where they were kindly feasted in the cabin; Japazaws treading often on the captain's foot to remind him he had played his part. The captain led Pocohontas to the gunroom and told her she must stay with them to help bring about peace with her father. Whereat old Japazaws and his wife with the kettle and other toys went merrily ashore, while Pocohontas was taken to Jamestown. A message was forthwith sent to Powhatan, saying he must ransom his daughter. Three months later he returned seven of our men, but we refused to return her until he sent back the rest of the arms which he had stolen.

FOLLOWING the consent of Powhatan to his daughter Pocohontas's marriage to Master John Rolfe, we had friendly trade and commerce with his people. Resulting from this, we made league with our next neighbours, the Chickahominys, a lusty and daring people, and free. They sent two messengers with presents to Sir Thomas Dale and offered him their services, saying that they would ever be King James's subjects and be called Tassautessus, as they call us. Sir Thomas Dale and Captain Argall went with fifty men to Chickahominia and concluded peace on these conditions: firstly, they should forever be called Englishmen and be true subjects to King James and his deputies; secondly, they would neither kill nor detain any of our men or cattle, but would bring them home; thirdly, they would always be ready to furnish us with three hundred men against the Spaniards, or any others; fourthly, they should not enter our towns, but send word they were new Englishmen; fifthly, that every fighting man should bring to our store at the beginning of harvest two bushels of corn for tribute, for which they should receive so many hatchets; and lastly, the eight chief men would see all this performed, or receive the punishment themselves. For their diligence they should have a red coat, a copper chain, and a picture of King James, and be accounted his noblemen.

Ralph Hamor tells how he was sent for Powhatan's other daughter

BEFORE my return to England it pleased Sir Thomas Dale to allow me to visit Powhatan and his court so that I should be able to speak of it from my own knowledge. I took with me young Thomas Savage for my interpreter, and two guides. We came to Matchot, where the king was. He knew Thomas Savage well, who had been with his people in exchange for his man Namoutack, and said to him 'My child I gave you leave, being my boy, to go to see your friends yet for these four years I have not seen my own man Namoutack I sent to England, though many ships have returned from there.'

Then he offered me a pipe of tobacco and asked how his brother Sir Thomas Dale did, and his daughter Pocohontas and his unknown son, and how they lived, loved and liked. I told him his brother was well and his daughter so contented that she would not live again with him, whereat he laughed and demanded the cause of my coming. I told him that Sir Thomas Dale, hearing the fame of his youngest daughter, desired he would send her to him in marriage and also because her sister Pocohontas desired to see her. Powhatan replied that his daughter had been sold a few days back to a great *weroans* three days journey away for two bushels of rawrenoke. No amount of persuasion would cause him to change his mind.

THE prologue to this tragedy is supposed to have been occasioned by Nemattonow, otherwise called Jack the Feather because he was commonly most strangely adorned with them. He was accounted their chief captain by the savages and was said to be immortal from any hurt done him by the English. This man had taken one Morgan to trade at Pamaucke and had returned without him saying he was dead. Jack was wearing Morgan's hat, seeing which the two youths who were his servants, thinking he had murdered him, shot him so that he fell to the ground. On the way to the governor Jack, finding the pangs of death upon him, begged the boys two things: that they would not make it known he had been slain by a bullet and to bury him among the English. At the loss of this savage, Openchankanough was much grieved and made great threats of revenge, but the English returned him such terrible answers that he cunningly dissembled with signs of love and peace, yet fourteen days later he acted as follows.

On the Friday morning of that fatal day they came unarmed as usual into our houses with deer, turkey, fish, fruits and other provisions to sell and in some places sat down to breakfast with our people. And then in one moment they seized on the weapons and tools of our people that were to hand and by this means there fell on that fatal morning under the bloody and barbarous hands of that perfidious and inhumane people, 347 men, women, and children, mostly by their own weapons. Not being content with their lives, the savages fell again upon the dead bodies making as well as they could a fresh murder, defacing, dragging and mangling their dead carcasses into many pieces, and carrying some parts away in derision, with base and brutal triumph.

Here, in New England, nature and liberty furnish us freely that which in England costs us dearly. Men, women and children, with a small hook and line, may take many kinds of excellent fish. Is it not pretty sport to pull up two pence, six pence, and twelve pence as fast as you can raise and lower a line; he is a very bad fisher who cannot kill in a day with his hook and line one, two or three hundred cod.

For gentlemen, what exercise should more delight them than ranging daily these unknown parts for fowling, fishing and hawking. And taking pleasure from seeing the wild hawks stoop six or seven times after one another in an hour or two at the fish in the fair harbours as those ashore at a fowl. For hunting, also, the woods, lakes and rivers afford not only sufficient chase for those that enjoy such pleasure, but such beasts as not only are their bodies delicate food but also their skins are so rich that they will recompense a day's work with a captain's pay.

Notes

The numbers heading the notes below are those of the pages on which the references occur.

17

French Cape North of modern St Augustine. The Indian name for the river was Seloy.

River of Dolphins See Le Moyne map – *'F. Delfinum Laudonnierus appulit'*, 'I named this River, the river of Dolphines, because that at mine arrivall, I saw there a great number of Dolphines, which were playing in the mouth thereof.' (Laudonnière)

Indian welcome Ribaut's description places the French already on land, whereas in de Bry's illustration he is in the bow of the boat when making his sign: 'While we were thus praying, they sitting upon the grownd, which was dressed and strewed with baye bowes, behelde and herkened to us very attentively, withowt eyther speaking or moving. And as I made a sygne unto there king, lifting up mine arme and streching owt one finger, only to make them loke up to hevenward, he likewise lifting up his arme towardes heven, put fourth two fingers wherby it semed that he would make us to understand that they worshipped the sonne and mone for godes, as afterward we understode yt so.' (Ribaut) *see 52*

Seated Indians 'Yt is there mannour to parle and bargayn sitting, and the chef of them to be aparte from the meaner sorte.' (Ribaut)

Ribaut's first impression of the Indians was enthusiastic: 'They be all naked and of a goodly stature, mighty, faire and as well shapen and proportioned of bodye as any people in all the worlde, very gentill, curtious and of a good nature. The most part of them cover their raynes and pryvie partes with faire hartes skins, paynted cunyngly with sondry collours, and with the fore parte of there bodye and armes paynted with pretye devised workes of azure, redd, and black, so well and so properly don as the best paynter of Europe could not amend yt. The wemen have there bodies covered with a certen herbe like unto moste, wherof the cedertrees and all other trees be alwaies covered. The men for pleasure do allwayes tryme themselves therwith, after sundry fasshions. They be of tawny collour, hawke nosed and of a pleasant countenaunce. The women be well favoured and modest and will not suffer that one approche them to nere.'

Animal skin Ribaut's account speaks only of a 'girdell made of red lether'. In exchange he gave 'gownes of blewe clothe garnished with yellowe flowers de luce'.

Ships Ribaut's two little ships, shown in the picture, are not named. They were 160 and 60 tons. The smaller craft, for navigating shallow waters, are referred to by Ribaut as 'two barges and a boat well trymmed'. Other writers refer to 'pinnesses and shallops'.

18

Mulberries 'Desiring to imploye the rest of the daye on the other side of this river, to veue and knowe those Indians we sawe there, we traversed thither and withowt any difficultye landed amonges them, who receaved us verry gentelly with great humanytie, putting us of there fruites, even in our boates, as mulberries, respices and suche other frutes as thay found redely by the waye.' (Ribaut)

Indian chief 'Sone after this there came thither there kynge with his brethern and others, with bowes and arrowes in there handes, using therewithall a good and grave fashion of bihaviour, right souldierlike with as warlike a bouldnes as might be. They were naked and paynted as thothers, there hear likewise long, and trussed up with a lace made of hearbes, to the top of there hedes, but they had neither there wives nor children in there company.' (Ribaut)

River of May St John's river.

19

Seine 'Because at the entrye yt is as broade as from Havre de Grace unto Honefleu.' (Ribaut) St Mary's river.

Fish traps Several can be seen in the picture – 'made in the watter with great redes, so well and cunyngly sett together, after the fashion of a labirinthe or maze, with so manny tourns and crokes, as yt is impossible to do yt with more cunning or industrye.' (Ribaut) *see 76*

Vines One of the vines on the right of the picture is growing up a rather small tree. Ribaut described 'the hiest, greatest and fairest vynes in all the wourld with grapes accordingly, which naturally and withowt mans helpe and tryming growe to the top of okes and other trees that be of a wonderfull greatnes and height.'

In the first seven plates de Bry makes an effort to represent the various species of tree in Florida described by Ribaut as 'okes, palme trees, cipers, cedars and bayes', as well as 'the highest, fayrerest and greatest ffirr trees that can be sene'.

20

Six rivers There is some doubt about the identity of these rivers. Benjamin F. French (*Hist. Coll. Louisiana and Florida* 1869) identifies the Seine as the St Mary, the Loire as the Altamaha, the Charente as the Newport, the Garonne as the Ogeechee, the Gironde as the Savannah, and the Grande as the Broad River.

21

Turkeys In the bottom right of de Bry's plate is a passable representation, the first on record, of the American turkey. 'As we passed thorow these woods we saw nothing but Turkeycocks flying in the Forrests.' (Laudonnière)

Other birds, reported by Ribaut but not represented by de Bry, were 'guinea foule and innumerable wildfoule of all sortes, and in a lyttell ilande at the entrye of this haven, on the est notherest side, there is so great a numbre of egrets that the bushes be all white and covered with them, so that one may take of the yong ones with his hande as many as he will carry awaye. There also be a nombre of other foule, as herons, bytters, curleux, and to be shorte, so many smale birdes that yt is a straung thing to be sene.'

Deer Ribaut reports finding 'innumerable numbre of fotestepes of hartes and hyndes of a wonderfull greatnes, the stepes beynge all freshe and newe. And yt semeth that the people do nurishe them like tame cattell, in great herdes. . . .'

Port Royal The present Port Royal Sound. 'In this porte are many armes of the sea depe and lardg, and here and there of all sides many rivers of a meane biggnes, where withowt danger all the shippes of the worlde might be harboured.' (Ribaut)

The vegetables on either side of the grapes are presumably pumpkins. Laudonnière refers to 'great Pumpions, much more excellent than those which we have in France.'

22

The Captain of the French raises a column The text on which this caption is based comes from Laudonnière.

23

Charlesfort Constructed in May 1962 on Parris Island on a branch of Port Royal Sound to house the French who chose to remain Florida after Ribaut's departure. 'Wherefore (my lorde) trusting you will not thinke yt amisse, considering the great good and comodyties that may be brought thence into France, if we leve a nombre of men there, that may fortifye and so provide themselves of thinges necessarye, for in all new discovers yt is the chef and best thinge that may be don at the begining, to fortify and people the country which is the true and chef possesion. I had not so sonne sett fourthe this thinge to our company, but many of them offered to tarry there, yea with such a good will and jolly curradg, that suche a nombre did thus offre themselves as we had muche ado to staye there importunytie, and namely of our shipmasters and principall pilottes, and of such as we could not spare . . . Howbeyt, we have leift there but to the nombre of XXX in all, of gentilmen, souldiers, and merryners . . . and further, by there adviz, choise and will, installed and fortified them in an iland on the northe est side, a place of strong scyctuation and comodyous, upon a river which we have called Chenonceau and the inhabytacion and fortresse Charle forte.' (Ribaut)

Ovadé and Covexis The Indians round Charlesfort were unable to provide food and claimed that 'it was needeful for them to retire themselves into the woods, to live on Mast and rootes untill the time of the harvest.' (Laudonnière) They advised the French to apply to these two neighbouring chiefs, whose territory was on the river Belle (*Bellum* on de Bry's map).

Canoe The French, apparently paddling in different directions, can be seen in the top right of the plate. Ribaut writes of the Indian canoes, which he later refers to as 'troughbotes': 'they make (them) but of one peece of a tree working yt hollow so cunnyngly and fittely, that they put in one of these thus shapen boates or rather great troughes, XV or XX persons, and go therwith verry swiftly. They that rowe stand upright having their owers short, made after the fashion of a peele.'

Crocodiles *see 43*

Carrying provisions Note the baskets being delivered to the canoe on the left. A similar type is shown on page 40.

24

Laudonnière Laudonnière reached the river of May from France on 25 June 1564. He was greeted by the local chief Satourioua with cries of 'Amy! Amy!' and taken to visit the column set up by Ribaut two years earlier. 'Being come to the place where it was set up, wee found the same crowned with crowns of Bay, and at the foote thereof many little baskets full of Mill which they call in their language *Tapaga Tapola*. Then when they came thither they kissed the same with great reverence and besought us to do the like, which we would not denie them, to the ende we might drawe them to be more in friendship with us.' (Laudonnière)

Athore Eldest son of Satourioua ('Monarch of the confines of the River of May'), he was also a chief, or *Paracoussy*. Laudonnière describes this noble, if incestuous, savage as 'a man, I dare say, perfect in beautie, wisedome, and honest sobrietie, shewing by his modest gravitie that he deserveth the name which he beareth, besids that he is gentle and tractable.' Note his long nails. He wears raccoon tails in his hair, one of a variety of items that de Bry depicts in their typical topknots. Note also the fish bladders in the ears; these are to be seen on both men and women in many of the plates. Other types of ear ornament include rings and birds' claws. De Bry does not seem to have drawn the small copper plates Ribaut writes of, which hung from the ears and 'with which they wipe the sweat from their bodies'.

Offerings In the foreground can be seen bow and arrows (the typical quiver made of a lynx skin), linked bottle-gourds (see Virginia p. 79), baskets of fruit and grain, a bundle of maize, various baskets including a back-basket probably containing the leaves of the *Ilex vomitoria* used in making their intoxicating drink *cassina*, and two wooden pannikins.

26

Fort Caroline Laudonnière's fort on the river of May. Satourioua seemed to have no objection to its construction on his territory and, though this is not shown in the plate, his men helped in the work. 'Paracoussy Satourioua, our neerest neighbour, & on whose ground wee built our Fort, came usually accompanyed with his two sonnes and a great number of Indians to offer to doe us all courtesie. . . . After that our Fort was brought into forme, I began to build a grange to retire my munition and things necessarie for the defence of our Fort: praying the Paracoussy to command his subjects to make us a covering of palm leaves. . . . Suddenly the Paracoussy commaunded in my presence all the Indians of his companie to dresse the next day morning so good a number of Palme leaves, that the Grange was covered in less than two days.' (Laudonnière)

The fort was named 'in honour of our Prince, King Charles' and 'was built in the forme of a triangle. The side toward the West, which was toward the lande, was inclosed with a little tranch and raised with turves made in the forme of a Battlement of nine foote high: the other side which was toward the river, was inclosed with a Pallisado of plankes of timber after the manner that Gabions are made. On the South side there was a kinde of bastion on which I caused a house for the munition to be built: it was all builded with fagots and sand, saving two or three foot high with turfes, whereof the battlements were made.' (Laudonnière)

Laudonnière's residence De Bry's fortress is conventionalized and it is difficult to identify Laudonnière's house with its gallery and river exit.

27
Neighbouring kings 'Satourioua hath under his obeysance thirtie other Paracoussies, whereof there were ten which were all his bretheren.' (Laudonnière)

The chiefs' headgears include feathers, the head of a bald eagle (with matching talons worn in the ears), a lynx (to judge by the pointed ear) with a tassel in its mouth, a leopard skin, and a sort of straw basket with feathers stuck in it. The hairstyle is common to the Timacuan Indians throughout the series.

Setting off for war They left with cries of '*He Thimogoa*' in the general direction of Outina's village on the May. (*Timoga* on de Bry's map).

28
Outina Olata Ouae Outina, arch-enemy of Satourioua. He was a powerful chief whose territory lay on the river May on the route to the Appalachians. The French wished to make an ally of him even at the expense of their friend Satourioua, in order to control his territory en route to the mountains where they had heard there was gold.

Ottigny Bernard d'Ottigny, Laudonnière's lieutenant.

Shield D'Ottigny's page seems to have got hold of an Indian breast-plate as worn by Outina and his warriors. Le Moyne writes of 'circular plates of gold and silver as large as a moderate-sized platter, such as they are accustomed to wear to protect the back and breast in war: much gold alloyed with brass, and silver not properly smelted.'

Ancient magician Laudonnière uses the Indian word *Jawa* or priest.

29
Potanou Enemy to Outina, he ruled an area near the foothills of the Appalachians, seen in the background.

Battle between Potanou and Outina 'Now because the custome of the Indians is alwayes to wage war by surprise, Utina resolved to take his enemie Potanou in the morning by the breake of day: to bring this to passe, hee made his men to travaile all the night, which might be in number two hundred persons, so well advised, that they prayed our French-shot to be in the fore-front, to the ende (as they saide) that the noyse of their pieces might astonish their enemies: notwithstanding they could not march so secretly, but that those of the village of Potanou, distant from the dwelling of Utina about five and twentie leagues, were ware of them: which suddenly employed and bestowed all their endevour to defend their village enclosed all with trees, and issued out in great companies: but finding themselves charged with shotte, (a thing wherewith they never had bene acquainted) also beholding the Captaine of their bande fall downe dead in the beginning of their skirmish, with a shot of a Harquebuse which strooke him in the forehead, discharged by the hand of Monsieur de Arlac, they left the place: and the Indians of Utina gate into the village, taking men, women, and children prisoners.' (Laudonnière)

Laudonnière later describes how the Indians would lie down whenever they saw an arquebus laid to the cheek. The major confrontation illustrated is untypical: most accounts of Indian fighting indicate surprise attacks, skirmishes, and retreats if observed.

30
Military formation Outina seems to be well protected by his square. The placing of the huts as described in this caption is a further indication of the veneration accorded by the Indians to their leaders.

34
Hermaphrodites Hakluyt refers to 'many Hermaphrodites which have the nature of both sexes', but such a creature is extremely rare in nature and it is likely that the elegant figures pictured, with their long wavy hair, flat chests and moss skirts, were male concubines, perhaps used by the priests, some of whom, according to Laudonnière, were 'sodomites'. Laudonnière says that the 'hermaphrodites' 'paint their faces much and stick their haire full of feathers or downe, that they may seem more terrible.'

The French were more tolerant than the Spaniards: Alvar Nuñez, an early visitor to Florida, wrote: 'I saw a most brutish and beastly custome, to wit, a man who was married to another, and these be certaine effeminate and impotent men, who go cloathed and attired like women, and perform the office of a woman: they carry no bowes, but bear very great and waightie burdens: and among them we saw many such effeminate persons, as I have said, and they are of greater lims and taller than the other men.' Balboa, in Darien, killed forty with his mastiffs.

'Terrible' or not, one of them served Laudonnière well: 'We met an Indian woman of tall stature, which was also an Hermaphrodite, who came before us with a great vessel full of cleere fountain water, wherewith she greatly refreshed us. For we were exceeding faint by reason of the ardent heate which molested us as we passed through those high woods. And I beleeve that without the succour of that Indian Hermaphrodite . . . we had taken up our lodging all night in the wood.'

It is possible that they were castrated, although there is no reference to this practice.

36
Mourning Laudonnière allows this ritual only to chiefs: 'When a King dyeth, they burie him very solemnly, and upon his grave they set the cuppe wherein he was woont to drinke: and round about the sayde grave they sticke many arrowes, and weepe and fast three days together without ceassing. All the kings which were his friends make the like mourning: and in token of love which they bare him, they cut off one halfe of their haire, as well the men as women.'

Weapons The flayed skin of an entire animal (jaguar?) has been used to cover the quivers. The bows are neatly attached with breechclouts.

Nails Long nails among the Timacua were not, it seems, put to the same use as the Choctaw 'turkey buzzard man', one of whose jobs was to strip the flesh from dead bodies.

Shell drinking cups Though not accurately delineated these would seem to be the nautilus (*Nautilus pompilius*).

37
Blood sucking This was common among Indians of

various tribes. The cone made by the end of a bison horn was sometimes used.

Tapaco Tobacco, the native variety of which was *Nicotiana rustica*. Spark, who visited the area with Hawkins, wrote: 'The Floridians when they travell, have a kinde of herbe dried, who with a cane and an earthern cup in the end, and the dried herbe put together doe sucke thorow the cane and smoke thereof, which smoke satisfieth their hunger, and therewith they live foure or five dayes without meat or drink, and this all the Frenchmen used for this purpose: yet they do hold opinion withall, that it causeth water & fleame to void from their stomacks.'

Pipes Bowls were normally made from clay or stone, and lobster claws were also sometimes used.

Venereal disease Laudonnière reports that 'Priests serve them instead of Physitions and Chirugions. They carry alwayes about them a full bag of herbes and drugs to cure the sicke diseased which for the most part are sick of the pocks, for they love women & maidens exceedingly.' The bark of the sassafras tree was supposed to be a cure for syphilis, and became in demand in Europe, also an infusion made from *lignum vitae*.

38

Hoes These could well have been made of either whale or manatee bone, though Laudonnière describes them as made of wood. 'They dig their ground with an instrument of wood which is fashioned like a broad mattocke, wherewith they dig their Vines in France, they put two graines of Maiz together.'

See also Ribaut: 'About there howses theye laboure and till there ground, sowing there fildes with a grayn called Mahis, wherof they make there meale, and in there gardens they plant beans, gourds, cowecumbers, citrons, peasen, and many other simples and rootes unknon to us. There spades and mattockes be of wood, so well and fyttely made as ys possible, which they make with certen stones, oister shelles, and mustelles.'

Winter season 'During the winter they retire themselves for three or foure moneths in the yeare into the woods, where they make little cotages of Palme boughes for their retraite, and live there of Maste, of fish which they take, of Oisters, of stagges, of Turkeycockes, and other beasts. (Laudonnière)

Sowing According to Hariot, the Algonquin Indians used similar methods: 'The ground they never fatten with mucke, doong, or any other thing, neither plow now digge it as we in England, but onely prepare it in sort as followeth. A few dayes before they sowe or set, the men with woodden instruments, made almost in forme of mattocks or hoes with long handles: the women with short peckers or parers, because they use them sitting, of a foot long and about five inches in bredth, doe onely breake the upper part of the ground to rayse up the weedes, grasse, and olde stubbes of corne stalkes with theyr roots. The which after a day or twoes drying in the Sunne, being scrapt up into many small heaps, to save them labour for carrying them away, they burne into ashes. (And whereas some may thinke that they use the ashes for to better the ground: I say that then they would either disperse the ashes abroad, which we observed they do not, except the heaps be too great; or els would take special care to set theyr corne where the ashes lie, which also we finde they are carelesse of.) And this is all the husbanding of theyr ground that they use.

Then theyr setting or sowing is after this manner. First for theyr corne, beginning in one corner of the plot, with a pecker they make a hole, wherein they put foure graines, with that care they touch not one another (about an inch asunder) and cover them with the moulde.

The ground thus being set according to the rate, by us experimented, an English acre conteining fortie pearches in length, and foure in bredth, doth there yeeld in croppe or ofcome of corne, beanes and peaze, at the least two hundreth London bushels: besides the Mococquer, Melden, and Planta solis: when as in England fortie bushels of our wheat yeelded out of such an acre, is thought to be much.'

In this strange Delvaux-like scene de Bry has represented two of the women workers adopting the European position for scattering grain. It is doubtful if they could have thus deposited the regulation four grains.

40

Game Presumably smoked. *see 41*

41

Smoked food 'They eate all their meate broyled on the coales, and dressed in the smoake, which in their language they calle Boucaned.' Various fish lie on the grating as well as a small alligator, a deer, a wolf or dog, and a snake – 'snakes foure foot in length, and sixe inches about, which the Indians eate for dainty meate, the skinnes whereof they use for girdles'. (Brereton) *see 106*

42

Deer skins See Strachey on Algonquin techniques in Virginia: 'On(e) savadge hunting alone useth the skyne of a deare slitt in the one side, and so put upon his arme through the neck, in that sort that the hand comes to the head, which is stuffed, and the hornes, head, eyes, eares, and every part as arteficyall counterfeited as they can devise; thus shrowding his body in the skynne, by stalking he approacheth the deere creeping on the ground from one tree to another; yf the deare chaunce to find fault, or stand at graze, he turneth his head with the hand to the best advantage to win his shoot; having shott him, he chaseth him by his blood and straine till he gett him.' *see 66*

43

Crocodile This was either the American crocodile (*Crocodylus acutus*) which ranged north into Florida and has been recorded at 23 feet in length, or the smaller alligator (*mississippiensis*) which has been known to reach 20 feet though it is rare today to find one over 12 feet. From its short snout it would appear to represent the former.

Nicholas le Challeux, the carpenter on Ribaut's expedition, made the following observations on the crocodile: 'There are crocodiles, especially, which are often seen coming up on the sand in search of prey. We have observed many – a dead one in particular, which we ate. The meat was tender, as white as veal, and had almost the same taste. It was killed by a gunshot, struck between two scales. Otherwise the crocodile is strong enough for any hits. His mouth is extremely large, his teeth straight, like the teeth of a comb. His body is twelve or thirteen feet long. His legs are short in proportion to his body, the claws strange and cruel. His tail is long and strong. His life depends upon his tail, for it is his principal means of defence. In the mouth I found no signs of a tongue. The lower jaw protrudes over the upper jaw, a monstrous thing; the mere sight of it strikes a man with fear'. A skin was sent to France, presumably from this beast. The specimen in the picture, compared to the scale of the humans, would be about thirty feet long, if such giants ever existed, though twenty-three foot specimens have been recorded. 'There is such an abundance of Crocodiles,' wrote Laudonnière, 'that oftentimes in swimming men are assayled by them.'

Hut The hut is no doubt an old watch-house as shown on page 47.

44

Women swimmers 'The agilitie of the women is so great, that they can swimme over the great Rivers bearing their children upon one of their armes. They climbe up also very nimbly the highest trees in the Countrey.' (Laudonnière)

45

Great age Laudonnière describes how the French were introduced to this extremely old gentleman. 'Our men, regarding his age, began to make much of him, using this speech, Amy, Amy, that is to say, friende, friende, whereat the old sier shewed himself ver glad. Afterward they questioned with him concerning his age: whereunto he made answere, shewing that he was the first living originall, from whence five generations were descended.' The Frenchman did not presumably accept this calculation, nevertheless it gave him a chance to moralize!

Feast The dish seems to be some sort of 'corn-meal mush' perhaps the 'straung thick pottage' described by Strachey – 'husked barley, lett boyle in an earthen pot three or foure howres.'

The objects in the foreground look like the metal discs worn by the warriors on page 28, though it is not clear why they are included in this scene.

46

Casina *Ilex vomitoria* – the Indians drank an infusion of its buds, leaves and tender branches; Alvar Nuñez gives a description of its preparation: 'Likewise they drink another thing which they take from the leaves of trees, like unto Mulberry trees, and boile it in certaine vessels on the fire, and after they have boyled it, they fill the vessels with water, and so keepe it over the fire, and when it has been twice boyled, they pour it out into certaine vessels, and coole it with halfe a goord, and when it gathereth much fome, they drink it as hot as they are able to suffer it, and while they put it out of the vessell, and untill they drinke it, they stand crying, who will drinke. . . . It is of the colour of Saffron, and they drinke it three days without eating, and every day they dronk one amphora, and an halfe.'

The monk San Miguel gives an early account of cassina drinking: 'Their bellies became like kettle drums and as they drank their bellies grew and swelled up: they continued thus for a while, and we thought to see the end of that fiesta, when we saw each one of them opening his mouth with much calmness throw out a great stream of water as clear as when he had drunk it. . . . Cacina is the name of a little shrub of the shape and form of the myrtle . . . its odour is like that of lye.' (op. cit. Swanton)

47

Indian houses 'There howses be fyttely made and close of woode, sett upright and covered with reed, the most parte of them after the fashion of a pavillion, but there was one amonges the rest verry great, long and broode, with settelles round abowte made of reedes, tremly couched together, which serve them both for bedds and seates; they be of hight two fote from the ground, sett upon great round pillers paynted with red, yellowe and blewe, well and trimly pullished.' (Ribaut)

Some of the huts illustrated are oval, others square or rectangular. They were windowless. 'We saw their houses made in circular or round forme 10 or 12 paces in compasse, made with halfe circles of timber, separate one from another without any order of building, covered with mattes of straw wrought cunningly together, which save them from the wind and raine; and if they had the order of building and perfect skil of workmanship as we have, there is no doubt but that they would make eftsoones great and stately buildings'. (Laudonnière)

49

Punishment In this instance death was not intended. See also Strachey on Powhatan's method of light punishment: 'His ordinary correction is to have an offender, whome he will only punish and not put to death, to be beaten with cudgells as the Turks doe. We have seene a man kneeling on his knees, and, at Powhatan's command, two men have beaten him on the bare skyn till the skyn have ben all bollen and blistered, and all on a goare blood, and till he hath fallen senceles in a swound, and yet never cryed, complayned, nor seemed to ask pardon, for that they seldom doe.'

51

Human sacrifice Fairly common among the Indians of S.E. America. Laudonnière learned of the custom of the Calusa Indians, further south, from a Spaniard who had been prisoner there: 'Every year, in the time of the harvest, this savage king sacrificed one man, which was kept expressley for this purpose, and taken out of the number of Spaniards, which, by tempest, were cast upon the coast.' Strachey describes a ceremony during which 'the okeus did suck the blood from the left breast of the child whose chance it was to be his by lott, till he were dead.'

Sun worship 'They have no knowledge of God, nor of any religion, saving of that which they see, as the Sunne and the Moone.' (Laudonnière)

'We understand they (Algonquin Indians) give great reverence to the sun; for which both at his early rising and late sitting, they couche themselves downe, and lift up their hands and eyes, and at certayne tymes make a round circle on the ground with tobacco, into which they reverently enter, and murmure certaine unhallowed words with many a deformed gesture.' (Strachey)

See also George Percy: 'William White (having lived with the natives) reported to us of their customes in the morning by breake of day, before they eate or drinke both men, women and children, that be above tenne yeeres of age runnes into the water, there washes themselves a good while till the Sunne riseth, then offer Sacrifice to it, strewing Tobacco on the water or Land, honouring the Sunne as their God, likewise they doe at the setting of the Sunne.' Percy describes them during this ceremony as 'making many Devillish gestures with a Hellish noise, foming at the mouth, staring with their eyes, wagging their heads and hands in such fashion and deformitie as it was monstrous to behold.' The Europeans may have recognized an early cult of their own – the 'Solar Stag'.

Note the French soldier holding a lighted tinder ready at the touch-hole of his arquebus – 'matche in cocke' as the expression had it. This habit seemed to alarm the natives – they complained to Laudonnière's Lieutenant that 'the women and young children were affraid out of all measure to see fire in their matches so neere their harquebuses: and that therefore they most earnestly besought them to put them out.'

53

Games 'They exercise their yong men to runne well, and they make a game among themselves, which he winneth that has the longeth breath. They also exercise themselves much in shooting. They play at ball in this manner: they set up in a tree in the middest of a place which is eight or nine fathom high, in the top whereof there is set a square mat made of reedes or Bulrushes, which whosoever hitteth in playing thereat, winneth the game'. (Laudonnière)

De Bry does not illustrate any goal-getting games, which were popular among the Indians, both with sticks and hand. The breechclout and the beads hanging from the tree are presumably the prizes referred to. Perhaps the archers are playing the game of shooting after an opponent's arrow: if the feathers were hit that arrow was kept.

Marriage There is little information about Timacuan marriage customs. We know from Strachey that the great Algonquin chief Powhatan had over a hundred wives. It seems that minor Timacuan chiefs were not expected to have more than two: 'They marry, and every one hath his wife, and it is lawfull for the King to have two or three: yet none but the first is honoured and acknowledged for Queene: and none but the children of the first wife inherite the goods and authoritie of the father. The women doe all the businesse at home. They keepe not house with them after they know they to be with child. And they eat not of that which they touch as long as they have the flowers.' (Laudonnière)

Laudonnière tells another story from the territory of the Calusa Indians, indicating marriage by abduction, not uncommon among primitive tribes: 'They are taken for the most warlike men of all that countrey, as they made good proofe when the king of Calos, having made alliance with Oathcaqua, was deprived of Oathcaqua's daughter, which he had promised to him in marriage. He tolde me the whole matter in this sort: As Oathcaqua well accompanied with his people carried one of his daughters, exceeding beautifull, according to the colour of the countrey, unto King Calos, to give her unto him for his wife, the inhabitants of this Isle advertised of the matter, layed ambush for him in a place where he should passe, and so behaved themselves, that Oathcaqua was discomfited, the betrothed young spouse taken, and all the damosels that accompanied her; which they caried unto their Isle: which thing in all the Indians countrey they esteeme to be the greatest victory: for afterward they marry these virgins, and love them above all measure.'

Fans These would seem to be made of the tail feathers of the turkey.

Trumpets This is the only illustration of the musical instruments of the Timacuan Indians, though le Moyne describes Satourioua's warriors as including 'twenty pipers, who produced the wildest kind of noise, without harmony or rhythm, each blowing with all his might to see who could blow the loudest. Their instruments were thick reeds, like organ pipes or whistles.' (Le Moyne)

Pearls The maidens seem to be rich in pearls, wearing them around ankles, legs, waists, arms and necks. According to Ribaut there was 'a great abundance of perles, which, as they declared unto us, they take owt of oysters, whereof there is taken every day among the riverside and amonges the reedes and in the marishes and in so marvelous aboundance as ys scant credeble. And we have perceved that ther be as many and as faire perles found there as in any contrey in the worlde.'

55
Pendants These are similar to those worn by the warriors on page 31. It is unlikely that they were made of gold or silver, more probably it was an alloy.

56
Moss Spanish moss is shown in several plates in the Florida series. 'The women have there bodies covered with a certen herbe like unto moste, whereof the ceder trees and all other trees be alwaies covered.' (Ribaut)

The 'azur blue' is shown in White's painting of a Florida lady in the British Museum, which may have been based on a le Moyne original. White has her sling her mossy garment over her shoulder in the manner of the maiden in this plate (see also pp 36, 51 and 57), though one breast is covered in the White drawing.

Tattooing Various ingredients were used by the Indians as dyes. Mention is made of soot of pitch-pine, and red of cinnebar. The 'special herb' referred to by le Moyne may have been an indigo or something like the woad used by the Ancient Britons (de Bry engraved several Ancient Britons and Picts very heavily tattooed, see pp 88 and 89). In the plates it will be seen that both men and women were tattooed in various linear designs on faces and bodies. There seem to be no pictorial representations as often found in other groups of Indians.

See also John Spark on Timacuan Indians: 'They do not omit to paint their bodies also with curious knots, or antike work, as every man in his own fancy deviseth, which painting, to make it continue the better, they use with a thorne to pricke their flesh, and dent in the same, whereby the painting may have a better hold.'

A later writer (Le Page du Pratz, 1758) enlarges on the fact that fever results from tattooing: 'It inflames the body considerably, sometimes gives a fever, and makes the tatooed person extremely sick if he is not very careful while the inflammation lasts to eat nothing but corn, drink nothing but water, and keep away from women.' The word 'tattoo', originating in Polynesia (*tatau*), did not of course come into English usage until the eighteenth century.

57
Burning of deceased's property The chief's house and its contents can be seen blazing in the village. This seems at variance with the plea of the Indian who helped Dominque de Gorgues, the avenger (see Introduction). The Indian, on being offered a present during the action against the Spanish, told de Gorgues to give it to his wife 'that if hee escaped not . . . she might bury the same with him, that thereby he might be better welcome into the village of the soules or spirits departed.' (Hakluyt)

58
Apalatcy The region of the Appalachians.

Gold, silver and copper See de Bry's map – 'in quibus aurum argentum et aes invenitur'.

Laudonnière was approached by emissaries of Hostaqua who occupied an area of the river of May in the Appalachian foothills to enlist his support against his enemies and thus control the mountains. 'This king', wrote Laudonnière, 'knew the passages unto the mountains of Apalatci, which the French men desired so greatly to atteine unto, and where the enemy of Hostaqua made his abode; which it was easie to be subdued, if so bee we would enter into league together. This king sent me a plate of a minerall that came out of this mountaine, out of the foote whereof there runneth a streame of golde or copper, as the Savages thinke, out of which they dig up the sand with an hollow and drie cane of reed untill the cane be full; afterward they shake it, and finde that there are many small graines of copper and silver among this sand: which gives them to understand, that some rich mine must needs be in the mountaine. And because the mountaine was not past five or six dayes journey from our fort, lying towards the Northwest, I determined as soone as our supply should come out of France, to remove our habitation unto some river more toward the North, that I might be neerer thereunto.'

59
Pierre Gambié Described by le Moyne as 'a strong and active young fellow', he had been brought up at the house of Admiral Coligny. Le Moyne says that he was tyrannical and hated by the natives because he demanded that they obtain impossible things. Laudonnière's version of the story suggests that the Indian king in question had commissioned the murder himself.

65
Roanoke The first description of the English landing in Virginia is found in the narrative of Captain Arthur Barlowe who, with Philip Amadas, reconnoitred the coast for Sir Walter Raleigh in 1584. 'The second of Iuly, we found shole water, which smelt so sweetely, and was so strong a smell, as if we had bene in the midst of some delicate garden, abounding with all kind of odiferous flowers, by which we were assured that the land could not be farre distant: and keeping good watch, and bearing but slacke sail, the fourth of the same moneth, we arrived upon the coast, which we supposed to be a continent, and firme lande, and wee sailed along the same, a hundred and twentie English miles, before wee could finde any entrance, or river issuing into the Sea. The first that appeared unto us, we entred, though not without some difficultie, and cast anker about three harquebushot within the havens mouth, on the left hande of the same: and after thankes given to God for our safe arrivall thither, we manned our boates, and went to view the land adioyning, and to take possession of the same, in the right of the Queenes most excellent Majestie, as rightfull Queene, and Princess of the same. . . . Which being performed . . . wee viewed the land about us, being whereas we first landed, very sandie, and lowe towards the water side, but so full of grapes, as the very beating, and surge of the Sea overflowed them, of which we found such plentie, as well there, as in all places else . . . as also climing towards the toppes of the high Cedars.'

Early visitors to the North American coast, from the Vikings onwards, tended to be impressed by the profusion of grapes. De Bry's vine looks as if it had been etched in as an afterthought. Hariot supplies more information: 'There are two kinds of grapes that the soile doth yeeld naturally: the one is small and sowre of the ordinarie bigness of ours in England: the other farre greater & of himselfe lushious sweet.' An effort to depict one climbing a cedar is to be seen on page 19.

Dangerous coast De Bry depicts the dangerous coast north of Cape Hatorask, with its line of sandy banks much further out than indicated, which forced larger ships to lie off. Such smaller craft as shallops, seen in the picture, were used to land men and navigate the inner waterways. The various wrecks imply general hazard.

Barlowe gives a more detailed account of the topography: 'Beyond this Island, called Croonoake, are many islands, very plentifull of fruites and other naturall increases, together with many Townes, and villages, along the side of the continent, some bounding upon the Islands, and some stretching up further into the land.

When we first had sight of this Countrey, some thought the firste lande we sawe, to be the continent: but after wee entred into the Haven, wee sawe before us another mightie long Sea: for there lieth along the coast a tracte of Islands, two hundreth miles in length, adioyning to the Ocean sea, and betweene the Islands, two or three entrances: when you are entred betweene them (these Islands being very narrowe, for the most part, as in most places sixe miles broad, in some places lesse, in fewe more) then there appeareth another great Sea, containing in bredth in some places, fortie, and in some fiftie, in some twentie miles over, before you come unto the continent: and in this inclosed Sea, there are about a hundreth Islands of divers bignesses, whereof one is sixteene miles long, at which we were.'

Babies Dolls, also referred to as 'babes' – one is reminded of the pedlar in Spenser's *Shepherd's Calender* with his 'truss of trifles As bells and babes, and glasses in his packe.'

66
Weroans 'In some places of the countrey one onely towne belongeth to the goverment of a Wiróans or chiefe Lorde, in other some two or three, and in some sixe, eight & more; the greatest Wiróans that yet we had dealing with had but eighteen townes in his government, and able to make not above seven or eight hundred fighting men at the most. The language of every government is different from any other, and the further they are distant the greater is the difference. . . . What subtilty soever be in the Wiroances and Priestes, this opinion worketh so much in manie of the common and simple people that it maketh them have great respect to their Governors, and also care what they do, to avoid torment after death, and to enjoy blisse; although notwithstanding there is a punishment ordained for melafactours, as stealers, whore-moongers, and other sortes of wicked doers; some punished with death, some with forfeitures, some with beating, according to the greatness of the factes.' (Hariot)

The English were in the habit of describing their Queen as the 'great Weroanza of England'.

The Weroans of the Roanoke Indians was called Wingina, and his territory Wingandacoa. He was later to call himself Pemispan. At first friendly, he turned against the English and was decapitated in a skirmish. The overlord, who formed a confederacy of tribes, was Powhatan.

'Every weroance knoweth his owne meeres and lymitts to fish, fowle, or hunt in (as before said), but they hold all of their great weroance Powhatan, unto whome they pay eight parts of ten tribute of all the commodities which their country yeldeth, as of wheat. pease, beanes, eight measures of ten, (and these measured out in litle cades or basketts, which the great king appoints) of the dying roots, eight measures of ten of all sorts of skyns, and furrs eight of ten; and so he robbes the people, in effect, of all they have, even to the deare's skyn wherewith they cover them from cold, in so much as they dare not dresse yt and put yt on untill he have seene yt and refused yt, for what he comaundeth they dare not disobey in the lest thinge.' (Strachey)

Pounce 'Coloured powder sprinkled over holes pricked in paper to form a pattern on paper underneath' (Chambers Dictionary). Strachey's description of the process involves searing rather than pricking. 'The women have their armes, breasts, thighes, shoulders, and faces, cuningly ymbrodered with divers workes, for pouncing or searing their skyns with a kind of instrument heated in the fier. They figure therin flowers and fruits of sondry lively kinds, as also snakes, serpents, eftes, &c., and this they doe by dropping uppon the seared flesh sondry coulers, which, rub'd into the stampe, will never be taken awaye agayne, because yt will not only be dryed into the flesh, but growe therein.' *see 56*

Bow and arrow 'The bowes are of some young plant, eyther of the locust-tree or of weech (witch-hazel), which they bring to the forme of ours by the scraping of a shell, and give them strings of a stagg's gutt, or thong of a deare's hide twisted. Their arrowes are made of some streight young spriggs, which they head with bone, two or three inches long, and these they use to shoote at squirrells and all kinds of fowle. Another sort of arrowes they use made of reedes: these are peeced with wood, headed with splinters of cristall or some sharp stone, with the spurrs of a turkey cock, or the bill of some bird, feathered with a turkey's feather, which with a knife (made of the splinter of a reed, which he will make as sharp as a surgeon's gamott) he cutts him into forme. . . . To make the notch of his arrowe, he hath the tooth of a bever sett in a stick, wherewith he grateth yt by degrees; his arrowe hedd he quickly maketh with a litle bone (which he ever weareth at his bracer, and which bracer is commonly of some beast's skynne, eyther of the woolf, badger, or black fox, etc.) of any splint of a stone, or peece of a deare's bone, of an oyster shell, or of cristall, in the forme of a heart, barb'd and jagged, and these they glue to the end of their arrowes with the synewes of deare and the topps of deare's horne boyled into a jelly, of which they make a glue that will not dissolve in cold water. Forty yards they will shoot levell, or very neere the marke, and one hundred and twenty is their best at random.' (Strachey)

De Bry's illustration is based on White's water-colour, which shows only the front view of the Weroans. Probably due to a reversal in printing, the bracer appears on the right wrist in de Bry and the archers in the background shoot left-handed. The quiver is secured by the animal's tail.

Deer hunting 'Deere, in some places there are great store: neere unto the Sea coast they are of the ordinarie bignes as ours in England, & some lesse: but further up into the countrey, where there is better feed, they are greater: they differ from ours onely in this, their tailes are longer, and the snags of theyr hornes looke backward.' (Hariot)

See also Strachey: 'In the tyme of hunting every man will strive to doe his best to shew his fortune and dexterity, for by their excelling therin they obteyne the favour of the women.

At their hunting in the desarts they are comonly two or three hundred togither. With the sun rising they call up on(e) another, and goe forth searching after the heard, which when they have found, they environ and circle with many fiers, and betwixt the fiers they place themselves, and there take up their stands, making the most terrible noise that they can. The deare being thus feared by the fires and their voices, betake them to their heeles, whome they chase so long within that circle, that many tymes they kill six, eight, ten, or fifteen in a morning. They use also to drive them into some narrow point of land, when they find that advantage, and so force them into the river where with their boats they have ambuscade to kill them. When they have shott a deare by land, they followe him (like bloodhounds) like the blood and straine, and often tymes so take him. Hares, partriges, turkeys, fatt or leane, young or old, in eggs, in breeding time, or however they devour, at no time sparing any that they can catch in their power.' *see 42*

67

Secota A village on the mainland (see pp 83–4). It was situated on the north bank of the Pamlico River (Beaufort, N. Carolina).

Wreath Barlowe describes a meeting with a royal lady 'of meane stature, and very bashfull' who wore about her forehead 'a broad band of white Corrall . . . in her eares she had bracelets of pearles, hanging down to her middle.'

68

Ear hangings These would seem to be of fur, possibly ermine tails.

Hares' skin More probably made of cottontail rabbit. Hariot writes: 'Those (conies) that we have seen & al that we can heare of are of a grey colour like unto hares: in some places there are such plentie that all the people of some townes make them mantles of the furre or flue of the skinnes of those they usually take.'

This plate, and four others in the series, are signed G. Veen, de Bry's assistant. His employment may be indicative of de Bry's haste to publish. A background, not present in White's original, has been added and presumably shows the sporting priests in action.

69

A young gentle woman White captioned his drawing on which this plate is based 'One of the wyves of Wyngyno.'

70

Chief The caption to White's drawing is 'A chiefe Herowan' and is thus likely to be a portrait of Wingina.

Hair 'For Barbers they use their women, who with two shels will grate away the haire, of any fashion they please.' (Smith)

71

Pomeiooc Local historians site it near the mouth of Gibbs Creek, Hyde Co., North Carolina.

Gourd The mother carries a large gourd such as a bottle gourd. The neck has been shaped to make a carrying handle, more clearly represented on page 79. The 'pleasant drink' might be such as Barlowe described: 'water, sodden with Ginger in it and Black Cinamon, and sometimes Sassaphras, and divers other wholesome, and medicinable hearbes and trees.'

Daughters In the original painting by White his caption gave the child's age as 'eight or ten'. Strachey allows little girls freedom from skirts until the age of twelve.

Twist In Elizabethan English it could mean a branching, in this case of the thighs, i.e. fork. Farmers still apply the word to livestock.

Moss Spanish moss.

72

Skins The large skin, with its shaggy lining, may be that of the buffalo. He is wearing skin shoes, or moccasins. These are not shown in White's original and are the only example of Indian footwear shown in the series.

73

Dasemonquepeuc White's painting states that this lady came from Pomeiooc.

74

Conjurer White captions his drawing 'The Flyer' and presumably illustrates a specific dance, though the bird on the head was a not unusual headgear. Medicine men and soothsayers, or as Hariot described them, 'coniuerers', were in a different class to the priests, but allied to them. The sporran-like object looks like an otter skin. Otters were shamanistic.

The 'Flyer's somewhat rigid posture is explained by Beverley's observation: 'The Conjuror is a partner with the Priests, not only in the Cheat, but in the advantages of it, and sometimes they officiate for one another. When this Artist is in the Act of Conjuration, or Pauwawing, as they term it, he always appears with an air of Haste, or else in some Convulsive posture, that seems to strain all the faculties, like the Sybils, when they pretended to be under the Power of Inspiration.' A 'convulsive' posture is also apparent in the priest shown on page 29.

75

Canoes Hariot calls the tree most favoured for boat building 'Rakiock.' 'Their boates are made of one tree, either of Pine, or of Pitch trees: a wood not commonly knowen to our people, nor found growing in England.'

76

Sea crab The King-crab, more correctly called horseshoe crab (*limulus polyphemus*). Two are visible in the bottom right of de Bry's engraving. Hariot calls it the Seékanhauk, and describes it as 'a kinde of crustie shel fishe which is good meate about a foote in breadth, having a crustie tayle, many legges like a crab; and her eyes in her backe.' The meat is now generally considered inedible.

Fish traps Strachey describes them as: 'certaine inclosures made of reedes, and framed in the fashion of a laborinth or maze sett a fathome deepe in the water, with divers chambers or bedds, out of which the entangled fish cannot returne or gett out, once being in. Well maye a great one, by chaunce, breake the reedes and so escape, otherwise he remaines a pray to the fishermen the next lowe water.' *see 19*

Fish species De Bry has tried to illustrate as many fish as possible based on White's original drawings, adding several others such as cat-fish and a sting ray. Species include hammer-headed shark, box fish, eel, gar (in canoe), and mullet.

Hariot describes the fishing scene and includes a reference to White's pictures: 'For foure moneths of the yeere, February, March, Aprill and May, there are plenty of Sturgeons. And also in the same monethes of Herrings, some of the ordinary bignesse as ours in England, but the most part farre greater, of eighteene, twentie inches, and some two foot in length and better; both these kindes of fish in those monethes are most plentifull, and in best season, which wee found to be most delicate and pleasaunt meate.

There are also Trouts: Porpoises: Rayes: Oldwives: Mullets: Plaice: and very many other sorts of excellent good fish, which we have taken & eaten, whose names I know not but in the countrey language; we have of twelve sorts more the pictures, as they were drawn in the countrey, with theyr names.

The inhabitants use to take them two manner of wayes, the one is by a kinde of wear made of reedes, which in that countrey are very strong. The other way, which is more strange, is with poles made sharpe at one ende, by shooting them into the fish after the maner as Irish men cast darts, either as they are rowing in theyr boats, or els as they are wading in the shallowes for the purpose.

There are also in many places plentie of these kindes which follow:

Sea Crabbes such as we have in England.

Oisters, some very great, and some small; some rounde, and some of a long shape: They are founde both in salt water and brackish, and those that we had out of salt water are far better than the other as in our owne countrey.

Also Muscles: Scalopes: Periwinkles: and Crevises. . . . There are many Tortoyses both of lande and sea kinde, theyr backs and bellies are shelled very thicke; theyr head, feet and taile, which are in appearance, seeme ougly, as though they were members of a serpent or venemous beasts: but notwithstanding they are very good meat, as also theyr egges. Some have been found of a yard in bredth and better.'

A net lies in the stern of the canoe. Two of the Indians wear an otter skin cincture. The fire, in this instance, is probably for warmth (see also page 59), but Beverley (1705) reproduces the White drawing on which de Bry's plate was based and describes the Virginian Indians' use of fire for night fishing: 'They have also another way of fishing, like those on the Euxine Sea, by the help of a Blazing Fire by Night.'

79

Former treatise Hariot wrote in *A briefe and true report*: 'Pagatowr, a kinde of graine so called by the inhabitants: the same in the West Indies is called Mayze: English men call it Guinny wheat, or Turkie wheate, according to the names of the countries from whence the like hath beene brought. The graine is about the bignesse of our ordinary English peaze, and not much different in forme and shape: but of divers colours: some white, some red, some yellow, and some blew. All of them yeeld a very white and sweete flowre: being used according to his kinde, it maketh a very good bread. Wee made of the same in the countrey some mault, whereof was bruwed as good Ale as was to bee desired. So likewise by the helpe of hops, thereof may be made as good Beere. It is a graine of marvellous great increase: of a thousand, fifteene hundred, and some two thousand folde. There are three sorts, of which two are ripe in eleven and twelve weeks at the most: sometimes in tenne, after the time they are set, and are then of height in stalke about sixe or seven foot. The other sort is ripe in foureteene, and is about tene foot high, of the stalkes, some beare foure heads, some three, some one, and two: every head conteining five, sixe, or seven hundred graines, within a few more or lesse. Of these graines, besides bread, the inhabitants make victuall, either by parching them, or seething them whole untill they be broken: or boiling the flowre with water into a pappe.'

How they eat In the foreground is to be seen a bottle gourd pot, a leather bag, a clay pipe, a walnut, a fish, corn-cobs and a shell. Walnut milk, according to Hariot, was sometimes added to their pottage.

81

Marks De Bry's engraving does not bring out the tribal emblems clearly visible in White's drawing – downward-pointing arrows, a small animal in a shield, and two arrows.

Rattles Used throughout the south eastern areas of North America. Also in South America (see page 107). Smith (1608) writes: 'the chiefe instruments are Rattels made of small gourds or Pumpion shels. Of these they have Base, Tenor, Countertenor, Meane and Trible. These mingled with their voices sometimes 20 or 30 togither, make such a terrible noise as would rather affright than delight any man.'

84

Pomeiooc White's picture is captioned 'The towne of Pomeiock and true forme of their howses, covered and enclosed some with matts, and some with barcks of trees. All compassed about with small poles stuck together instedd of a wall.'

Within the houses can be seen raised platforms, their bedsteads, which, according to Strachey, 'are thick short posts stalkt into the ground, a foot high and somewhat more, and for the sydes small poles layed along, with a hurdle of reeds cast over, wherein they rowle downe a fyne white matte or twoo (as for a bedd) when they goe to sleepe, and the which they rowle up againe in the morning when they rise, as we doe our palletts, and upon these, round about the howse, they lie . . . especially making a fier before them in the midst of the house, as they doe usually every night, and some one of them by agreement maynteynes the fier for all that night long; some of them, when they lye downe to sleepe, cover them with matts, some with skinns, and some lye stark naked on the grownd, from six to twentie in a house, as doe the Irish.'

Tobacco 'There is an herbe which is sowed apart by it selfe & is called by the inhabitants *uppowoc*. In the West Indies it hath divers names, according to the severall places and countreys where it groweth and is used: The Spaniardes generally call it Tobacco. The leaves thereof being dried and brought into pouder, they use to take the fume or smoke thereof by sucking it thorough pipes made of claie, into their stomacke and heade; from whence it purgeth superfluous fleame & other grosse humors, openeth all the pores & passages of the body: by which meanes the use thereof, not only preserveth the body from obstructions; but also if any be, so that they have not beene of too long continuance, in short time breaketh them: wherby their bodies are notably preserved in health, & know not many greevous diseases wherewithall wee in England are oftentimes afflicted. . . .' (Hariot)

Beside the tobacco plants sunflowers can be seen growing, also outside Pomeiooc in the preceding plate.

Corn The three fields of corn in various stages of growth are labelled by White in his painting 'Their rype corne', 'their greene corne' and 'corne newly sprung'. Laudonnière refers to a birdscarers' hut in Florida: 'There was a house built for their lodging, which keepe and garde the mill: for there are such numbers of Cornish choughes in this Countrey, which continually devoure and spoyle the mill, that the Indians are contrained to keepe and watch it, otherwise they should be deceived of their harvest.'

85

Kiwasa 'They thinke that all the gods are of humane shape, and therefore they represent them by images in the formes of men, which they call Kewasowok, one alone is called Kewas: them they place in houses appropriate or temples, which they call Machicomucke, where they worship, pray, sing, and make many times offering unto them. In some Machicomuck wee have seene but one Keewas, in some two, and in other some three. The common sort thinke them to bee also gods.

They beleeve also the immortalitie of the soule, that after this life as soon as the soule is departed from the bodie, according to the workes it hath done, it is eyther caried to heaven the habitacle of gods, there to enjoy perpetuall blisse and hapinesse, or els to a great pitte or hole, which they thinke to be in the furtherest partes of their part of the world towarde the Sunne set, there to burne continually: the place they call Popogusso.' (Hariot)

Head See section on Florida. The hair style is the same as Le Moyne's Timacuan Indians.

Flesh-coloured face The white skins of the Europeans may have given the Indians the idea that they were in some way related to their God.

86

Tomb This scene represents the interior of a similar building to that marked A on page 83. Strachey writes: 'Only to the priests the case of these temples and holy internments are comitted, and these temples are to them as solitary Asseteria colledges or ministers to exercise themselves in contemplation, for they are seldome out of them, and therefore often lye in them and mayntayne continuall fier in the same, upon a hearth somewhat neere the east end.'

White's painting, on which de Bry's plate is based, is captioned 'The Tombe of their Cherounes or cheife personages, their flesh clene taken from the bones save the shynn and heare of theire heads which flesh is dried and enfolded in matts laid at theire feete, their bones also being made dry or covered with deare skynn not altering their forme or proportion. With their Kywash, which is an Image of woode keeping the deade.'

87

Tribal marks Some of these marks are to be seen in White's painting of the dance engraved by de Bry (see page 81). The swastika was a common sign among North American Indians.

The method of attaching the quiver with the animal tail is clearly shown. In this engraving the chief wears his bracer on the more appropriate wrist.

92

Campon Kampen, now a holiday resort on the German island of Sylt.

Sanct Tual Setubal, about 20 miles S.E. of Lisbon.

White Moors Black Africans were generally referred to as 'Moors'. White Moors were Arabs or Berbers.

Prisoners Many of the early colonizers of Brazil were exiles, bankrupts and convicts. These 'degradados' had previously been sent to Africa and India.

93

Cap de Gel Arzillas, a small port near Tangier.

Albakor The albacore, a species of tunny.

Bonitte Bonito – a tunny, also known as 'Spanish Mackerell'.

Durado Bottle-nosed dolphin.

Pisce bolador Flying fish. There is a charming description of these creatures in *A Treatise of Brasil*: 'The flying fishes are ordinarily of a spanne long or little more, it hath the eies verie faire, of a certaine verie gallant picture, that beautifies it much, and doe seeme precious stones, the head is also very faire, it hath wings like Reere-mice (bats), but of a silver hue; they are much persecuted of the other fishes, and for to escape they flie in flockes, like Stares (starlings), or Sparrowes, but they flie not verie high, they are also good to eat, and when they flie they glad the Sailors, and many times they fall in the ship, and come in at the Cabbin windowes.'

Cape de Sanct Augustin Cabo de Santo Augustino, also mentioned by Vespucci, was a favoured landfall for navigators. Pernambuco lies about 50 miles to the north.

Brannenbucke Staden's rendering of Pernambuco.

Marin Olinda.

Artokeslio Staden's proper names are frequently corrupt. De Bry writes Artokoelio, but this must refer to Duarte Coelho Peirera, Captain General of Pernambuco.

94

Garasu Iguarassu was one of the first sugar factories. It was founded by Coehlo on the river of that name.

Tamaraka The island of Itamaracca, colonized by the Portuguese in 1535.

Pepper The Indians were presumably burning the wild species of capiscum (*frutescens*), a perennial native to a large part of South America.

Bows and Arrows 'These Arrows to one's sight seem a thing of mockerie, but are verie cruel weapons and pierce quilted breast-plates or curates; and striking a stick they cleave it asunder, and sometimes happen to goe through a man and sticke on the ground. Since the Frenchmen and the Portugals came into those Countreyes, the Barbarians, after their manner have accustomed to strengthen their Arrowes with Iron heads, or at least, with verie sharpe Nailes'. (De Léry)

For aerial shots the Indians would sometimes lie on their backs to draw their bows, though de Bry does not depict this. There are many accounts of the accuracy of the bowmen and their rapid rate of fire. 'They shoot so speedily, and so certainely', wrote de Léry, 'that (bee it spoken by the Englishmens leave, who are yet accounted the most skilfull Archers) putting their Arrowes in the hand wherewith they hold their Bow, twelve may sooner be shot by them, then sixe by the Englishmen'.

Mandioca Manioc, the root that produces cassava and tapioca, was the staple diet of the Indians and settlers.

95

Buttugaris Presumably Staden means that the harbour was in the country of the Petyguaras, allies of the French against the Portuguese-backed Tanyaras. According to Schnirdel (Schmidt) they had the best Brasil wood, and were great friends with the French, 'and did contract with them untill now, marrying their daughters with them.'

Brazil wood The hard reddish wood of the *sappan*, an East Indian tree used in dyeing. In the eastern trade it was known as *brasileum*. When a similar wood was discovered in S. America the country became known as *terra de brasil*. De Léry writes: 'The Brasil tree is the most famous of all that soile (from whence also that Countrie hath taken the name) especially for the colour which our Dyers make therewith. This tree is called by the Barbarians Araboutan, and equalleth our Oake in height and plentie of Boughes. Some of these are found, the thicknesse whereof containeth full as much as three men can fathome.'

Porta Santa Maria Porto di Santa Maria, in the Azores.

Civilien Seville.

Rio de Platta The River Plate.

Pirau Peru.

Sancta Catherina An island of southern Brazil.

Carios Staden locates the Carios in the colder country south of the Tropic of Capricorn, and has them clothing themselves in skins. The women made 'garments of cotton yarn, like a sack below and open above, and they wear these garments and call them Typpoy.'

Schnirdel (Schmidt) has them naked: 'These people of Carios inhabit a large Countrie, extending it selfe three hundred leagues in length, and breadth: they are men of short stature, and thicke, and more able to indure work and labour then the rest. The men have a little hole in their lippes, and yellow Christall therein (which in their language they call Parabol) of two spannes long, and of thicknesse of a quill or reede. The men and women both in this Countrie, goe all naked, as they were created of God. Amongst these Indians the father sells the daughter, the husband the wife. They value a Woman at a Shirt, a Knife, a Hatchet, or some other thinge of this kinde. These Carios also eate mans flesh, if they can get it. For when they take any in the warres, whether they be men or women, yong or old, they fatten them, no otherwise then we doe Hogges. But they keepe a woman some yeeres, if she be yong, and of a commendable beautie, but if in the meane time, she apply not her selfe to all their desires, they kill, and eate her, making a solemne banquet, as marriages are wont to be celebrated with us. But they keepe an old woman, till she dye of her owne accord.'

Tuppin Ikins More will be heard in Staden's narrative of the Tupinikin and the Tupinamba, rival tribes of the Tupi nation, supposed to have originated in Uruguay. The former were allied to the French and the latter to the Portuguese. Anthony Knivet (Purchas XVI) gives us an oblique glimpse of the Tupinikin: 'The Topinaques inhabite at Saint Vincents, they are men of good stature, and of reasonable good complexion; their women are all painted with divers colours, and on their heads, they weare a thin barque of a tree like a Ribband: the Canibals eate mans flesh as other Canibals doe, they adore no Idoll, neither have they any kinde of Religion, onely when they kill any man they all paint their bodies with a kinde of fruit, called Janipavo, and all their heads are set with feathers, and great stones in their under-lips, with Rattles in their hands, and thus they will dance for three dayes together. I was amased to see how they would drinke a filthy drinke without breaking of their bellies, and asked them how they were able to stand so long and drink so much of that filthy drinke: they answered me, that Tabacco did make them as fresh as if they had done nothing.'

96

Rio de San Francisco Not to be confused with the large river of the same name further north. Burton describes it as a 'disappointing stream'.

Canoes De Bry's canoes look as if they were dug-outs. In fact, as will be seen from Staden's description (see page 99) and de Léry's, which follows, they were made of bark: 'If, which often happeneth, they please to undertake a Voyage, against the Enemie, by Boat, they passe along the shoares, and commit not themselves unto the maine Sea. They order themselves in their Boats, which they call Ygat, everyone whereof consisteth of the barke, taken off, and appointed to this use.'

La Soncion Ascunçion, capital of Paraguay.

97

Johann Ferdinando, a Buschkeyner from Bilka Otherwise Juan Fernandez, a Basque from Bilbao.

98

Insulae de Alkatrases 'Pelican' Islands, about 45 miles E.S.E. of Santos. An alcatraz is a brown pelican (*Pelicanus occidentalis carolinensis*).

San Vincente An island formed by the tidal channel of the river on which Santos now stands. It was the first Portuguese colony in Brazil.

Tome de Susse Thomé de Souza, first governor of Brazil (Bahia).

99

Club This may have been the ceremonial club *Iwara Pemme* described on pp 109 and 111. More probably it was an undecorated weapon such as they carried in battle. De Léry described the hefty instrument as follows: 'They have Tacapes, that is Clubs, or Swords made some of redde, and some of blacke wood: they are commonly the length of five or sixe feete, round at the ends, or of an ovall shape, of the breadth of a foote, and of the thicknesse of a Thumbe in the middest, but the edges are verie finely sharpened, for they are made of verie heavie wood, such as Boxe is, and are little inferior to the edge of a verie sharpe Axe: so that I easily beleeve, that one Toupinambaultian armed with such a Clubbe, and inraged with furie, would bee able to put two of our Countrie Fencers to much trouble, and drive them to their shifts.'

Perot Possibly the Tupinambas were insulting them with the Spanish word *pero*, or dog.

Kawewi Pepicke *Kawaway* was their fermented liquor. It was made of manioc chewed, steeped and fermented. In old French there was a word *caouinage* meaning a drinking bout. Burton suggests that *Pepicke* signifies revenge.

Yga Ywera *A Treatise of Brasil* mentions 'Groves, wherein are found trees of great bignesse and length, whereof they make great Canoas of seven or eight spannes and more in length, which bear a load like a great Barke, and doe carrie twentie or thirtie Rowers of a side; they make likewise great Beames for the Sugar-mills.' According to Levi-Strauss (B.A.E. Bull. 143) the Tupinambas probably used the bark of the jatoba (*Hymanaea courbaril)* for their canoes.

100

Uwara The Guara, or scarlet ibis (*Endocimus ruber*) – the Tupis wore the feathers on their headresses and skirts.

Blowpipes Staden does not enlarge on the use of the blowpipe among the Tupis, nor does de Bry represent it in the illustrations.

101

Inni See Staden (Ch. VI) on the *inni*, or hammocks: 'They are made of cotton yarn and they tie them to two poles above the ground, and at night they burn their fires between them. They do not willingly go out from their huts at night for any reason without fire, so greatly do they fear the devil whom they call Ingange and often see.'

102

Tammeraka The maracca, a gourd or other hollow container attached to a stick and filled with stones or seeds for rattling. They seem to have been the Tupis' main object of veneration, with powers of prophecy (see page 107). Human hair or the scarlet feathers of the Guara were fastened to the top and a mouth-like slit was cut in the gourd.

103

Cotton Staden writes: 'The cotton grows on trees about a fathom high with many branches. When it blooms the flowers turn into balls. When they are about to ripen they open and the wool is found round black kernels which are the seeds. The shrubs are full of these balls.'

French alliance On a later occasion the French, in order to secure an alliance with a Brazilian tribe, are said to have imported West African negroes for them to eat.

104 and 105

Bratti Grey mullet.

Meire Humane *Meire*, presumably the local pronunciation of *Monsieur* or *Maître*, was the standard native way of addressing a Frenchman. Meire Humane was said to be St Thomas, a legend that was encouraged by the Catholic Church. Certainly some ecclesiastic, possibly shipwrecked, seems to have been at large in the area before the arrival of the conquerors and may have inspired his Indian flock to adopt his tonsured hair style.

In *A Treatise of Brasil*, we read: 'They let no hair grow in the parts of the body, but they pull them out, only the head excepted, which they cut in many fashions, for some weare them long with a halfe Moone shaven before, and they say they took this use from Saint Thomas, and it seemeth that they had some notice of him, though confusedly.'

Knivet (Purchas XVI) describes a place called Etaoca, or 'Stone House', where the Indians claimed that 'Saint Thomas did Preach to their forefathers: hard by standeth a Stone as bigge as foure great Canons' which the Saint by a miracle had turned into wood. Knivet claimed that nearby he had seen 'great Rockes upon which I saw a great store of prints of the footing of bare feet; all of which prints were of one bignesse. They say that the Saint called the Fishes of the Sea, and they heard him.'

Feathers Knivet writes: 'When I saw them first (the Cannibals) I thought they had beene borne with feathers on their heads and bodies, like fowles of the aire, they had anointed their bodies with gumme of the oiletusees of Balsome, and covered themselves so artificially with the feathers of divers colours, in such order, that you could not see a spot of their skins but their legs.' The feathers encircling the posteriors of the Indians seem somewhat embellished by de Bry and came from the rhea (*Rhea americana*) the three-toed ostrich of America.

106

Salting Staden writes (Ch. XI): 'There are many tribes of savages who do not eat salt. Some of those among whom I was a prisoner ate salt, which they had seen used by the French who trade with them. But they told me of a nation called Karaya, whose country adjoins theirs, lying inland from the sea, who make salt from palm trees and eat it. They prepare the salt as follows, for I saw and helped them do it. They cut down a thick palm tree and split it into small slivers, then they made a stand of dried wood on which they burn the splinters to ashes. From this they make a solution of lye which they boil until the salt separates. I thought at first it must be saltpetre, and tried it in the fire, but it was not. It tasted like salt and was grey in colour.' Palms used in the making of salt would have been the jara (*Leopoldina major*), using the fibres and fruits or the leaves of such species as *Mauritia flexuosa*.

Smoked meat The grid for smoking or roasting over an open fire was called *boucan*. The pirates, or 'buccaneers', were so called because they adopted this custom. De Léry writes: 'The Americans fastning foure woodden forks in the ground, of the thicknesse of an arme, three foote asunder, in the figure of a square, and almost of the equall height of three feet, lay stickes acrosse over them two fingers distant each from other, and so make a woodden Grate: this, in their language, they name Boucan. They have many such Grates in their houses, whereon they lay flesh cut into gobbets or pieces, and making a soft fire of dry wood, that there may bee no smoake almost at all, they suffer them to bee broyled as long as they please, after this manner, having twice turned them in the space of an houre. . . . You shall behold these Grates filled with mans flesh, which, I thinke, they bring as spoyles taken from the conquered enemies, to be slaine and eaten.'

Generous behaviour See *A Treatise of Brasil*: 'They eate all that they have and devide it among their friends, in sort that of one fish they have they devide it to all, and they hold for a great honour and gallantrie to be liberall and thereby they get great fame and honour.'

109 and 111
Face painting Staden refers elsewhere to a tree called *Juni Papeeywa*, which is the pawpaw tree, 'whereupon a fruit grows not unlike an apple. The savages chew this fruit and squeeze the juice into a vessel and paint themselves with it. At first it looks like water on the skin but after a time the skin becomes as black as ink. It remains so until the ninth day when it disappears, but not before, however much they may wash themselves.'

Mackukawa eggs Probably the eggs of the chacalaca, the *macucagua* of *A Treatise of Brasil*: 'The Macucagua is greater than any Henne of Portugall, it resembleth a Feasant, and so the Portugals doe call it; it hath three skinnes one over another, and much flesh, and verie savourie, they lay twice a yeere, and at everie time thirteene or fifteene egges.'

Killing ceremonies *A Treatise of Brasil* gives a more detailed account of cannibalistic rites. It concludes: 'hee striketh till he hitteth and that is enough, for assoone as he is downe he giveth him so many blowes till he batters his head (though one man was seene that had it so hard that they could never breake it, for as they goe bare-head, they have them so hard that ours in comparison of theirs are like a Pompion, and when they will injurie any White man, they call him soft-head.' Oviedo warns the Spaniards to aim elsewhere with their swords: 'for so many swords have been broken on their heads with little hurt done'.

A Treatise of Brasil adds that after the execution: 'The killer stands all that day with so much silence as if he had some astonishment in him, and carrying to present thither the head of the dead, they pull out one of eies, and with the strings and sinewes of it they anoint his pulses, and cutting off his mouth whole, they put it on his arme as a Bracelet, and then he layeth downe in his Net as a sicke man, and certainly hee is sicke for feare, that if he doe not accomplish the Rites perfectly, the soul of the dead will kill him.' Written in 1601 this account confirms Staden's though clearly in no way deriving from it.

Additional names Under the ironic heading: 'Of their creating Gentlemen' *A Treatise of Brasil* says: 'Of all the honours and pleasures of this life, none is so great for this people as to kill and get a name on the heads of their Adversaries.'

Konyan Bebe Thevet has left a romantic description of the cannibal potentate whom he called Quoniambe and compared to Menelaus. His 'palace' is described as being decorated with the heads of Portuguese and defended by captured cannon.

114
Attack by the Tupiniki De Bry's illustration is the only one in the series to depict a shield and a trumpet. De Léry writes: 'They have Targets of Hide of Tapiroussou (tapir), broad, plaine, and rounde, like to the bottome of a Germane Drumme, with these they cover not themselves in fight, after the manner that our Souldiers use, but fighting, receive the Arrowes of the Enemies with them. . . . There are some, who with hornes, which they call Inubia, of the length of an elle and an halfe, and of the thicknesse of our Country Speare, of the bredth of an hand at the lower end like a trumpet, raise the soldiers.'

115
Weeping welcome *A Treatise of Brasil*, gives an account of this 'weeping welcome' often described by early travellers: 'When any guest does come to the house, the honour they make him is to bewaile him; Now the guest being come into the house they set him in the Net, & after he is set without speaking any word to him, the wife and the daughters, and the other friends do sit them downe round about him with their haire loose, touching with the hand the partie: they all beginne to weepe with a high voice and a great abundance of teares, and there they tell in a versified prose all things that have happened since they saw one another to that houre, and manie other which they invent, and the troubles that the guest hath suffered in his journie; and all things else that may provoke pitie and tears. The guest all this time speaketh not one word, but after they have bewailed him a good while they wipe the teares, and remaine so quiet, so modest, so pleasant and merrie that it seemeth they never wept.'

Burial In the picture, the body is about to be lowered into a circular grave. Thevet describes, and illustrates, a similar hole with the dead man seated at the bottom. He refers to an excavation, round like a well, about the same depth as a man's height.

116
Brascupas Braz Cubas, founder of Santos (here 'Sanctus'). He died in 1592 and is buried there.

117
Backe The paca – a small pig-like rodent of which de Léry writes: 'Pag, or Pague . . . is a wilde beast of the indifferent height of an Hound, with a deformed head, the flesh comming neere unto the taste of Veale, with a very faire skinne, distinguished with white, russet, and blacke spots, so that it would be of great price with us, if they were to be gotten.'

A Treatise of Brasil adds: 'The Pacai are like Pigs, there are great abundance of them; the flesh is pleasant, but it is heavie. They never bring forth but one at once. There bee others very white; these be rare, they are found in the river of Saint Francis.'

119
Mamelukes In this context Staden means the offspring of a white man and an Indian woman.

126
Cubagua A small island just off Margarita Island, about twenty miles off the north coast of Venezuela. It was the centre of the pearl fishing industry. According to Benzoni the island was flat, sterile, waterless and full of rabbits. Las Casas, the worthy monk who became a bishop and did so much to bring Spanish misgovernment to the notice of the authorities, appears on Cubagua in a controversial role. Las Casas had persuaded Charles V to grant him the governorship of Cumana, so that he might re-organize the pearl fisheries on more humanitarian lines. He arrived at Cumana with his men, but the local military commander, Diego d'Ocampo, refused to recognize him. 'Thus' says Benzoni, 'with biting words and mocking each other, several days elapsed, till the doctor, seeing that Ocampo would not obey the orders and laughed at him, determined to go to San Domingo to complain. . . .' Las Casas built a wooden house at Cumana where he left his stores and followers. Meanwhile d'Ocampo and his men left the scene, quarreling about the division of their haul of pearls.

El Dorado Putatively sited in Guiana (see Raleigh in Guiana).

127
Cumana An early Spanish settlement on the north coast of Venezuela, built to protect the old pearl fishery. When Benzoni arrived the original mud fortress had been destroyed by flood but a wooden one had been contructed to guard the watering point of shipping from the Pearl Islands.

Indians The local Indians, or what was left of them, were Caribs. 'Out of the great multitude of Indians that there used to be, there remained only a few petty chiefs, whom the Spaniards had spared for their own wants. Others had retired to some uninhabited places, only to escape from the domination of the Christians.' (Benzoni)

Distended ears Stretched ears, sometimes with large discs inserted, is a not uncommon tribal fashion. Harcourt writes of 'a Nation of Charibes having great eares of an extraordinary bignes, hard to bee beleeved.' Alvar Nuñez Cabeza de Vaca, a governor of the River Plate, describes the Orejones who 'pierce holes in their ears large enough to pass a fist through: in these they insert gourds of a medium size, afterwards replacing them by larger, distending the lobe of the ear till it hangs down to the shoulder. When they fight, they take these gourds or discs out of their ears and roll them up, or else tie their ears behind their heads.'

Black teeth According to Benzoni, the uglier the local women became, the handsomer they thought themselves to be. He describes their method of blackening teeth: 'They make a certain mixture to preserve the teeth with oyster shells, of the sort that produce pearls, burning them with leaves of the *laxi* and adding a little water so that the mixture looks like the whitest lime. This they spread over the teeth which become black as charcoal, and thus they are preserved for good, without pain.'

130
C This was presumably to mark them as the property of the King of Spain, Charles V, though in fact only one in five would belong to him.

131
Hispaniola Haiti – the most exploited of the Caribbean islands from the time of Columbus onwards.

Spanish cruelties Benzoni's account was useful ammunition for the propagandists working against Spanish domination of the Indies; but the strongest campaigner for reform was the Spanish priest Bartolomeo de las Casas, whose description de Bry used in the picture of Indian 'sodomites' being savaged by mastiffs. Las Casas' diatribe deserves quoting at some length: 'The Spaniards with their horses, their Spears and Lances, began to commit murders, and strange cruelties: they entered into Townes, Borowes, and villages, sparing neither children nor old men, neither women with childe, neither them that lay In, but that they ripped their bellies, and cut them in peeces, as if they had beene opening of Lambes shut up in their fold. They laid wagers with such as with one thrust of a sword would paunch or bowell a man in the middest, or with one blow of a sword would most readily and most deliverly cut off his head, or that would best pierce his entrals at one stroake. They tooke the little soules by the heeles ramping them from their mothers dugges, and crushed their heads against the clifts. Others they cast into the Rivers laughing and mocking and when they tumbled into the water, they said, now shift for thy selfe such a ones corpes. They put others, together with their mothers, and all that they met, to the edge of the sword.' Las Casas gave three million Indians as having perished on Hispaniola. Oviedo puts the number at 1,600,000.

132
Sodomy Sodomy, cannibalism and idolatry were the cardinal sins of the Indians according to the Church. That the Indians also regarded the former as heinous is suggested by a passage in de Léry, who was in Brazil in the days of Hans Staden: 'I have observed that the younger sort both men and women are not very much given to lust: and I would that our Countrey people could moderate themselves as well in this behalfe. But that I may attribute no more unto them then than is meete, I remember, that often in their brawling they used to object to this reproach Tyvire, that is Buggerers, unto one another, whereby we may conjecture, that that hainous and abominable wickednesse raigneth amongst them.' The French in Florida seem to have been less critical than their priestly confrere.

134
The doctor Las Casas.

Amaracapanna Piritu, near Cumana. Note the clubs as in the Staden series.

135
San Juan de Porto-Rico Puerto Rico – the Indian name was Borichiù.

Human flesh The Carib tribes were mostly cannibals, whereas the Arawak Indians were not. This picture indicates that the Caribs were not always the 'Lambes so meeke' that Las Casas claimed them to be.

138 and 139
Law of Baiona Promulgated at Burgos in 1512, it regulated the employment of slaves.

Cimaroni Descendants of these Cimaroons or 'maroons' are still to be found on West Indian islands. Negroes were first introduced in the days of Columbus when it was found that the Indians were unable to tolerate the hard working conditions.

Sugar mill The plate (pp 140–1) gives an excellent visual description of the workings of a sugar mill; from the cutting of the cane, via the water driven crushing wheel, to the boiling vats and the carrying away of the molasses.

142
Goldsmiths 'The Art or Science of Gold-smiths, among them is the most curious, and very good workmanship engraven of tools made of flint, or in mold. They will cast a platter in mold with eight corners, and every corner of several metall, that is to say, the one of gold, and the other of silver, without any kind of solder: they will also founder cast a little caldron with loose handles hanging thereat, as we use to cast a bell: they also cast in a mold a fish of metall with one scale of silver on his backe, and other of gold: they will make a Parret or Popinjay of metall, that his tongue shall shale, and his head moove, and his wings flutter: they will cast an Ape in a mold, that both hands and feet shall stirre, and hold a spindle in his hand seeming to spin, yea and an Apple in his hand, as though he would eate it. Our Spaniards were not a little amazed at the sight of these things. For our Gold-smiths are not to be compared unto them.' (Francisco Lopez de Gómara)

The illustrator seems to have based his ideas on a European goldsmith's shop, with its scales, tools, and somewhat baroque objects. The casting process mentioned above is shown on page 172.

143
Sibolla West of Mexico City.

Pedro de Alvarado One of Cortez's captains – his *soul* presumably afflicted him on account of former cruelties to the Indians.

Salisco Xalisco – north west of Mexico City.

Niquesa and Hodeida Diego de Nicuesa and Alfonso Ojeda were sent out to the Indies with instructions to enforce morality upon the natives on pain of enslavement. They instituted a reign of terror culminating in a reaction in Spain that led to the freeing of slaves. They were governors of Veragua and Carthagena respectively.

146
Balboa Vasco Nuñez de Balboa. Having crossed the isthmus of Panama in 1513, Balboa had his first sight of the 'Southern Sea', the Pacific Ocean. 'Panciaco' is being baptized in the right of the picture.

147
Turtles The turtles illustrated hardly seem to be of immense size. They look more like what Oviedo describes as 'Tortoises of the common sort' as opposed to his 'great Tortoises (which are certain shell fishes) of such bignesse that ten or fifteene men are scarsly able to lift one of them out of the water, as I have beene informed of credible persons dwelling in the same Iland.'

The Governor Diego Gutierrez. The right half of the picture does not show him taking pleasure, or umbrage, in conversing with Benzoni, but an earlier incident when some Indian chiefs presented him with alloyed gold and fish, fruit and smoked boar's flesh.

148
Santa Martha Santa Marta mountains, Columbia. Benzoni writes of the nearby Rio Magdalena, 'which falls into the sea with such violence, especially during winter, that passing ships can easily collect fresh water from the surface.'

Barter 'Each man took only what he wanted, without conditions or avarice, saying: "You take this, and give me that in exchange." The articles they most esteem are eatables.' (Benzoni)

149
Don Gonzalo Many Indians adopted, or were gratuitously given, Spanish names after the conquest, especially after they had been christened.

150
Guacci Perhaps a sort of frog referred to in *A Treatise of Brasil* as *guararici*: 'The feare that the Indians have thereof is a wonderfull thing, that of the onely hearing it they die, and tell them never so much they have no other remedie, but let themselves die, so great is the imagination.'

151
Poisoned arrows Raleigh gives a realistic description of their effect: 'There was nothing whereof I was more curious, than to finde out the true remedies of these poisoned arrows, for besides the mortalitie of the wound they make, the partie shot indureth the most insufferable torment in the world, and abideth a most uglie and lamentable death, sometimes dying starke mad, sometimes their bowels breaking out of their bellies, and are presently discolored, as blacke as pitch, and unsavery, as no man can endure to cure or attend to them.'

155
Tunal Tree A cactus, upon which perched an eagle surrounded by the feathers of birds it had devoured. Here, according to legend, the wandering Mexicans founded the city of Tenochtitlan, 'place of the cactus fruit'.

Azcapuzalco The region ruled over by Tezozómoc. De Bry has included in the same plate the story of the tribute demanded by Tezozómoc who, to test his tributaries, commanded them, on pain of death, to bring him a floating garden with a wild duck and a heron sitting on eggs which would hatch on their arrival before him. The raft was said to be sown with maize, corn, chile, amaranth, beans, gourds and roses. They added for good measure cakes of the red worms that swarmed in the lagoons.

156
Mexican dancing Acosta describes how in their dances they would represent various trades – shepherds, labourers, fishermen and hunters. Sometimes they would imitate the devil. The men who danced on the shoulders of others, which was also a popular dance in Portugal, were called *paellas*. De Bry does not illustrate their 'casting up and receiving againe a heavie blocke on their hams'.

Musical instruments 'They use sundry sortes of instruments whereof some are like flutes or little lutes, others like drummes, and others like shells: but commonly they sing all with the voyce, and first one or two sing the song, then all the rest answer them. Some of these songs were very wittily composed, contayning histories, and others were full of superstitions, and some were meere follies.' (Acosta)

157
Llama According to Acosta 'They do not finde that they multiply much: and therefore the Kings Inguas did defend the hunting of the Vicugnes. . . . Some complaine, that since the Spaniards entred there, they have given too much libertie to hunt the Vicugnes, and by this means they are much diminished.'

158
Potosi The richest silver mine of the Spanish empire, it was in Bolivia, formerly part of the Kingdom of Peru.

159
Cuyoacan Before the battle the Mexicans had their revenge by 'laying at the gates certaine things which smoaked, by meanes whereof many women were delivered before their time, and many fell sicke.'

162
Devil's dress The disguised priest, visible in the background of the picture, is described by Acosta as 'having mouthes upon every joint of him, and many eyes of glasse, holding a great staffe with the which he did mingle all the ashes very boldly and with so terrible a gesture, as he terrified all the assistants.'

163
Incense Probably *copal.*

Wooden devices Acosta says they used bodkins made of *maguay*, the Mexican aloe.

Castigation They would also sometimes 'slit their members in the midst'.

Statue of their god According to Acosta this was an idol made of pastry and honey with eyes of green glass and teeth of maize.

166
Prisoner The victim can be seen in the background carrying a flute, which he sounded from time to time to let people know he was passing. Other scenes from his unhappy progress are featured in the plate – the cage, the sword-fight, the flaying, and the displaying of the skin.

167
Whales The blackfish, or pilot whale, is not uncommon off Florida and can come into shallow waters to feed or mate. The story related by Acosta is also told by Monardes (*Joyfull Newes out of the newe found Worlde*, 1577) and repeated by Fr San Miguel writing about his experiences in St Augustine in 1595.

Rafts Acosta enjoyed watching the large number of fishermen on their rafts off Callao 'every one set on horsebacke, cutting the waves of the sea, which in their place of fishing are great and furious, resembling the Tritons or Neptunes.' De Bry, who has combined two regional methods of fishing in one plate, cannot be said to have done justice to the Indians' skill in reed-boat manufacture, if the specimens still in use on nearby Lake Titicaca are comparable.

170
Puerto de los Espanoles Port of Spain, Trinidad.

De Berreo Antonio de Berreo y Oruna was an elderly Spaniard who had married the niece of the conquistador Quesada. From his concession in Trinidad he had made several journeys in search of 'El Dorado'. Being taken prisoner by Raleigh he tried to discourage him from the venture. According to Raleigh: 'this Berreo is a gent. well descended . . . of great assuredness, and of a great heart: I used him according to his estate and worth in all things I could, according to the small meanes I had.'

172
Amazons Columbus told the same story about the inhabitants of the island of Madanino (Montserrat). Strabo placed them in Scythia. The story was told by a number of explorers of South America. The right breasts were supposedly cut off to facilitate the drawing of a bow. Thevet (1558) has an illustration of them emerging from barricades of turtle shells.

Ewaiponoma Herodotus tells of the Acephali of Libya who 'had their mouths in their breasts'. Mandeville reported similar monsters. Shakespeare, who probably read Raleigh's account, makes Othello relate the wonders he had seen, including 'the cannibals, that each other eat, The Anthropopagi, and men whose heads Do grow beneath their shoulders.'

173
Cacique A local chief or head man. Having at first treated them with some ceremony the Spaniards down-graded them to 'non-officer status'. Raleigh noted that since the English, French and Spanish had come among them 'they cal themselves *Capitaynes*, because they perceive that the chiefest of every ship is called by that name.'

Toparimaca Raleigh always seemed to get on well with the Indians. His description of his meeting with this local chief is typical of a number of his confrontations. Having given him some Spanish wine ('which above all things they love'), Raleigh and his captains caroused with the Indians and drank their wine which was 'very strong with pepper, and the juice of divers herbes, and fruits digested and purged.' They kept it in great earthen pots of ten or twelve gallons and were 'the greatest garousers and drunkards of the world.' Raleigh cast an interested eye on the wife of the visiting *cacique*: 'In all my life I have seldome seene a better favoured woman: She was of good stature, with black eies, fat of body, of an excellent countenance, hir haire almost as long as hir selfe, tied up againe in pretie knots, and it seemed she stood not in aw of hir husband, as the rest, for she spake and discourst, and dranke among the gentlemen and captaines, and was very pleasant, knowing her own comelines, and taking great pride therein. I have seene a Lady in England so like hir, as but for the difference of colour I would have sworn she might have been the same.'

Gold sand Raleigh did not witness this practice when visiting Toparimaca, nor probably on any other occasion. His version of the story runs as follows: 'At the times of their solemn feasts when the Emperor carowseth with his Captayns, tributories, and governours, the manner is thus. All those that pledge him are first stripped naked, and their bodies anoynted al over with a kinde of *Balsamum* (by them called *Curcai*) of which there is great plenty yet very deare amongst them, and it is of all other the most pretious, whereof we have had good experience: when they are annointed all over, certaine servants of the Emperor having prepared gold made into fine powder blow it thorow hollow canes upon their naked bodies, untill they be al shining from the foote to the head, and in this sort they sit drinking by twenties and hundreds and continue in drunkennes sometimes sixe or seven daies together.' This tale derived from the Indian legend of the 'golden man' – *el dorado*.

Drink According to Raleigh: 'Those Guianians and also the borderers, and all others in that tract which I have seen are marveylous great drunkardes, in which vice I think no nation can compare with them.'

Manoa Raleigh's imagined El Dorado on its huge 'lake', which was probably flood water. It can be seen at the south of his map 'Manoa, or Dorado, this is the largest town in the whole world.'

176
Morequito Probably San Miguel, about 160 miles up the Orinoco. (Raleigh places it 300 miles up).

Pinas The pineapple – the wild species, such as Raleigh would have met in Guiana, is small and yellow rather than golden. The first description of the pineapple comes from Columbus on Hispaniola.

Paraquitos 'The Tuins are a kinde of Parot very small, of the bignesse of a Sparrow, they are greene, sprinkled with other divers colours, they are much esteemed, as well for their beautie, as because they prattle much, and well, and are very tame. They are so small, that they skip everywhere on a man, on his hands, his breast, his shoulders and his head; and with his bill hee will cleanse ones teeth, and will take the meate out of the mouth of him that brings them up, and make many gambols; they are alwaies speaking or singing after their owne fashion.' (*A Treatise of Brasil*)

177
Tiuitiuas These were Guaraunos Indians living in the 'broken islands and drowned lands' of the Orinoco delta. Sir Walter Raleigh met them while in Guiana and describes them as 'a verie goodlie people and verie valiant, and have the most manlie speech and most deliberate that ever I heard of what nation soever. . . .' They were forced to live on high ground during six months of the year when the Orinoco flooded and lived mostly on the mountain cabbage or Palmetto.

Capuri and Macuri According to Raleigh they were 'for the most part Carpenters of Canoas'. He adds that the Arawak Indians were in the habit of beating their chiefs' bones into powder and mixing it with their drinks.

180
Boat removed This presumably refers to the *Zee-Meeuw*. The crew had mutinied; but after the mutineers got drunk the officers recovered the ship, and ordered the guilty thrown overboard.

Five boats The *Zon*, the *Halve Naen*, the *Aeolus*, the *Morghensterre* and the *Jagher*.

Man on shore 'They here saw a man of Giantly stature, climbing the hils to take view of them. This was in the land of Fogo, or Fire, which is South of the strait.' (Purchas).

Dutchmen killed 'Some of the companie going on May day on shore, to take certaine goodly Birds, were surprized by some of the Savages, and two slain.' (Purchas)

Spanish wine 'They conferred with the Savages, and gave them Sacke, and certaine Knives, for Pearles joyned together in fashion of hornes.' (Purchas).

It will be noticed that this 'narrative-map', a clever device of the illustrator, indicates North to the bottom of the page.

182
Giants Giants were reported by many travellers in the area of the Magellan Straits: Magellan, Hawkins, Sarmiento and even Byron in the eighteenth century claim to have encountered these jolly, if unpredictable people. Magellan called them Patagonians, on account of their big feet; Cavendish, at Port Desire, measured footprints eighteen inches long. Pigafetta, chronicler of Magellan, describes a dancing and singing giant who was so big that 'the head of one of our men, of a meane stature, came but to his Waste.' His hair was painted white, his face yellow with red circles round the eyes and hearts on his cheeks. Another giant, who was also always singing and dancing, they named John and taught him to say words 'even as wee doe, but with a bigger voice.' Magellan's men shackled two more giants; one managed to escape, but first 'did eate at one meale a Basket of Bisket and drunke a Bowle of water at a draught.' The other, who they baptized and christened Paul, died in the heat when they reached the equator. According to Pigafetta they wore skins, cut their hair 'like Fryers' and were very jealous of their women. When they had stomach-ache 'they put an Arrow halfe a yard or more down the Throat, which makes them vomit greene choler and bloud'. Because of the cold they 'trusse themselves so, as the genitall member is hidden within the body.'

There is no reason to assume that the giants ate 'man's flesh': Pigafetta says they ate raw flesh, presumably guanaco, and 'a certaine sweet Root, which they call Capar,' though from other observations (see note to page 189) a taste for human flesh has also been suggested. See also Cavendish, who mentions others, apparently not giants, who ate some Spaniards left behind by Sarmiento to garrison the Straits. 'They were men-eaters, and fedde altogether upon rawe flesh, and other filthie foode.' From the conversation with the boy who learned to speak Dutch it was learned that the giants were called 'Tirimenen' and their territory 'Coin'.

183
Penguins 'Having salted them they continued good some two moneths, and served insteed of Befe'. (Hawkins)

This salting process was not always reliable. Cavendish, who took on 14,000 penguins from the same place (Drake took 3,000), found that they began to corrupt and 'there bred in them a most loathsome and ugly worm, of an inch long. They multiplied in a most extraordinary degree, and devoured not only provisions and clothes, but ate into the timbers of the ship. At the last we could not sleep for them, but they would eat our flesh.'

Port Desire Named by Cavendish in 1586 after one of his ships.

Danger to ships 'The ground was slippery stones, for about halfe an houre after, the winde blowing hard North West, both our ships lying with two Anchors a Peece out: presently drave upon the South shoare, for there five and twentie anchors could not have holden them so that wee verily thought both our Ships would there bee cast away. The great Ship sate with her side upon the Cliffes, and shoke with the falling water somewhat lower and still kept stanch.' (Purchas)

Bird Island 'Our men went on shore into the island, which was almost covered with egges; for a man standing still on his feete, with his hands might reach to fiftie foure nests, each having three or foure egges a piece, much like (but somewhat greayer) than Sea-Mues egges, the birds were blackish Sea-Mues, we carried thousands of them aboord, and eate them.' (Purchas)

Ship burns 'The "Horne" was laid on shore . . . to make it cleane . . . we burnt reeds under it when the flame of the fire sodainly got into the Ship, and presently tooke such hold thereof, that in the twinckling of an eye it was so great, that we could by no meanes quench it.' (Purchas) Thus they lost the smaller of their two ships, a galliot of 110 tons.

Graves 'Upon the highest part of the hilles wee found some burying places, which were heapes of stones, and we not knowing what that meant, pulled the stones off from one of them, and found mens bones of tenne and eleven foot long: they buried the dead upon the top of the hils, flat on the ground, and cover them also with stones, which keepes them from being devoured by beasts or birds.' (Purchas)

Cavendish reported a grave at Port Desire 'made all with great stones of great length and bignesse, being set all along full of the dead mans darts whiche he used when he was living. And they colour both their Darts and their Graves with a red colour which they use in colouring of themselves.'

Sea Lions 'Yong sea Lyons which we eate, and are of a reasonable good tast.' (Purchas)

Peacocks A misnomer for the rhea, the South American ostrich.

Stag-like animal Presumably the guanaco. Pigafetta, who accompanied Magellan, describes the guanaco as having 'the head and ears of the size of a mule, and the neck and body of the fashion of a camel, the legs of a deer, and the tail like that of a horse, and it neighs like a horse.'

Stone fort A natural feature known today as Tower Rock.

186

Patagonian woman This unfortunate lady must have been a survivor of van Noort's savage slaughter (see page 182), which had taken place seven weeks before. This would explain the reference to the dead, and the binding of the wrists of the man in the foreground. De Weert gave her a knife but left her on the island despite her pleas to be removed to the mainland.

187

Women and children De Weert let this unfortunate woman go, giving her a cap, a cloak and some beads. The younger child was sent off with a green dress, but the four-year-old girl was kept on board and brought back to Amsterdam, where she soon died.

188

Fuegans These are presumably the Alcalufs. They are described as having teeth as 'thin and sharp as the edge of a knife.' The Dutch did not have a high opinion of them: 'as to their manners, they are rather beasts than men; for they tear human bodies to pieces, and eat the flesh, raw and bloody as it is. There is not the least spark of religion or policy to be observed amongst them: On the contrary, in every respect, brutal; in so much that, if any have occasion to make water, they let fly against any one that is near them, if he does not get out of their way.' (Callander)

Throwing rope The *bola*, a length of rope with a stone ball attached to the end, designed to fly through the air and wrap round the legs of game or cattle.

Canoes The ends of these 'gondolas' seem unduly curved in the illustration. Later representations, made during the passage of the *Beagle*, indicate a similar craft but with a less pronounced silhouette. An illustration in Beauchesne's *Voyage à la Mer Pacifique* (1702) shows a gondola-like craft with a fire burning in it.

189

Giants These do not sound like the giants of Pigafetta's description, but several different groups were reported in the area. L'Hermite left nineteen men on shore for the night and returned to find only two alive. 'The savages had come down upon them as soon as it grew dark, and had knocked seventeen on the head, with their slings and wooden clubs. . . . There were only five dead bodies found on the shore, among which were those of the pilot and two boys. The latter were cut into quarters and the former strangely mangled; but the savages carried off all the rest, in order, as it was supposed, to eat them.' (Decker in Callander)

194

Captain Gosnold Bartholomew Gosnold visited Virginia in 1602. He had only one ship, though the illustration shows three. It was intended to leave twenty-four settlers but the plan was abandoned.

Marthaes Vineyard Martha's Vineyard. 'The place most pleasant . . . we went ashore, and found it full of Wood, Vines, Gooseberrie bushes, Hurtberies, Raspices, Eglentine, &c.' (Gosnold)

Elizabeth's Island 'Touching the fertilitie of the soyle by our owne experience made, we found it to be excellent for sowing some English pulse it sprowted out in one fortnight almost half a foot. . . . We laboured in getting of Sassafrage, rubbishing our little Fort or Ilet, new keeling our shallop; and making a Punt or Flat bottome Boate to passe to and fro our Fort over the fresh water, the powder of Sassafrage in twelve houres cured one of our Company that had taken a great Surfet by eating the bellies of Dog-fish, a very delicious meate'. (Gosnold) They actually landed on Cuttyhunk, Elizabeth Isle being the name now applied to the whole group.

Sassafras A kind of laurel with a reddish-brown wood. Popular in Europe at the time as a stimulant, sudorific, and diuretic, with a reputation as a cure for syphilis.

195

Compass 'Much they marvailed at the playing of the Fly and Needle, which they could see so plainely, and yet not touch it, because of the glasse that covered them.' (John Smith)

Powhatan Indians The figures in the foreground wear 'certain fowles' leggs . . . with beasts' clawes, beares, arrahacounes, squirrells etc. The clawes thrust through they let hang upon the cheeke to full view, and some of their men there be who will weare in these holes a small greene and yellow-couloured live snake, neere half a yard in length, which crawling and lapping himself about his neck oftentymes familiarly, he suffereth to kisse his lippes. Others weare a dead ratt tyed by the tayle, and such like conundrums.' (Strachey)

Captain Argall Samuel Argall was appointed to the Council in Virginia under Lord De La Warr in 1610. In 1613 he was sent to expel the French who had settled in the Virginia Company's territory. He razed their settlements on the Acadian Peninsula (re-named Nova Scotia) and was also involved in ousting the Dutch from Manhattan. In 1617 he became Admiral for New England and knighted by James I.

199

Chickahominys A stalwart tribe of Indians occupying an enclave within the Powhatan confederacy though not owing total allegiance. Fear of Powhatan was to some extent their reason for subjecting themselves to the English.

200

Ralph Hamor Secretary to the Virginia Colony.

Rawrenoke Roanoke – shell currency.

201

Openchankanough Powhatan's brother. Powhatan had died in 1618.

Some relevant dates

1492–3	Columbus's first voyage
1497–8	Cabot to Newfoundland
1500	Cabral to Brazil
1501	Vespucci explores the east coast of S. America
1513	Ponce de Leon to Florida
1513	Balboa views the Pacific
1520	Magellan through the Straits of Magellan
1521	Cortez overthrows the Aztecs
1524	Verrazano explores the east coast of N. America
1533	Pizarro overthrows the Incas
1534–42	Cartier's expeditions in Canada
1541–56	Benzoni in the New World
1548–54	Hans Staden in the New World
1562–5	French Huguenots in Florida
1577–80	Drake's circumnavigation
1584–8	First English settlement in Virginia
1588	Defeat of the Spanish Armada
1590	Publication of the de Bry edition of Hariot's Virginia
1595	Raleigh's first explorations in Guiana
1598	Death of Theodore de Bry
1598–1601	Van Noort's circumnavigation
1603	Death of Queen Elizabeth and accession of James I
1607	Foundation of Jamestown
1610–11	Hudson to Hudson's Bay
1614–17	Spilbergen's circumnavigation
1616	Schouten and Le Maire round Cape Horn
1618	Execution of Raleigh
1620	*Mayflower* lands at Plymouth, New England
1624	'Nassau Fleet' rounds Cape Horn
1634	Final volume of *America* published

Select Bibliography

Acosta, José de	*Historia natural y moral de las Indias* (1590) Purchas
Anon	*A Treatise of Brasil, written by a Portugall which had long lived there* (1601) Purchas
Barlowe, Arthur	*The first voyage made to the coasts of America* . . . Hakluyt
Benzoni, Girolamo	*La Historia del Mondo Nuovo* (1565)
Beverley, Robert	*The History and Present State of Virginia* (1705)
Bry, Theodore de	*Grands Voyages – Historia Americae* (1590–1634)
Callander, John	*Terra Australis Cognita* (1766–8)
Gómara, Francisco Lopez de	*La Istoria de Las Indias, y Conquista de Mexico* (1552)
Gosnold, Bartholomew	*A Briefe and true Relation of the Discoverie of the North part of Virginia* (1602)
Hakluyt, Richard	*The Principall Navigations, Voiages and discoveries of the English Nation* (1589)
Hamor, Ralph	*A true discourse of the present estate of Virginia* (1615)
Hariot, Thomas	*A briefe and true report of the new found land of Virginia* (1588)
Hawkins, Richard	*The Observations* . . . (1593) Purchas
Knivet, Anthony	*The admirable adventure and strange fortunes* . . . Purchas
Las Casas, Bartolomé de	*Brevissima relación de la destruyccíon de las Indias* (1552)
Laudonnière, René de	*A notable historie* . . . (1587) Hakluyt
Le Moyne, Jacques	*Brevis narratio* . . . (1591)
Léry, Jean de	*Histoire d'un Voyage Faict en la Terre du Brésil* . . . (1578)
Martire d'Angleria, Pietro (Peter Martyr)	*De Orbe Novo Decades* (1493–1525)
Monardes, Nicolas	*Joyfull Newes out of the newe founde Worlde* (1577)
Noort, Oliver van	*The Voyage of Oliver Noort about the Globe* Purchas
Nuñez Cabeza de Vaca, Alvar	*Commentaries* (1555) Hakluyt Soc. Ed. Dominguez L. (1891)
Oviedo y Valdés, Gonzalo Fernandez de	*Historia general y natural de las Indias* (1537–47) Purchas
Percy, George	*Observations gathered out of a Discourse of the Plantation of the Southerne colonie in Virginia* Purchas
Pigafetta, Antonio	*Of Fernandus Magalianes* Purchas
Purchas, Samuel	*Hakluytus Posthumus or Purchas His Pilgrimes* (1625)
Raleigh, Walter	*The Discoverie of the Large, Rich, and Bewtiful Empyre of Guiana* (1596) Hakluyt Soc. (1848)
Ribaut, Jean	*The whole and true discoverie of Terra Florida* (1563)
Schnirdel, Huldrike (Schmidt, Ulrich)	*The travels . . . from 1534 to 1554* Purchas
Smith, John	*The Generall Historie of Virginia, New England & The Summer Isles* (1624)
Spark, John	*The second voyage of Sir John Hawkins* (1564) Hakluyt
Staden, Hans	*Warhaftige Historia und beschreibung eyner Landtschafft der Wilden* (1557)
Strachey, William	*The Historie of travaile into Virginia Britannia* Hakluyt Soc. (1849)
Swanton, John R.	*The Indians of the Southeastern United States* (1946) Smithsonian Institute
Thevet, André	*Les Singularitez de la France Antarctique* (1558)
White, John	*Portfolio of water colour paintings* (British Museum Prints and Drawings Department)

Many of the above books are most easily referred to in the excellent publications of the Hakluyt Society. The best modern versions of Hakluyt and Purchas were published by MacLehose & Sons in 1904 and 1906 respectively.

Index

The numbers in *italic* refer to notes.

295
300
305
LA FLORIDA
Lacus & Insula Sarrope
Golfo Mexicano
Sinus Ioanis Ponce
Rio Canotes
Rio Pacis
Aquatio
CALOS
Calos
Insulæ dictæ Testudines
Scopuli dicti Martires
Circulus Cancri
C. de Crutz
Rio de S. Spirito
Phoudor de Medavo
Rio de flores
P. de S. Ioan navidad
Sinus Morguel
Mocossou
C. de Canareal
Bimini
Roques
P. Florida
CVBA INSVLA
Hauana
Portus Matancas
Cauana
Portus principis
Ysabella
Guanaguarico
S. Trinitatis
S. Iacobi
Baya honda
Ins. Pinnorum
Iardines scopuli nauigantibus formidabiles
Caymut
Bamco mos
IAMAICA
Seuilla
Oristan
Caquay
Port fornica rum
Hoc loco prima dissensio orta, et pugna commissa inter Hispanos
Nipeca
Cuerno
Xaquaes
Atalta
Seuilla
Salamanque
Maranga
IVCATAN
Merida
C. Cateche
Champaton
Ins. Mulierum
Xiculenca
Casta
Chetemal
CAPS
C. S. Maria
S. Pier
C. de gracias a dios
FONDVRA
Rio d'Vllua
Port de Cauala
Quicuri
Trugillo
Malinca
Tapatan
Val. d'Olanchio
Nico
S. Iacques
HISPANIA NOVA
Nata
Huc quarta & postrema Nauigatione peruenit Columbus
C. de Comagre
Guanaxo
Cap de Honduras
Coste Riche
C. de Marmol
Cap de Marmol
GOLFA D'VRAVA
R. de Suere
CARTAGENA
Mompox
Comagre
Caribana
El Cemi
Ancerma
Ancon
DA
VRAVA
Antiochia
Rio de la Laguna poblada
Nicaragua
Xunqui
HIGVERA
GVATTIMALA
Granada
Olanchio
Leon
NICARAGVA
Nicoya
Chira
Costa braua
Pari
Recilejo
Quicare
C. Berica
Mapelo
VERAGVA
Nombre de Dios
Caribã
PANAMA
La Castille de l'or
Laculaca
S. Fe
Caly
Cartago
S. Miguel
Popayan
Arma
Timana
Labuenaua
Cabo de baxas
P. de Peru
Past
Villa Viciosa
Los Quillacigas
C. de S. Francesco
R. de S. Tiago
S. tiago
Bahia
S. Mat.
Pasto